WANDER WOMEN

ALEXANDRA BLANCHARD
ALEX HOWLETT

Wander Women

*Tales of Transgression
in a Bordered World*

HURST & COMPANY, LONDON

First published in the United Kingdom in 2022 by
C. Hurst & Co. (Publishers) Ltd.,
New Wing, Somerset House, Strand, London, WC2R 1LA
© Alexandra Blanchard and Alex Howlett, 2022

Distributed in the United States, Canada and Latin America by
Oxford University Press, 198 Madison Avenue, New York, NY 10016,
United States of America.

A Cataloguing-in-Publication data record for this book
is available from the British Library.

ISBN: 9781787387973

www.hurstpublishers.com

Illustrations by Emmy Lupin

Printed in Great Britain by Bell and Bain Ltd, Glasgow

CONTENTS

ACKNOWLEDGMENTS

Thank you to all the women, trans and non-binary people who shared their stories. You made this book. Thank you to all our loved ones, the women in our families and our friends, who have shared their own important stories with us and showed us just how powerful storytelling can be.

Special thanks to our editor Lara Weisweiller-Wu and the team at Hurst, who have done such an incredible job at both editing and embracing our chaos.

Wander Women is for anyone confronting and resisting the borders of their world.

INTRODUCTION

Borders can manifest in many different guises.

In this book, we look at the borders of countries, of laws and policy, stories of seeking refuge and asylum. But in the stories we are sharing, borders also appear in many different and unexpected forms. For Jessi, who is a wheelchair user, their barriers can be physical—a pavement or stairs. Barriers can also come in the form of policy: the benefits they receive to pay someone to help them move through the world. For Alphare, her reasons for migrating as well as her borders to migration are her gender identity. She is transgender, putting her at risk of much persecution in her home country and in places of refuge.

Skin colour and even just coming from a 'foreign' place was a huge border to belonging to British society in the 1960s, and we learn about how those prejudices have altered in a more modern context. Patrice, Ranjan, Ari and Elizabeth all migrated because of their husbands, and we explore how freedom can be limited within the home as well as outside the home, but simultaneously, how those borders can be resisted. In the stories of Syrian activists, Holocaust survivors and Saharawi politicians, we learn about how women survive conflict to find purpose and accomplish change.

Women's migration, volunteering and activism is so often enacted around family and children. We also look at the particular way in which women's migration, volunteering and activism is an act of movement between these roles and roles within the domestic; and we explore how such fluidity can be condemned as transgressing gender norms in many societies—both the expectation that a woman's priority should be her children, and the expectation that a woman's influence should be in the home, not in politics.

Many of the people we spoke to arranged their work and their interviews with us around school days or around looking after children. Interviews were punctuated by interruptions, apologies and mothering. Motherhood is central to so many of the stories in this book, and the home is often a crucial space for activist work. Aminatou was nominated for a Nobel Peace Prize, and carries out much of her work advising activists from the heart of homes, around her children; Eva was carried to term by her mother through some of the most feared death camps of the Holocaust—Auschwitz and Mauthausen; Ari summoned the courage to leave her husband and seek refuge because of her children, who, in her own words, give her wings; Najat gave us overwhelming descriptions of the refugee camp in Iraq that centre around her children and household chores, finding food and washing clothes.

The house and the domestic are often seen as a private sphere, and as such, often remain as invisible as the labour carried out there. There are silences in and around many of the stories we share: people whose names have been changed, stories that have been avoided or rewritten by memory. This is, by the very nature of oral storytelling, a book of many flaws. There have also been many moments of intense emotion during our interviews, where people have been radically honest about their experiences, and shared stories of great weight.

INTRODUCTION

As part of our introduction, we are sharing the story of Piretta, who wanted to speak to us not about her personal story, but to shed light on certain gendered cultural practices and reasons for migration, as well as the unstable and precarious nature of asylum seeking.[1] Her reasons for keeping her personal story to herself were just as revealing. Piretta has a huge amount of fear around speaking out. This is a fear that originates from a multitude of places, including where she has come from. Her story is incredibly traumatic and difficult for her to relive. It was a stark reminder of the bravery and resilience of every person who has shared their story with us in this book, and of just why we so urgently need to seek out, make space for, and listen to those voices wherever we can find them.

Piretta mentioned embarrassment and shame as reasons for keeping quiet, not wanting her community to know what she had endured. Piretta told us that, in the UK, if she shared her story she might be considered 'brave', but in her society and culture, in the Gambia, they see it as the individual's fault for 'not following the rules of your parents' and community. Piretta also doesn't want her children to be saddled with the stigma of what she has been through. Piretta reflects on these first-generation silences, talking about how it deprives children of their family history. 'Most of us have beautiful stories but we do not share them because of the way that we feel and it's very hard to break that feeling. Even stories the children need to hear.'

She gives the rough outline that she migrated due to a forced marriage and female genital mutilation (FGM). She tells us that the family into which she was marrying expected her to be circumcised and that refusing is seen as a disgrace. 'It's a big celebration if you have done it and it's a big shame if you haven't done it,' she explains.

'If you're not strong enough and these types of things happen to you', she tells us, 'your mental health can be worse. It did

3

affect me sometimes, all the time actually. It traumatised my brain. That is why I cannot accept things and why the reflection is too much. I'm just trying to be strong and brave.'

Piretta says one of the things that she values most in Britain is the freedom of speech. She believes that this is integral to her mental health. In the Gambia, she says, 'Who are you going to talk to? You've got no one to talk to. You have it in your mind, that's just in there. You cannot share. It's traumatising you. You talk to yourself every day.' She tells us about her mum, who has recently come to the UK. She was imprisoned for eight months (Piretta doesn't tell us why, but she does say that she was innocent) and is very traumatised. But now she is healing because, Piretta believes, she is getting the right support and is talking to people.

Piretta suggests that many men leave the Gambia because of violence and most women migrate from the Gambia due to FGM or child marriages, despite the difficulty and expense. She says that even though FGM was banned by the government in the Republic of the Gambia in 2015, the culture remains. 'Sometimes children will be taken without the mother knowing, sometimes it's women around 30 or 40.' Figures show that, in the Gambia, FGM is most commonly practised between the ages of 0 and 9,[2] with around 76 per cent of women between 15 and 49 having undergone FGM.[3] In some countries, such as Somalia and Guinea, FGM is 'almost universal', with 'levels around 90 per cent'.[4]

'Many have lost their lives.' FGM can also be accompanied by a myriad of health problems, depending on the procedure. Piretta believes that Gambian people living in the UK are often quite afraid of returning to the Gambia on holiday in case it happens to their children. Piretta hasn't returned to the Gambia since she left. Despite this, more than half of the female population of the Gambia think the practice of FGM should continue.[5]

INTRODUCTION

Piretta is from a very religious and strict background, but although she is religious, she sees a big difference between religion and culture; for her, FGM and early marriages are an issue of culture, not religion. She points to lack of education for the prevalence of FGM. Education is expensive, especially if there are a lot of children in a household and, according to Piretta, not widely approved of in the Gambia, as it can lead to children questioning their elders. Piretta says that she had a little bit of education, and that this allowed her to shake her head and say no sometimes. She also believes that feminism hasn't been established firmly in the Gambia yet, and that that contributes to the culture of FGM. 'The men still think they own the power. It's difficult if the women are not heard and respected... It's going to be difficult to fight.'

This is not the only cultural difference that Piretta noted between the Gambia and Britain. When she went before a British judge for her asylum seeking process, she kept her eyes down when she was recounting her experiences. Later, her lawyer came to her and said that the judge didn't believe her because she didn't look him in the eye while she was telling him her story. Piretta laughs. 'In my culture, this is a sign of respect, but in your culture it is a sign of telling lies.'

Another cultural difference that Piretta found funny was the way in which British children would tell the story of how their parents met. Piretta exclaims, 'But for us, that's rude! How your parents met, that's rude!' She laughs heartily, before continuing more sombrely. 'So I will never know how my parents met. They will never tell me.' But in the UK, Piretta loves hearing people's stories of how they met; she thinks they're beautiful.

***

There is also a community nature to storytelling. One refugee we spoke with, Azade, told us that despite the difficulty of sharing her story because of the feelings it brings up, she does talk about it with her community of women. In a living room setting, at home, the stories of her friends, both dark and beautiful, are shared. Piretta echoes this sentiment, saying that sometimes it is important to talk about and yet sometimes you can see in your friends' eyes that they can't. This privacy and intimacy of storytelling, in a domestic and female-led space, is something that reverberates through the book.

As well as feeling culturally embarrassed and ashamed of their stories, Azade and Piretta have another, more telling reason for their silences. Both Azade and Piretta have managed to claim asylum legally in the UK. Yet for them, there is still a hangover and stigma from that precarious time of seeking asylum. Azade feared that telling her story would somehow impact her right to stay or get her in trouble. This fear is a direct result of the suspicious culture in today's asylum seeking process.

The whole period of seeking asylum is deeply unsettling and upsetting. Reports suggest that 'Uncertainty of the future, deprivation and feelings of powerlessness are commonly reported by asylum-seekers', as well as a feeling of not belonging.[6,7,8] Ari, a woman whose story we tell later, spoke about the fear of constantly feeling like she was fighting: fighting the authorities, fighting for her rights and fighting with her mental health as a result. Reports also suggest that 'rates of depression and anxiety were as high as rates of PTSD, affecting on average one out of three asylum seekers and refugees'.[9] In Norway, 19 per cent of refugee women are likely to have a psychological consultation, compared with 12.3 per cent of non-refugee women, with refugee women around 8.2 per cent more likely 'to have purchased at least one type of psychotropic medicine'.[10] These results stem from both the asylum seeking process as well as the exposure to trauma, depending on the circumstances of their leaving.

Piretta believes statistics about mental health like these are not only to do with the traumatic experiences but to do with the fact that most asylum seekers aren't allowed to work while their applications are being considered. This is due to the fact that, according to the UK government, 'entering the country for economic reasons is not the same as seeking asylum, and it is important to keep the two separate'.[11] In a new country, there might be language and cultural barriers, and asylum seekers are often left reeling from the circumstances from which they have fled. On top of this, without work which provides a chance to feel like a functional part of a new community, many asylum seekers feel purposeless or lost. Piretta tells us that she felt so trapped not being able to work and being alone. 'Coming from Africa, not seeing anyone in the morning was like a prison for me'. The biggest support she was given in her asylum seeking process was that of a busy host family whose lively atmosphere made her feel alive.

This sense of purposelessness doesn't only affect adults. There have been studies into a phenomena affecting hundreds of children in Sweden called resignation syndrome. Symptoms often start as anxiety and depression. The children become more withdrawn into themselves, speaking less and less, and eventually taking to bed. The children don't wake to eat, acknowledge pain or discomfort, despite brain-wave recordings noting that their brains are not unconscious. More than 400 cases were reported in the two years from 2003 to 2005.[12]

This phenomenon, resignation syndrome, generally only affects families seeking asylum. This is not an illness or a disease as much as it is a societal problem. The instability and hopelessness provoked by asylum seeker status, either the demoralising effects of a drawn-out process designed to find failures in applications, or the threat of returning to the place or situation from which the families have fled, is enough to cause children to shut down completely into states of apparent unconsciousness. Some children recover after a few months or a few years, but generally it is not medical intervention that aids this recovery but a completion of the asylum process.

Piretta shared a story that exemplifies the instability and feelings of danger while seeking asylum. At certain stages within the asylum seeking process, either before a decision has been made or after a claim has been refused, asylum seekers may be asked to sign in with immigration offices as regularly as every week. In the UK, this might be in a police station or a branch of the Home Office, whichever is closest. At this appointment, asylum seekers are at risk of being detained suddenly and without warning. Detention can also happen at the homes of asylum seekers, again without warning, and most often at night or dawn. Detention centres are essentially prisons, where freedom of movement is limited. Most crucially, adults can be held indefinitely. These are not prisoners. These are people who have applied for asylum, had their cases considered and refused.

Piretta had to sign in monthly at the police station, and this check-in caused a considerable amount of fear for Piretta and her friends. Her friends told her stories of other asylum seekers who were handcuffed and detained at sign-ins. Piretta says they were really scary. Every time she went to the police station, Piretta felt 'uncomfortable' and 'unhappy'. The mother of Piretta's host family used to come with her to the station to make her feel more comfortable. Piretta said that it made her feel better to know that there was someone who had her back.

Once, Piretta went with a friend who needed to sign in at the police station. At the station, her friend was suddenly arrested. Piretta was waiting for her, sitting on one of the benches. A police officer came over to her and said, 'You can go home now. She's not coming out.' Piretta kept asking the officer 'But why?'

The officer replied, 'She. Is. Not. Coming. Back.'

A little while later, Piretta received a call from her friend. She asked Piretta if she could bring her coat, because she was freezing. She told Piretta that she had been moved to the station nearer their house. Piretta brought her coat and some essential items to this station. When she got to the station, she told the officer there that she was looking for her friend. The officer told her that she wasn't allowed to see her. Piretta said, 'Even if I can't see her, can you give her her coat? Because she is freezing cold.'

Piretta described the way that the police officers spoke to her, in an intimidating way to make her feel scared. But Piretta just sat on the bench. The police officers asked her what she was doing and Piretta told them that either she was going to see her friend or they were going to give the coat to her friend. They weren't very happy with her sitting there, or her declaration, but, Piretta tells us, 'That's just me. I'm not going to be scared off, even though I was scared.'

When they brought Piretta's friend down, she was handcuffed and she was crying. Piretta handed her her things. She tells us that:

> Until today, I don't know where she is. I don't know if she's been deported. I haven't got her contact details. And I can't forget about her. And every time I went to sign in, I would remember that. Even today, if I go past a police station, it's still in my mind. You cannot forget about them.

Piretta heard rumours that her friend's application for refugee status had been denied but Piretta asked, 'If she failed her asylum, is this the way they should treat her?' She suggested that they treated her like she had killed somebody, like she was a criminal.

Piretta was discussing this with friends who were also asylum seekers, and they told her that she shouldn't talk like that because they were scared. Piretta refers to the conversation that we were having saying that they would never have spoken to us because they would be afraid of our conversation finding its way to the authorities. When homes can be raided and teachers are part of border control, it is understandable to feel like every aspect of the world is threatening deportation. Piretta tells us that her friends would stay over at each other's houses and not sleep in their rooms because they were afraid of the police coming in the middle of the night. They would only go back to their houses during the day.

Piretta tells us that the threat of deportation was the scariest part of her journey. The government knows that the public wouldn't approve of how humans seeking asylum—refuge—are being treated. But, so long as they are kept out of sight and out of society until they are deported, they will remain reduced to labels that are twisted and vilified by politicians and media: 'illegal', 'criminal'.

Wander Women is a book very much in the business of questioning and discarding labels; our chosen method for doing this is recovering and sharing with you the experiences and voices of women, non-binary and transgender people.[13] These stories have a habit of falling through the gaps, whether they are stories of migration across borders or stories of the obstacles women and trans people have fought to dismantle.

In Britain, for example, where both authors of this book are based, media representations of migration and the so-called 'refugee crisis' facing the UK often focus solely on male migration from France to the UK.[14] It is equally important to cover women and trans people's experiences of migration and, crucially, the lives of the women and trans people who are less able or less willing to migrate and the reasons why.

***

There is immense privilege involved with who is allowed to settle and why. The difference between the two terms 'immigrant' and 'migrant' is marginal and yet crucial. 'Migrant' is defined as someone with a tendency to move from place to place in order to find better living conditions or work, while 'immigrant' is a term defined as someone who comes to live permanently in a foreign country. The words 'immigrant' and 'migrant' might, for some, summon ideas of young men leaving their home in search of opportunity or adventure or jobs, marking them an 'economic migrant'.

Though these terms are often used interchangeably, 'illegal' is generally only fixed onto the term 'immigrant'—so much so that they have become a permanent compound noun. This is perhaps because it is the threat of settling permanently that is more frightening and therefore more criminalised than the idea of someone passing through for work or opportunities.

However, immigrants with privilege, either that of money or whiteness or even the privilege of being highly skilled, are afforded different labels. An expatriate, or expat for short, is someone who is living in a country other than their native country. The term 'expat' is predominantly applied to Western people, and often white Western people, who live abroad and, crucially, not vice versa. It is possible to buy citizenship to many countries, amongst them the UK, the US, Canada, Cyprus, Australia, Singapore and Spain. If you are wealthy enough, you can afford to be a citizen and not an illegal immigrant.

The term 'refugee' is more readily associated with women. The connotations of 'refugee' are often more one-dimensional than representations of a 'migrant'; refugees are limited to being the victims. Dina Nayeri discusses the concept of a refugee:

> Who is a true refugee? It makes me chuckle, this notion that 'refugee' is a sacred category, a people hallowed by evading hell. Thus they can't acknowledge a shred of joy left behind or they risk becoming migrants again.[15]

She draws the implied distinction between 'refugee' and 'economic migrant' as that of agency and threat, suggesting that a 'refugee' is more acceptable because they are seen as broken and pitiable, i.e. non-threatening. These labels dehumanise, turning people who move into stereotypes and caricatures without faces, while also being a false dichotomy. They suggest that, if a refugee has left their country of origin because of economic troubles, they aren't a 'real' refugee, or if an asylum seeker aspires to have economic success in their host country then this renders their application fraudulent. By this logic, economic migrants therefore cannot also be those fleeing and seeking safety. The purpose of this book is to show the many faces of migration, the multitude of reasons for people's movement and the myriad of journeys they have along the way.

During the years we spent researching and writing this book, our home country, the UK, was obsessed with a 'Channel migrant crisis'. The way this crisis has been discussed by politicians and the public, and covered by the press, is a mirror or microcosm to rhetoric around the broader 'European migrant/refugee crisis' provoked by the aftermath of the Arab Spring in the Middle East and North Africa.

In the late 2010s and early 2020s, press depictions of those arriving (in 'unprecedented' numbers) on English shores via boat from the European mainland have oscillated between fearful portrayals of hordes swarming across the Channel to take jobs and abuse the NHS, and tragic depictions of drowning bodies. The language used by tabloid and right-wing newspapers in the UK to describe migration topics is almost always hyperbolic, with the purpose of inciting fear. If you search for articles about migration on the website of mainstream newspaper *The Sun*, they are grouped under the heading 'UK immigration crisis'.[16]

The word 'crisis' is repeated throughout their articles. One article refers to the 'dangerous foreign criminals' who will no longer be able to avoid deportation by utilising a clause in the European Convention of Human Rights that includes a right to family life.[17] This sits next to an article that asks 'DID THEY DROWN?', regarding a family that had attempted to cross the Channel to Dover looking for a 'good life'.[18] For the 28.4 million people who read *The Sun* every month, a migrant can be a victim or a criminal, but rarely a person.[19]

One purpose of this book is to question the dehumanising labels overused in the media, such as 'economic migrant', 'flood of migrants' or 'migrant crisis', and promote the understanding that migration is a natural part of human evolution. This understanding is particularly important when significant inequalities between the global north and south have necessitated movement, both economically and in terms of war and climate change.

This kind of attitude in the media is exacerbated by government policies.

Governments worldwide are continually reacting in xenophobic and fearful ways to otherness, from the UK's use of the military to make the Channel an 'unviable' crossing for migrants to China's recent annexation of Hong Kong and Morocco's occupation of Western Sahara. Actions by political bodies such as these, under guises of protection and lawfulness, create persecution away from which people migrate, and simultaneously make movement vulnerable to exploitation and danger.

Around the world, rich countries have drawn up their bridges and built up their walls, further criminalising those who move across borders. Now, more than ever, it is vital to switch off the often reductive noise about people that move, and instead hear their own, hugely divergent voices. That is what we're seeking to do in this book.

Part of the issue with immigration policy is not only that it dehumanises and criminalises migrants in general, but that it increasingly seeks to turn away those with an internationally recognised legal right to claim safety: many of those crossing the Channel have fled war zones. According to the UNHCR, the definition of a refugee is someone who has fled war, violence, conflict or persecution and has crossed an international border to find safety in another country.[20] The UNHCR's definition of an asylum seeker does not specify the cause of seeking asylum beyond that they are 'usually' fleeing conflict or; they are defined by their seeking of sanctuary that has not yet been processed or granted.[21]

The attitude of previous Home Secretary, Priti Patel, towards migrants has been particularly cruel and dismissive. Patel's actions have included the implementation of a new Nationality and Borders Bill that the government declares will 'fix the broken asylum system'[22] and that has been called 'racist'[23] and an 'Affront to Humanity';[24] it is also known as the Anti-Refugee Bill.[25] This bill specifies measures such as the removal of asylum seekers to a safe third country while their application is pending. One such proposed third place for offshore asylum processing is Rwanda, though this is, at the time of writing, being met by legal challenges.

Another element of the bill is allowing Border Force to stop and seize small boats crossing the Channel, while giving 'Border Force staff who commit criminal offences while pushing back boats immunity from prosecution'.[26] The reasoning for this is that 'The British public have had enough of seeing people die in the Channel'.[27] That is a direct quote from the government website. It further criminalises migrants who cross the Channel, despite the fact that 'the majority of people who arrive by small boat are likely to be granted protection' '(either refugee status or humanitarian protection)'.[28] How can there be such a thing as an illegal asylum seeker?

Crucially, the bill creates a two-tier system for refugees depending on the route they take to get to the UK. Group 1 refugees are those who come directly to the UK via safe and legal routes, and Group 2 are those who have migrated to the UK by irregular routes. The difference in treatment between these two groups of refugees may include 'length of leave, requirements for settlement, family reunion, and recourse to public funds'.[29] This is intended to 'influence the choices that migrants may make when leaving their country of origin', including encouraging them not to take 'dangerous journeys and instead use safe and legal routes'.[30] However, the Geneva Convention specifies that 'subject to specific exceptions, refugees should not be penalised for their illegal entries or stays'.[31]

This differentiation between refugees will only succeed in making refugees more vulnerable. Asylum can only be claimed by people once they reach the UK and yet, other than various nationality-specific resettlement schemes such as those for Ukrainians and Afghans, there are no visas for coming to the UK to claim asylum. It is a catch-22 that only harms the people it professes to protect. A report from the Refugee Council 'predicts more than 19,000 people a year fleeing war, conflict, and bloodshed could face years in UK prisons for attempting to find safety'.[32]

This only represents the hostile environment created by the government of a single European country. States across the world echo these unwelcoming policies; the scale of hostility and welcome oscillates depending on the country, its position in the world and its culture, but it is rare for this hostility to be absent entirely from the policies drawn up by any given country's government.

Our journey

In 2018, we met Hamdi Bueha, UK representative of the Polisario Front, at a quiet café in west London. Hamdi is Saharawi—from

Western Sahara, a resource-rich disputed region in north-west Africa—and works for their government. The Polisario Front campaigns for the self-determination of the Western Sahara region, which is currently largely colonised by Morocco. In October of that year, we hosted a film screening at the university where we met as students, King's College London.

The film was called *Life is Waiting: Resistance and Referendum in Western Sahara*, and was directed by filmmaker Iara Lee, whose story we share later in this book. Much like Iara, we were fascinated by the use of creative pursuits, such as poetry, art and filmmaking, as a means of resistance to colonialism and power. But our main interest was the place that women hold within political and activist spheres in Saharawi life and those hierarchies of power.

At this stage, we loosely decided to initiate a sort of community based on research, interviews, screenings and events that would have one thing in common: tales of women's lives. Speaking over cups of elaborately made tea at the Polisario headquarters in London with Hamdi's colleague Sidi, we discussed how we could show our support for the Saharawi cause and, more relevantly, speak to some female Saharawi campaigners and politicians.

This led to a conversation with Nobel Peace Prize nominee Aminatou Haidar and leading female Saharawi politicians about the unique and empowered place Saharawi women hold in both their political sphere and more generally in the refugee camps in Algeria. As a result of these meetings, we started focusing on transforming our research into a book. However, one interview with the Secretary General of the National Union of Saharawi Women, Minatu Larabis, gave us a different idea. Minatu told us that:

> It's a challenge for women in other societies. There are challenges for other women around the globe that we don't have. But we do have our own struggles.

INTRODUCTION

We realised that aligning the differing lived experiences of women globally would do more to further conversations about borders, migration and women's roles—and could be utilised to enact change. We also wanted to go further, to discuss not only geographical borders but also the often invisible borders linked to gender, disability, race or sexuality. By including these varying borders, we examine the different political and legal changes that have affected the migratory journeys of women and transgender people—beyond just the visible borders of nations.

We build upon and include the more often discussed stories of migration, which include conflict and border-crossings, but we also go a step further, by including the voices of those redefining the meaning of 'woman', 'migrant' and 'border'. In doing so, we wanted to show how the importance of a person's story is not defined by how far they have travelled or the countries they have been to. A person who has never left their home country has experienced journeys and boundaries that equally reveal their vulnerabilities and strengths. The importance of seeing these struggles side by side is decisive in revealing patterns of exclusion.

Wander Women is filled with verbatim interviews with people about their stories of movement with further context and history.

In Chapter 1, we look at the journeys of two transgender people, Alphare and Paddy, their reasons for migration and their experiences of migration, both across borders and within communities. We explore the treatment of trans people in detention centres and refugee camps, as well as in their home countries.

The next chapter focuses on the intersection between traumatic historical events and women's movement, exploring the impact of colonialism in Ireland on women's rights, particularly focusing on the lack of abortion rights, precipitating a movement for Irish women. We also tell the stories of Jewish women who were displaced by the Second World War. One of these stories is that of Anka, who gave birth in a concentration camp, and the other is that of a photographer, Dorothy, who managed to escape the Nazis and used creativity as a means of exploring or resisting borders.

The next two chapters focus on specific conflicts: the fight for self-determination in Western Sahara and the Syrian Civil War. We talk to politicians and activists in Western Sahara, exploring the role of women as matriarchs in Saharawi society and in the refugee camps. We talk to researchers and activists who have worked to better women's rights in Syria during the conflict, as well as two women who made a prolonged escape from both the war and Syria's long-standing ethnic tensions; the first explains life in a refugee camp as a mother of small children, while the latter recalls how solidarity among women can alleviate those challenges.

The theme of motherhood continues in the next chapter, as we tell the stories of four women whose migration was precipitated by their husbands and how they found life beyond their marriage contracts. Patrice, Elizabeth and Ranjan's stories explore the macro- and micro-aggressions of racism in British society in the 1960s and, combined with Ari's story of domestic abuse, expose the inherent vulnerability of being dependent on a partner, particularly as an immigrant.

In our penultimate chapter, we look at the movement-disabling structures of cities, from London to Jeddah. We discuss the borders to movement created by the architecture of cities for wheelchair users, as well as the barriers that are created by architectures of ableist policy. We explore how the gendering of urban public space can enforce limits on the freedoms of women and trans people, but simultaneously discover how the size and anonymity of a city can confound or even be used to subvert patriarchal expectations. Sharing women's stories from Hong Kong reveals the extent to which women in the city have sacrificed their personal safety and security in order to protect their political and civil freedoms. Brief moments of freedom and protest on the streets are followed by stints in custody and lengthy prison sentences.

We finish by looking at activists all over the world working to rescue migrants from boats, to build camps and playgrounds for children, to give legal advice to those caught by Russia's invisible cities, to break blockades and provide help where they can. Voices of women volunteering within both refugee camps and on search and rescue missions add an important perspective to the consequences of political situations in Europe and Africa. These inspiring women end the book with optimism, reminding us to hope, and that change is possible.

Within these stories—although demonstrating the injustices in the lives of women and trans people caused by limiting social and political structures—self-acceptance and joy is also palpable in the re-telling of their life stories. Our interviewees' ages range from 24 to 96, and their stories incorporate different perspectives. We aim to challenge and develop the reader's ideas of gender and borders. There is a desire for unlearning and change in the current climate. This book weaponises storytelling as a means of resistance.

We examine the links between government policies and the impact they have on the lives of women and trans migrants, including the necessitation of sex work or the risks of human trafficking. Juno Mac and Molly Smith believe that there is a huge overlap between people smuggling and people trafficking. They suggest that often 'smuggling becomes trafficking', particularly when the migrant is more vulnerable and has to take on debt to pay their smuggler, and that 'by viewing trafficking as conceptually akin to kidnap, anti-trafficking activists, NGOs and governments can sidestep broader questions of safe migration.'[33] They assert that many people who find themselves trapped in exploitative situations 'were seeking to migrate', emphasising that *'borders make people vulnerable'*.[34]

People who migrate without documents are vulnerable to ending up in exploitative work situations as a result of 'debt bondage' (owing a debt to a smuggler), or simply because they cannot assert their labour rights because of their lack of documentation. For women and trans people, that work might involve farm work, domestic work or hospitality, as well as sex work (or rape if they are being forced into sex work).[35]

We explore women's roles within the political structures defining migration through research and interviews. According to World Bank data, women make up just over 49 per cent of the world's population.[36] Yet research conducted by UN Women shows that only 25 per cent of all national parliamentarians are women.[37] Women and marginalised people are disproportionately affected by the decisions made by men in seats of power in countries across the world where governing bodies are used to police the bodies and rights of women and trans people.

In our interviews, stories feature the 'double discrimination' experienced by people who move, but their narratives are usually more defined by the choices they have made. The ways in which people have presented their narratives to us have been retained as much as possible in our text and, in doing so, we have prioritised their self-determination.

The potential for positive change is story-led. The potency of this book lies in the collective strength of the stories and the current thirst for centring previously unheard or overlooked voices. The more we know and understand, the more empathy and change we can enact.

People are increasingly aware of how different identities cross over, with intersectionality becoming more mainstream; in *Wander Women*, these stories of movement and gender—the experiences of mothers, writers, lawyers, artists, activists and academics—combine, and something quite new emerges. Their experiences are insightful, facilitating the inclusion of important statistics, history and policy. While each tale of crossing and transgressing borders is unique, at the core of each story are universal tenets; our interviewees are united by their strength and their determination.

The journeys that the chapters follow belong to women and trans people we have met through our personal or professional lives, through volunteering, work, family and friends. The regions and issues covered in the book felt very separate for a long time, based as they were on different friendships or meetings over a period of four years, but placed side by side the parallels and connections are so evident.

Here is the result of these years of work. This is the product of endless conversations with wonderful and wanderful women and trans people—not only the ones whose names appear in this book as interviewees, but also with friends, family members, neighbours, colleagues and strangers down the pub. We hope this book acts as a celebration of those voices.

Alphare

1

BEYOND THE BINARY

When we first sat down to plan this book, we realised we wanted to look beyond the physical and geographical borders of countries, to the obscured boundaries that might not be immediately obvious. If we're examining labels and their connotations, we must also understand how people's identities are weaponised by the powerful to control and limit freedoms. It became obvious that we were restricting the scope of this exploration in a different—and perhaps problematic—way. Cisgender women are not the only ones limited because of their gender, and we have spoken to transgender and non-binary individuals whose lives and movements have been shaped by how others perceive their gender.

It is crucial to include stories from transgender and non-binary perspectives not only due to the layers of danger that can limit movement within cities and across borders but because trans and non-binary people are often discussed across media. These discussions are very rarely from the perspectives of the individuals whose own identities are the subject at hand.

The UNHCR is working to improve the treatment of trans individuals and acknowledges the shocking level of discrimination migrants are likely to experience if they are transgender. In a discussion paper on the subject, the UNHCR point out that 'without an accurate understanding of the situation faced by transgender and gender non-conforming people, asylum adjudicators may regard transgender persons as opportunistic cisgender "cross-dressers" without serious protection needs'.[1] The stories in this chapter are the life experiences of two very different trans individuals who exemplify the varied ways one's gender identity can impact the way you move around the world.

'I can't get justice'

Alphare loves basketball. She played the game in her hometown in Uganda, where she lived with her father. In fact, she was so good at basketball that she managed to study at university on a basketball scholarship. Alongside her studies, she also started up a cleaning company to make enough income. These are all the markers of a success story: someone who has come from a poor background with the smarts and the skills to educate themselves and make a better life. It is the kind of story we see retold in films, books, adverts—the universally appreciated 'bootstraps' stories.

Except Alphare wasn't afforded this future; it is a future that she feels is held in suspension, waiting for her, endlessly delayed. 'I have my own dreams, I have my own career,' she says over the phone, speaking from a reception centre, at the Kakuma Refugee Camp in Kenya. She finds herself there because she left Uganda at the beginning of 2022 to find safety.

She was facing persecution in Uganda because Alphare is transgender. Her own father wouldn't speak to her. A friend of hers said that if she travelled to Nairobi in Kenya and found a specific organisation that her friend knew about, she would be provided temporary accommodation while she entered into a resettlement process. But when she arrived, the organisation couldn't offer her accommodation or work. The only option left for Alphare was the refugee camp, Kakuma. She soon realised that this would be anything but the safe haven from persecution she was looking for.

In June 2021, the UNHCR held a global roundtable on 'Protection and Solutions for Lesbian, Gay, Bisexual, Transgender, Intersex and Queer People in Forced Displacement'. A discussion paper attached to this event identifies how:

> LGBTIQ+ people frequently experience continued harm during the onset of an emergency situation, while in transit and upon arrival in places of asylum. This harm includes but is not limited to: Stigmatization, sexual and gender-based violence, abuse by or lack of protection from security forces, arbitrary detention [refoulement] and exclusion from access to basic services.[2]

This reads like a checklist of the human rights abuses Alphare has lived through since arriving at the refugee camp. When we speak to her, she has been living there for five months, and she is losing hope. 'Being in a refugee camp shouldn't be the end of everything,' she says, but she explains that it is increasingly feeling that way. 'I'm desperate for hope,' she tells us.

> People are trying to attack me all the time. The stress makes me sick. I lock myself away. People stare at me. The attitude here is even worse [than in her home country]. The police have no jurisdiction, which I think the other refugees realised.

When Alphare started to experience physical threats from other people living in the camp, she went to the police for help. Instead, the police officers tried to taser her, 'to show I'm nothing to them'. Instead of investigating the violence perpetrated against Alphare, the police told her to 'go back where you come from'.

Instead of the other refugees, who were threatening and mocking her, having their behaviour investigated by the police, Alphare had to find another way to protect herself. She realised that, by spending her days in the reception centre at the refugee camp, she was putting a boundary and a gate between herself and the rest of the community—isolating herself but also ensuring her temporary safety.

In their discussion paper, the UNHCR describe how they are making continued efforts to improve the living conditions and treatment of the LGBTIQ+ community. They also claim that the 'UNHCR undertakes continuous engagement with human rights mechanisms and advocacy on behalf of LGBTIQ+ persons'.[3] We reached out to the Gay and Lesbian Coalition of Kenya to see how the organisation might be able to help Alphare. They took action and contacted partner refugee organisations, who explained that they had already linked Alphare to support at the camp in Kakuma.

However, according to Alphare, a representative from the UNHCR had visited her once and never returned. 'I am losing hope,' she repeats.

Yet still, she resists. For a while, other refugees would call her discriminatory names every time she walked past, including a Swahili equivalent for 'sugar', which is considered a derogatory term for queer people in Kenya. She said she ignored them and eventually they stopped. Instead, they started to try and attack her, and she had to run away. Nobody helped her. Now she hides in her room, afraid to go outside. She doesn't see how her situation will change without any support.

Transgender respondents to the UNHCR paper reported that they 'experience severe marginalisation throughout the entire displacement cycle', and that forms of persecution and disadvantage include sexual violence, discrimination, exclusion from formal education, health care, legal employment and housing. The extent of the obstacles transgender migrants face often forces them to turn to survival sex work.

The list of challenges continues: borders are complicated by legal documents not matching identities, leading to invasive body searches and detention; trans migrants may no longer be able to access necessary hormone treatments in their countries of arrival; the UNHCR also claims that 'mainstream transgender rights organisations may not prioritise their concerns and have been reported to provide them with less support than is available from mainstream umbrella LGBTIQ+ support organisations who work with displaced and stateless people'.[4]

The attitude of the UK government towards trans migrants exemplifies the international lack of consideration for their well-being. Between 2004 and 2010, 'individuals who claimed asylum in the UK on account of their sexual orientation or gender identity were not considered in need of international protection if it would be "reasonable" to expect them to be "discreet" on return to their home country'.[5] This might have applied to Alphare's situation, despite the threat to safety and barriers to accessing health care in the refugee camp.

While UK law now reads that 'it is not reasonable to expect a transgender man or woman to conceal his or her gender identity in order to survive',[6] the Home Office have still called into question persecution in countries like Uganda, where 'the asylum seeker's country of nationality has criminalised homosexuality but there is inconsistent application of this law'.[7] Between 2016 and 2018, over 3,100 claims of asylum were refused by the UK from LGBTIQ+ 'nationals from countries where consensual same-sex acts are criminalised'.[8]

Criminalisation of homosexuality in Uganda has fluctuated greatly over the last fifteen years; most recently, in 2021, a bill criminalising same-sex relationships and sex work was passed by an out-going legislator but then, swiftly, not granted assent by the newly formed parliament, which refused to progress the bill. The bill would not have been given assent by the ruling government, which had received previous condemnations from the international community for its past criminalisation of homosexuality.[9]

The changeable relationship between Uganda and its criminalisation of homosexuality reveals the extremes of opinion that are held about LGBTIQ+ individuals in Uganda and the dangers that these opinions might pose for someone like Alphare.

Furthermore, detention centres are notoriously difficult places for both trans migrants and migrants in general. In the UK, for example, with one exception, all detention centres are run by private companies that receive a fixed sum per detainee. Leah Cowan notes that 'any savings on that amount... can be pocketed by the business'.[10] This goes a long way towards explaining the many reports detailing the limited health care and substandard food found in detention centres. There are many reports of sexual abuse and violence in detention centres as well as during deportations.

These horrific environments, alongside the indefinite holding times, make for incredibly damaging conditions for mental health. Deaths by suicide rise from 0.01 per cent in the general population to 36 per cent in detention.[11] Not only do 'trans asylum seekers face particular threats of violence in detention', but poor medical care can mean that access to crucial medication, including hormones, is halted or the drugs confiscated, having a huge impact on the mental and physical health of trans detainees.[12] Indeed, the prison sector and detention centres have much in common, including the housing of trans and non-binary people in centres that do not suit their gender identity. This too can have hugely damaging implications, on both physical safety and mental well-being.

There are many similar reports, from the US and from Australia's notorious offshore system, about the condition of detention centres and treatment of detainees, including trans people. Human Rights Watch 'found serious and disturbing allegations of sexual harassment and abuse, of mistreatment, of the dangers of being placed with the male population, and [lack of access] to medical treatment' from trans women in US Immigration and Customs Enforcement detention.[13] The report stated that a number of the 'substantiated incidents of sexual assault in US immigration detention facilities' involved 'trans women who were sexually assaulted by male guards'.[14]

For the most part, the only crime committed by people incarcerated in detention centres (for indefinite periods of time in poor conditions) is that of movement.

Life is not much better for those trying to move to the UK, either without papers or via a worker visa. Emily Kenway suggests that 'this hostile environment not only pushes undocumented people into riskier parts of our economy but also prevents them from seeking help safely when they experience exploitation'.[15] Often, undocumented migrants will feel forced to stay in exploitative 'jobs', with their employees holding their precarious status as a threat over their head. They are stuck with the choice of remaining in an exploitative situation, running away or risking deportation if they speak to authorities.

An even more explicitly state-sanctioned form of exploitation is that of the UK 'Overseas Domestic Worker' visa, also known as the 'tied visa' in its post-April 2012 to pre-April 2016 form, because of the way it tied these 'workers' to their employers. The law used to prevent workers from leaving their employer and from renewing their visas; leaving the employment altogether violated the visa, making the person undocumented, or 'illegal' in the eyes of the government.[16] This visa has now been amended to allow workers to change their employers. However, the worker must then, at short notice and for potentially a limited time (depending on the length of time left on the visa), find a new employer.[16]

In reality, while it is legal to change employers, workers are still 'tied' to their employer, because of the difficulty of finding new work. People on these visas are left incredibly vulnerable to exploitation or abuse. Although Alphare isn't trying to come to the UK, these dangerous options and the rigged game of asylum-seeking reveal the lack of choices for someone persecuted in both their home country and the refugee camp in which they have sought refuge.

At the time of writing, it has been almost half a year since Alphare arrived in the camp. With every day that passes her health worsens, and yet nothing changes. Alongside hundreds of other refugees, her life exists in a suspended state, but unlike hundreds of others, she has no access to community or humanity, persecuted by those who live alongside her. A week after we speak, she texts asking how we are. She tells us that she is not so fine. 'The longer I stay here, the more sick I get. I feel my life is reducing like a phone battery day by day.'

Alphare's story is left feeling unfinished precisely because the interruption to her migratory journey has also led to the interruption to her life journey, with devastating consequences to her mental health. Her story cannot be neatly finished or written up while she is being held interminably at a red light.

Paddy, a non-binary trans person living in London, and our next interviewee, shares stories about their own differing journey. Their freedom of movement is less impinged upon by their identity. Instead, they describe how, although their movement is not so restricted, their freedom to present themselves in their entirety to whomever they meet as they migrate from place to place is instead restricted. Safety comes into consideration for transgender people on the move, no matter who they are or where they are.

***

A few years ago, Paddy was going out with a couple of friends to a queer venue, G-A-Y Bar in central London. At one point in the night, Paddy went to the toilets with their friends. Since both of the friends were men and Paddy is non-binary, it made sense that they went into the men's toilets together.

Straight away, a bouncer working at the venue approached Paddy and told them to use the women's toilets instead. Paddy tried to explain that they weren't a woman, they were non-binary, and as such could use both the men's and the women's toilets. The bouncer continued to refuse to let them use the toilet, and the situation escalated. Eventually, the manager of G-A-Y joined the conversation, but only to defend themselves. They explained that, since the bouncers were outsourced and not employed directly by G-A-Y, this was a good enough reason for the bouncer to not respect Paddy's gender identity.

For Paddy, this was no excuse. 'The bouncers still worked for them and they should make sure they reflect their values. [G-A-Y] is supposed to be a queer safe space, but they're not. It's just a queer safe space for cisgender people.'[17]

Paddy had known they weren't a girl 'for [their] whole life'. But the specific words and knowledge to accurately identify themselves were decades away from becoming common knowledge. 'I knew trans was a thing, but I thought you had to be either one or the other.'

Paddy didn't identify as a girl, but they also didn't identify as a boy. Eventually, upon moving to London after university, Paddy integrated in the queer community there and discovered that there was was an alternative term to describe their identity: non-binary. At the age of 25, Paddy started their medical transition.

While they have reached a point where they feel comfortable with their gender identity and they are surrounded by a like-minded and supportive community, it isn't easy. Paddy describes how now, at the age of 28, many people see them as a man.

When they walk around with their girlfriend, people assume they are a straight couple. They exist in a world where they have little control over how they are perceived. They often can't correct people who misgender them when the consequences can be dangerous, as negative attitudes towards trans and non-binary people remain prevalent. Paddy explains why they sometimes don't explain that they are actually non-binary to people who assume they are a man. 'If they realise I'm not a guy, that's when it becomes unsafe. With men, it's sometimes more dangerous if they feel like they've been tricked or they got it wrong. That's when it could turn potentially unsafe,' they explain.

In her book *The Transgender Issue*, Shon Faye charts the rise of trans coverage in the British media through the 2010s to present day. She links this to the increasingly violent attitudes towards trans people in the general public. Despite less than 1 per cent of the population in the UK being trans,[18] today it is seen as a divisive culture war, which often becomes intergenerational.

Very few of the conversations around transgender people are actually started by those who are trans. An infamously frequent commentator on trans rights is J.K. Rowling, a cisgender woman and fiction writer with no strong links to the trans community. Rowling is one of many 'gender critical feminists' who believe biological gender identity should take precedent above marginalised genders and who have often dominated the debate over trans rights.[19]

> By the end of the 2010s, trans people weren't the occasional freak show in the pages of a red-top tabloid. Rather, we were in the headlines of almost every major newspaper every single day. We were no longer portrayed as the ridiculous but unthreatening provincial mechanic who [had] a 'sex swap'; now, we were depicted as the proponents of a powerful new 'ideology' that was capturing institutions and dominating public life. No longer something to be jeered at, we were instead something to be feared.[20]

In 2020 alone, *The Times* and the *Sunday Times* published over 300 articles on trans topics, which amounted to almost one a day.[21]

These shifts in public attitudes are reflected in the personal lives of trans people and how their freedom of movement has often been severely limited by threats to their safety. According to a Stonewall report on British transgender experiences, 41 per cent of transgender people and 31 per cent of non-binary people experienced a hate crime or incident in 2018, when the report was published.[22] This violence reaches into the daily lives of trans people, with 12 per cent being physically attacked by colleagues or customers in the workplace, and 40 per cent of trans people and 52 per cent of non-binary people admitting they adjust the way they dress for fear of discrimination or harassment.

Paddy describes adjusting the way they move through the world to be compatible with the views of those around them, whether this is how they are misgendered at airport security or by the male waiters at a restaurant in Bali. While speaking about their home of London, they emphasise that their experiences are—comparative to those of other genderqueer people—fairly positive, as they have found a varied and welcoming community in the city, one that is characterised by understanding.

But, outside of this community, they still have to be wary of how they are perceived. They tell us that 'people's perception of me has changed [since they have transitioned], and that in turn has affected how I navigate situations. I have to adapt to how people see me. It feels a little bit sad that people don't see me for being a non-binary person. They only see me if I'm a guy or a girl. If you're in the middle bit, you're not seen so much.'

Paddy is in the unique position of having experienced both the social privilege of being perceived as a man and the restrictions caused by being seen as a woman. 'It's a lot easier for me to move around and exist when people think I'm a guy.

I look more male now and I've noticed that change from people perceiving me as a woman to perceiving me as a man. I feel so much safer, unbelievably safer. I don't feel the same fear that I used to,' they say.

Our conversation with Paddy reveals the sliding scales of danger and trauma that result from different gender identities. Despite the nuances and differences, all of this is a consequence of attitudes that urgently need to be reformed. Internationally, commonplace discrimination of transgender and non-binary communities is reflected by governments' inaction and absence of progressive policies.

Now, because Paddy appears as masculine, when they are walking along the street at night behind a woman, they will try to let the woman know that they aren't a threat. Either they will cross the road, or pretend to be on the phone and will 'camp myself up a bit'. They explain that they 'know how it feels for women or more femme people especially' to feel afraid while travelling through public space because of their gender and appearance. Hopefully the day will come when that same level of respect and consequential visibility will be reciprocated for the non-binary and trans communities.

Dorothy

2

BATTLE SCARS

HISTORIES OF TRAUMA

Authoritarian regimes usually negatively shape the lives of women and marginalised people most. This can be seen replicated by governments across every continent. With the stories of Anka, Dorothy and Irish women in general, we hone in on the impact historical and ongoing regimes have had in European countries, from Germany to Ireland. They begin to demonstrate how the choices of women can be limited by political events, from the persecution of the Jewish population in much of Europe by the Nazis to the formation of the Republic of Ireland and the rise of the Catholic Church.

We can see how each woman has reacted to these violations of their freedoms and their bodily autonomy. There are scars—marks left by these experiences. But there's also a sense of humour to their retelling of these histories: a liveliness within the darkness and an underscoring of anger that promises better futures, as they each resist in their own way.

The act of creation was, for Dorothy, vitally important as a way of exploring her feelings of otherness and displacement, as an outsider looking into different worlds. For Anka, finding joy in a trip to the cinema after the horrors she experienced in Nazi death camps was itself an act of resistance, and Countess Markievicz, sentenced to death for her participation in the Easter Rising, had revolution at her core.

'Women were at the forefront of the revolution'

In 2019, Professor Bill Rolston from the University of Ulster wrote a blogpost for the London School of Economics summarising the history of the colonisation of Ireland. He points out that 'it is not simply about the past':

> For all that Ireland is not a developing country, it bears scars similar to those of other post-colonial countries in the Global South. It was colonised, and the legacy of colonialism continues to disrupt democratic processes to the present day. The process of decolonisation remains incomplete, most obviously in Northern Ireland but also in the Republic. As Brexit threatens the economics and politics of these two neighbours, Britain and Ireland, there are many commentators who now argue that Ireland's economic development and political health depend on the ending of partition and the reunification of the country within the European Union. This would be a significant step on the road to decolonisation.[1]

Rolston's article focuses on how the continued partition of Ireland—North and South, Unionist and Republican, Protestant and Catholic—is also a continuation of the country's colonisation. He comments on how this colonisation, traced back to the twelfth-century invasion by the Normans, has impacted the economy of the country.

The Irish Gaelic language has been gradually stamped out by laws initiated by English rulers for as long as 700 years. In 1367, Article III of the Statute of Kilkenny banned English colonists from speaking the Irish language and also prohibited Irish people from using their language when communicating with the English. This was developed particularly by the 1737 Administration of Justice Act, which banned the speaking of Irish in courts and the writing of legal documents in Irish. Those who attempted to speak Irish in any court would be fined £20.

Northern Ireland retains these same rules in court. In the 1998 Good Friday Agreement, the British government committed to respect the 'linguistic diversity' in Ireland—but there is little evidence of this newfound respect. In Northern Ireland, the only legal protection of the Irish language comes from the European Charter for Regional and Minority Languages. Because of the EU referendum vote and the British public's decision to leave the EU, the Irish language will lose this singular legal protection.

Catholics, the 'descendants of the original displaced indigenous' people of Ireland, have been displaced by the settlers coming from the UK since the seventeenth century.[2] What could the quality of life in Ireland be if this pattern had not begun centuries ago, if the famine hadn't occurred and Britain hadn't simultaneously benefited economically from its ownership of Ireland, yet failed to support it through years of acute crises? As Rolston points out, 'to this day' the population of Ireland is not yet at pre-famine levels, as over two million people either died or emigrated at the time, and many more continue to emigrate to London, New York, Australia and beyond as a result of the lack of employment opportunities.

This has impacted—and continues to impact—the women who have lived in Ireland over the centuries; the reverberations are as immeasurable as estimating how life for Irish Catholics could have been different if they had not been displaced over

170 years ago. The religious and ethnic identities of Irish women and men continue to shape their lives today, demonstrated most literally by the border dividing the island into two nations. But anecdotally, insight can be gained from women's experiences of living in both Northern Ireland and the Republic.

The religious, political and social divides have moulded women's lives in dramatically different ways—on an island that is only 171 miles wide. This also has a negative knock-on effect for the ethnic minorities living in the country. If the dominant ethnic populations and their quality of life has been impacted by civil war, how much does this push minorities into the margins and how can this be seen by the distribution of economic opportunities, housing and resources?

One religious tradition that continues to cause tensions in Northern Ireland is the 'Orange Walk', an annual event where members of the Orange Order march in the run-up to 12 July to commemorate when Prince William of Orange defeated King James II and VII at the Battle of the Boyne in 1690. Despite many Orange Walkers' protestations that they only march as part of a tradition, many Catholics, Nationalists and outsiders see the Orange Walk as a means of claiming public space by, for example, marching through Catholic-majority areas, encouraging sectarianism, and as a source of further conflict.

The Troubles has shaped people's lives in the city of Derry and beyond since the Battle of Bogside in 1969. In 1972, sectarian violence between the Catholic population, Protestants and the British Army reached a crescendo when members of the British Army shot twenty-six unarmed protestors dead on a day that became known as Bloody Sunday. Since the army believed there would be an IRA sniper at the event, the British battalion received an order to fire live rounds. The soldiers apparently interpreted this quite liberally. They fired directly into a crowd of fleeing civilians, killing twelve further people.

Women's documented perspectives on the civil war that dominated the twentieth century in Ireland are as essential as they are sparse. Author Flynn Berry points out the way in which significant IRA members such as Mairéad Farrell and events such as a hunger strike in a women's jail (in which force-feeding caused the death of a striker) were accorded much less space in non-fiction books written about the IRA.[3] An exception to the rule is the IRA volunteer and bomber Dolours Price, 'known for her extreme devotion to the cause and her inherently violent nature', who was eventually sentenced to life in prison.[4]

During our interview with academic and activist Camilla Fitzsimons, we use the phrase from Bill Rolston's article, 'colonial hangover', to describe the continuing impacts of Britain's rule on both sides of the border. Camilla interrupts: 'It's not a hangover'. She makes it very clear that, as far as she sees it, the colonisation of Ireland is very much not something of the past, as Northern Ireland continues to exist under English rule. But it goes beyond this obvious fact; she mentions that the anniversary of Bloody Sunday, in Derry, occurred only days before our call. That loss, grief and anger continue to exist in the living memories of many Irish people—and those memories and the accompanying feelings are very far from fading.

She points out that historical traumas with ongoing legacies in Northern Ireland concern not only the civil war but also women's rights. Camilla describes the lengthy and fraught history of the grassroots battle for reproductive rights in Ireland. She gives us the light-touch, condensed history of the thirty-five-year struggle, and it's still heavy: a bloody battle with lives unnecessarily lost. Up until the very recent and restricted legalisation of some abortions in Northern Ireland, people's only option was to travel abroad—largely to Britain—to terminate their pregnancies.

This created further limitations on the freedoms and rights of Irish women and marginalised people. Those who couldn't afford to travel to England for their abortions didn't have the choice. Despite both Northern Ireland and England being part of the same 'United Kingdom', this necessary journey so many women were forced to make from one country to the other exposes the gendered inequalities existing between these united islands.

In comparison to the ongoing difficulties in the Republic of Ireland—'it's one of the worst laws in Europe. Abortion is still illegal, but they offer circumstances under which you can do it'— Northern Ireland is better.

As Camilla puts it, in Northern Ireland, the legalisation of abortion 'came through Westminster'. In 2017, under Theresa May's ('of all people', Camilla adds) Conservative government in England, new abortion legalisation was drafted, permitting NHS-funded abortions for Northern Irish people in Britain.

The decades in the run-up to the legalisation of abortion in Northern Ireland were marked by resistance from its political party, the Democratic Unionist Party, as well as from many citizens in Northern Ireland.

In October 2012, Marie Stopes opened the first ever Northern Irish private abortion clinic, in Belfast. In a 2017 interview with the *Irish Times*, ex-MP Dawn Purvis, who helped to set up the clinic, described how 'from day one the protesters were there and the tactic was to harass and intimidate and publicly shame the women who were coming to use services, but similarly to intimidate staff on a daily basis'.[5]

Over the years since 2016, external pressures began to mount against the Stormont Assembly.[6] By February 2018, the issue had caught the attention of the United Nations. A report was released that identified that Northern Ireland's anti-abortion laws 'breached women's rights'.[7]

The proposal drawn up by Labour MP Stella Creasy in the summer of 2019 was the straw that broke the camel's back, with 332 MPs in Britain's parliament voting in support of her proposal to decriminalise abortion in Northern Ireland, and 99 MPs voting against. Pro-abortion activists celebrated. However, the critiques resulting from the proposal were raised not only by anti-abortion activists but also by many who saw this as a move by the British government to inflict direct rule over Northern Ireland.

In light of this law being introduced 'through Westminster', if Britain was responsible for initiating the decriminalisation of abortion and in so doing advancing women's rights in Ireland, how is it possible that Britain can simultaneously be responsible for the ongoing women's rights issues both sides of the border in Ireland today?

This is a question we put to Camilla. Is Britain responsible for gender inequality in modern-day Ireland? Her answer is quick and absolute. Yes. In her response, she maps out the history of modern-day Ireland from the 1916 Easter Rising and explains exactly how Britain's colonisation continues, even since rule officially ending in 1949 in the Republic:

> There was a coalition with the Church and the state. People often use the comparison that when the British empire left Ireland, when colonialism in that sense ended, we were then colonised by the Catholic Church. It wasn't a seamless transition, but the Irish state emerged from revolution in 1916. The very first proclamation of Ireland spoke about equality, spoke about all citizens, women were at the forefront of the revolution, Countess Markievicz, for example.
>
> But then we had a brand-new constitution, which enshrined women's place in the home. It's still in the constitution that a woman's place is at home.[8] There was a shift from British rule to Catholic—almost theocratic—rule. Many people would argue

it's still happening, as the Church has control of our schools and a lot of our hospitals.

The famine happened because of policies [in Britain]. When they executed the leaders of the Rising [this] swayed public opinion towards a Republic, but also very strongly against Britain. When Britain pulled out, Ireland was a very poor country with very few resources. The Church came and said, 'We will educate you. We will provide resources.'

As the remaining institution able to provide services for the people, the Catholic Church was empowered culturally. There is a clear link between the Church, churchgoers and limited reproductive rights in Ireland; in 2018, over half of regular churchgoers, according to the Pew Research Center, believed abortion should be illegal. Out of those who don't regularly attend church, eight out of ten people favour abortion.[9]

For women, the suffering caused by the Irish past is two-fold. The loss of cultural identity, language and history is as present as it is for the men of Ireland. But this sits alongside a loss of basic human rights—a loss of freedom to choose your role and freedom to choose what to do with your own body.

Speaking on this, Camilla turns to her own personal history. Her mother had ten children. She explains that the Church shaped her mother's life in a way it did for most:

The biggest border from an Irish perspective has been the Catholic Church. It's really hard to explain to people just how it wasn't even an invisible border. It was so powerful and strong. My mother used to say things like, 'If you don't go to Mass you'll be struck by lightning'. The priest would give out to people from the pulpit.

But it isn't just women whose rights have been restricted in Ireland. Camilla notes that the description 'women's reproductive rights' is reductive by both excluding trans men and gender-nonconforming people, as well as being difficult for women for whom reproduction is not an option. This careful use of language is not observed in the Republic of Ireland's the Health (Regulation of Termination of Pregnancy) Act 2018. This defines a 'foetus' in relation to a 'pregnancy' as 'an embryo or a foetus during the period of time commencing after implantation in the uterus of a woman and ending on the complete emergence of the foetus from the body of the woman'.[10] A woman is further defined as 'a female person of any age'.[11]

The new abortion law of 2018 is concerned with repealing sections of acts dating from 1929 through to 2013, which is a huge step forward for the Republic of Ireland.[12] However, it also then stipulates the very specific situations in which a pregnant person could be legally granted an abortion, or in their language, a 'termination of pregnancy'.[13] This is, as Camilla points out, 'one of the most conservative abortion regimes in Europe'.[14]

Further, in the Republic of Ireland the law allows medical practitioners—nurses, midwives and doctors—to refuse to carry out an abortion if they consciously object, as long as they 'make such arrangements for the transfer of care of the pregnant woman concerned as may be necessary to enable the woman to avail of the termination of pregnancy concerned'.[15] And this is not a marginal problem: the majority of clinicians still seem to be against providing these services.

Only 10 per cent of GPs have signed up to MyOptions.ie scheme, a government scheme that offers free, confidential, non-directive counselling and information services, as well as a clinical advice helpline for people undergoing early medical abortion, and only ten out of nineteen maternity services are offering full abortion services.[16]

Camilla explains how this creates invisible borders to accessing abortions:

These barriers, both legalistic and accessibility related, mostly affect people with very little money, including low-income migrants. Restrictions also disproportionately affect people with disabilities, those living with violence and coercion, those with heavy care loads, people who can't take time off work, and also those with irregular periods.[17]

Further, the language of 'conscientious objector', just as the language of 'pro-life' used around anti-abortion campaigns, is intentional and misleading. 'Conscientious objector' has historically applied to people refusing military service for ethical or religious reasons, and thus has very decisive links to peace and abstinence from violence. Linking an abortion with violence, or even war, is clearly loaded, and the balance of individual rights of conscience against the duty to serve others is obviously not equivalent. A country's loss of one soldier's contribution to an entire war effort is nothing compared with one woman's loss of control over her own life and body. To consciously object is to prioritise the life of a foetus over the rights of a pregnant person. To legally support conscious objection 'honours the values of the conscious objector over the rights of the pregnant person'.[18]

Irish women have always been the makers of their own futures. But, as Camilla points out, there was only a brief moment in the twentieth century where their constitutional equality had the potential to be rewritten. This was in the struggle for independence from the UK, when the 'very first proclamation of Ireland spoke about equality'. Countess Markievicz was nominated to stand as a political candidate for Sinn Féin in 1918—despite sitting in a prison cell in London's Holloway Prison—at the same time as the Bolshevik Revolution in Russia. Employees at Holloway Prison recorded her saying at the time:

Freedom has dawned in the East; the light that was lit by the Russian democracy has illuminated Central Europe, [and] is flowing Westward. Nations are being reborn, peoples are coming into their own and Ireland's day is coming.[19]

It is arguable whether Ireland's day has come, when a colonial border continues to exist and women's rights continue to be denied, despite hard battles fought. But much progress has been made since those words were uttered and generations of Irish people have since worked to gradually improve both civil rights and human rights in the country.

Markievicz called for women to 'dress suitably in short skirts and strong boots, leave your jewels in the bank, and buy a revolver'. In 1918, the Irish countess wrote: 'we may hope that our road to Freedom will be a peaceful and bloodless one'.[20] It was neither. As Camilla points out, freedoms for women are increasing. And it is essential that this fight continues to be intersectional, fighting with and for those that are facing multiple barriers of accessibility to have freedom over their bodies.

As women and people carrying babies in Ireland have been denied safe abortions for much of the country's history, the following story of Holocaust survivor Anka, told by her daughter Eva, also demonstrates the unsafety of childbearing for so many women. Where an Irish woman might not have the option to terminate a pregnancy, it was not an option for Anka to carry one through. Despite this not seemingly being a possibility—due to the overwhelming danger to her life any pregnancy would cause—she found a way.

'His death meant my life'

Eva has the authority of someone who has been a teacher all their life. Her frozen face smiles through patchy Wi-Fi, a tedious symptom of interviews during Covid. 'This will not do,' she decides.

One cannot help but admire someone willing to stand up with authority and firmness to the caprices of Wi-Fi itself. She would not endure a dodgy connection and why should she?

We arranged to meet at a later date.

Eva tells us that she's had a very easy life and she questions whether her story would be of any use to our book. But Eva's life is a miracle.

Eva is the daughter of Anka Nathan and Bernhard 'Bernd' Nathan. She was conceived in Terezim, a Jewish ghetto used as a holding camp for Auschwitz, borne through Auschwitz-Berkenau and a slave labour factory in Freiburg and born inside the gates of Mauthausen on the eve of its liberation.

Anka was born in 1917 in what is now the Czech Republic, to Stanislav Kauder and Ida Kauderová. Her parents were committed Czechs, who owned a tannery and leather factory in Třebechovice pod Orebem. To their family, being Jewish was incidental. Stanislav saw himself as a humanist and Anka believed that, 'We happened to be Jewish and that was that'.[21] Eva remembers her mother, Anka, attending the synagogue on High Holy days before heading home and cooking the Czech national dish, which was roast pork.

Similarly, Bernd, Eva's father, considered himself German first and Jewish second. Eva isn't sure that her father ever set foot in a synagogue. They suffered at the hands of the Nazis because of their ethnicity rather than their faith.

When Hitler came to power in 1933 and the antisemitic rhetoric began to rise, both sides of Eva's family began to leave for more neutral countries. An aunt left for Sydney; one uncle fled to the Netherlands, then again to Switzerland after the Nazis invaded the Netherlands; another uncle, Tom, escaped occupied Czechoslovakia and joined the British army in 1939. His wife and child were given a visa to follow, but Tom's wife, Ruzena, refused to follow, because they had a very unhappy marriage and she thought that she would be fine staying with her parents. Eva believes that this was the attitude of many Jews in occupied countries; nobody had any idea of the gravity of what was to come, let alone slave labour camps, concentration camps and death camps.

'They just thought that if they kept a low profile and more or less stuck to those rules and regulations, they would be okay. That is human nature. You hope for the best,' said Eva.

Eva's mother, Anka, was also offered options to leave on a couple of occasions. In 1939, Anka and a friend met some English journalists in a café.[22] Within a matter of minutes, they had asked Anka and her friend to marry them. While Anka laughed and said no, Anka's friend was married within six weeks. On another occasion, she was offered a *Durchlassschein*, or exit permit, through a job as a nurse in England. However, according to Eva, her mother felt invincible, like the war and the antisemitism wouldn't affect her. Her gilded childhood left her naïve to the intentions of the Germans until it was too late.

The reality of Hitler's rise to power became apparent when the Germans annexed Austria in 1938 and, in March 1939, Czechoslovakia. Anka, who was living in Prague, remembers watching tanks rolling into Prague with horror. It was the biggest shock to Anka, as her country that she had known and loved for twenty years began to disappear.

The Nuremberg Laws stripped Jewish Germans of their basic rights such as citizenship, and it had a huge social impact, creating a social boycott of Jews and their businesses, which in turn had a devastating economic impact. Jews were encouraged to emigrate from the Reich, but upon leaving, they were forced to pay a tax of 90 per cent of their wealth, leaving the vast majority of émigrés impoverished.[23]

The term that most often gets used for people who migrated, particularly around the world wars, is this French word, 'émigré'; Anka uses 'émigré' to describe her migration. This means much the same as refugee and immigrant, but while 'immigrant' suggests a focus on the place to which you are going, 'émigré' looks backwards, towards the place from which you have come.

Anka experienced the Nazis' legal restrictions as a progression of losses, all serving to slowly dehumanise the Jews. For Anka, the world got smaller and smaller as her family's car was taken and she was forced to drop out of university. Anka was studying Law, and the Nazis closed all Czech universities. Anka decided to get a job as an apprentice to a milliner.

It was against this backdrop of antisemitism and slowly tightening laws that Anka and Bernd met and married. Bernd had moved to Prague in 1933, after Hitler's rise to power; he thought that in Prague, he would be safe from the Nazi regime. He was an architect and interior designer, but in Prague, he worked for a furniture manufacturer, and for a film studio, building and designing film sets.

Anka and Bernd met in November 1939 and were married on 15 May 1940, a year or so into the occupation of Czechoslovakia. Eva has a photo of her parents, looking luminous on their wedding day. Their love was a whirlwind, striking them from the moment they saw each other. They were married within six months in a very small ceremony without even telling Anka's parents. Bernd looked German and spoke German with a Berlin accent, affording him certain privileges with the Nazi soldiers; he worked for and socialised with them.

Anka described the restrictions as 'pinpricks' on her newly married bliss with Bernd.[24] Anka was eternally optimistic, and this spirit remained with her throughout the war and after. She was known as 'the Smiling Anka'.

Anka and Bernd used to test the restrictions placed on their freedom of movement. Anka was a very keen cinema-goer, and decided to break the restrictions and go to see a film. Mid-way through, the film was stopped and Nazi soldiers began checking papers. They started at the back of the cinema, checking ID cards for anyone, like Anka, who shouldn't be there. They went row by row. Anka was terrified, thinking about the large 'J' on her papers that made her visit to the cinema illegal.

One row before the row in which Anka was sitting, the soldiers stopped, and left the cinema. This close shave was so frightening that Anka never remembered the name of the film for which she risked so much. This was just the beginning. After the war, when Anka came to the UK, she would go to the cinema almost every single day. Eva believes that it was such a light relief from the horrors of what she had been through, 'she had this need, it was almost an obsession to catch up on the frivolous things of life'.

Later on, the Nazis found a way to monitor and restrict the movement of Jews constantly and on sight, rather than having to stop them and check their papers: the yellow star that was embroidered with the German word 'Jude', meaning Jew. Anyone aged six and above who was considered to be a Jew had to buy and wear the yellow star.

Anka remembered the dark-green skirt, tan suede jacket and hat and gloves that she was wearing the first day she had to wear her yellow star to the shops. She said it didn't look too bad on the suede jacket, but she was very apprehensive about how people would react to her. In fact, people ignored her completely, whereas many other people faced a lot of abuse. Anka and Eva speculated that perhaps it was because she was a self-confident young woman, unwilling to be cowed or bullied by anyone.

We probably all have very clear ideas of what being taken to a camp might look like, from the shocking violence and abruptness of the Kristallnacht pogrom, to the paralysing silence and waiting of Anne Frank's experience.[25] Yet Anka's experience was very different.

At the end of November 1941, Bernd received a card in the post and it gave a time and a date where they would have to report to a warehouse in Prague, near one of the mainland railway stations. Eva tells us that they were advised to take warm clothing and pots and pans. This gave the impression that they were heading somewhere where they could take care of themselves. Bernd left with a small suitcase.

Anka received her card a few days later. As well as bringing her small suitcase and her best handbag, Anka was carrying with her a large cardboard box in which she had two or three dozen doughnuts, a favourite of Bernd's, and was dressed in her finest green suit and hat. She spent three days and three nights in the warehouse with hundreds of others, without much food or water, sleeping on the floor. Anka tried her best to keep her appearance together. She was going to see her husband and 'wanted to look her best for the man she loved'.[26]

They were marched to the railway station, along a route lined with young German officers. Eva suggests they were around eighteen or nineteen. One of these officers could see that Anka was struggling to carry her bags with her limp box of old doughnuts so he yelled out to her in German, 'I couldn't give a shit whether the box comes with you or not', implying that it wasn't going to do her much good where she was going. Anka ignored him and got on the train shakily. The doughnuts arrived, a little stale, in Terezin.

Terezin, to where Anka and Bernd first went, was peddled as a 'spa town'. It was seen as a retirement home and Jewish ghetto but no one expected its reality. Terezin, the Czech name for Theresienstadt, situated forty miles outside Prague, was a garrison town where Czech soldiers were stationed before the war. This was turned into a ghetto, transit camp and concentration camp after the Germans invaded and disbanded the Czech army. More than 150,000 Jews were sent to Terezin from all over Europe.[27] Many of these were then sent east from Terezin to concentration camps and death camps.

The conditions were extremely cramped, with thousands of people living there. They slept in bunks, crowded with the few personal belongings that they had managed to bring with them. Families arriving in Terezin were split up, men from women, and the elderly and children confined to separate sections again. There were moments when these groups mixed, but they largely lived separate lives. Anka was found by some of her girlfriends who were already living there, and who brought Anka to their room. Anka almost felt like she was on an adventure, having her friends there. She found Bernd that night and gave him the battered box of stale doughnuts.

Eva's parents were young and strong and able to work, which meant that they remained in Terezin for three years. This was an unusually long period of time; those who were less capable or more vulnerable were sent east to the death camps more quickly.

The hardships that Anka and Bernd faced in Terezin were made more bearable by the fact that they had each other. However, for Anka and many other women, the companionship of men came with great risks—that of pregnancy. Accurate statistics on pregnancy in the camps are difficult to come by, as women would hide their pregnancies, miscarriages happened often due to the brutality of conditions and women had their pregnancies aborted if they could. However, one Polish midwife, Stanislawa Leszczyńska, suggests that during her two-year internment at Auschwitz, she helped to deliver around 3,000 babies.[28]

Eva was not the only child Anka bore while living in Terezin. Before conceiving Eva, Anka discovered, in 1943, a couple of years into her stay in Terezin, that she was pregnant. Anka told

Eva that, 'It was very, very, very dangerous, but your father and I got together secretly as and when we could and to hell with the consequences. End of story.' The brief moments of passion that Bernd and Anka managed to steal in the concentration camp had very serious consequences, considered by the Nazis to be a crime punishable by death.

Anka was found to be pregnant by the Nazis, along with four other women. The Nazis made them all sign a document agreeing that, when the babies were born, they would be handed over to be euthanised—murdered. Anka gave birth to a little baby called Jiri in February 1944. Anka and Eva aren't sure what happened to the other babies when they were born. Jiri was not, however, taken away from Anka and Bernd by the Nazis, for reasons that are unknown. Sadly, Jiri died of pneumonia when he was two months old.

Eva says, 'his death meant my life, which is a very strange thing to say, but my brother's death meant my life and my mother's life. Had my mother arrived in Auschwitz holding my brother in her arms, she would have been sent straight to the gas chamber.'

At the end of September 1944, Bernd was sent to Auschwitz. The very next day, Anka volunteered to follow him, without truly understanding where he had been sent. As an eternal optimist, Anka thought, 'We've survived three years together. How could it get any worse?' But Anka never saw Bernd again.

The trains to Auschwitz weren't ordinary train carriages; they were cattle trucks. People were packed in so closely that they couldn't sit, there was barely any air, no food, no water, no toilet facilities except maybe a bucket. When they arrived in Auschwitz, people were in a very poor mental and physical condition, particularly children and the elderly.

Anka survived the selection as, despite being malnourished, she was still strong enough to work. Nobody knew she was pregnant with Eva when she arrived in Auschwitz. She passed by Dr Josef Mengele and remembers him saying, 'This time we have very good material in front of us'. He did not consider the people queuing in front of him as human beings.

She was told, with the others who made it through the selection, to put any luggage she had in a pile with her name on it. They were sent into showers, unaware at this point of the threat of the shower blocks, and had their heads shaved. They were given a striped uniform and, if they were lucky, a pair of shoes. Finally, they were tattooed before being sent to their new accommodations, filthy and crowded huts that stretched into the distance.

Anka and her friends were so frightened and bewildered as they shuffled into their packed hut, as they couldn't work out what this place was. They asked the women already living in the huts, 'What happens here? What goes on here? When will we see our families again?' The women there laughed, incredulous that they had arrived without knowing what happened in Auschwitz. One woman told them, 'We'll all go up in smoke and you'll never see your families again.'

With this ominous truth, Anka began her life in Auschwitz. There was very little sustenance for Anka, or for Eva growing inside her. They were given a liquid in the morning called 'coffee' and another liquid in the evening called 'soup' and one piece of bread. The way in which Eva describes these liquids suggests that they barely resembled the name they were given. Eva says that sometimes, if they were very lucky, there would be a piece of potato peel in their soup. It was a common occurrence for Anka to wake up with corpses on either side of her, of women who had died of starvation.

The camps were not only a place to confine Jews and others; they were also places within which movement and activity was rigidly controlled. Twice daily, there was an *Appelle*, a registration, in which all the prisoners would have to stand and be counted until the numbers tallied, or there was an explanation for why they didn't. Anka said that, 'It was very, very hard to stand stock still for hours and hours on end, regardless of the weather.' Eva tells us that you would try to keep as low a profile as you could because you had no idea how the Nazis would react to you.

Anka fainted more than once during *Appelle*, but when she came round, she found that she was being held up by the women around her, her friends, which meant that she hadn't sunk to the ground in a way that would have drawn attention to herself. Eva repeats the phrase she has already used a number of times while telling Anka's story: 'she lived to see another day'.

Because Anka was considered strong enough for work, she was sent to a slave labour factory, an armament factory, in Freiburg, near Dresden in Germany. She was set to work making V1s, unmanned flying bombs.

Anka spent six months in Freiburg, from October 1944 to the beginning of April 1945, working on the wings of V1s. The end of the war in Europe came on 8 May 1945. Eva tells us that, during those six months, 'Anka was becoming more and more starved and more and more obviously pregnant, which was very, very dangerous for her'. Fortunately, none of the Germans realised she was pregnant until it was too late to send her back to Auschwitz, because Auschwitz had been liberated. There were cases when pregnant women were sent back to Auschwitz, where Mengele took 'the most unspeakable revenge on those women', because, as Eva explains, 'he felt they had got away with it'.

Wendy Holden gives a horrifying example of this revenge in her historical account, *Born Survivors*. Ruth Huppert had her breasts strapped to her chest to prevent her feeding her child, because Mengele wanted to see 'how long a baby could survive without food'. Wendy says that 'For eight days, feverish and with her breasts swollen with milk, she and her baby lay helplessly together as Mengele visited daily'.[29] After watching her baby starve in front of her eyes, Ruth was eventually given morphine with which to inject her child, to end the slow demise.

In the beginning of April 1945, the Germans, realising they were losing the war, began to evacuate camps of the inmates in order to prevent them from falling into Allied hands. Eva tells us this was also to remove living witnesses to the horrors that had been occurring in the camps.

The Germans began to move anyone who was still strong enough to other camps on trains and long marches that were known as 'Death Marches'. All of those who had been forcibly displaced into camps were now forced to move once more, just as their liberation approached. Some of these marches were as long as 250 km. Many prisoners died from fatigue or exposure, while SS guards shot anyone who tried to escape or couldn't keep up. Thousands of prisoners died. Many more were massacred along evacuation routes.

Anka was evacuated from Freiburg with over 2,000 other women on a train of open coal wagons. These were filthy and open to the skies. She was on this open coal wagon for seventeen days with no food and barely any water. Other similar trains were discovered after the war with piles of corpses in them. These were other prisoners who hadn't been so lucky.

Anka's train was stopped periodically, and the bodies of women who had died were thrown out. At one of these stops, a farmer walked by and locked eyes with Anka. Anka said that she never forgot the expression of shock on his face. She described herself as looking like 'a scarcely living, pregnant skeleton'. She weighed around five stone, and she was nine months pregnant.

This farmer brought her a glass of milk. A Nazi officer who was standing near her raised his whip to shoulder height as though to whip Anka if she accepted the glass of milk. But he didn't. Instead he lowered his arm, without saying a word. Anka maintains that that glass of milk saved her life. Eva tells us, 'Perhaps it did'.

The train, after seventeen days, arrived in an Austrian town called Mauthausen. Eva tells us 'it is a beautiful village on the River Danube'. This picturesque village was hiding behind it, up a very steep hill, a concentration camp. In comparison with her arrival in Auschwitz, Anka had heard of the atrocities at Mauthausen from very early in the war.

The main form of slave labour and torture in Mauthausen was working in a stone quarry. Prisoners who had been starved for months or years in this camp had to dig out huge blocks of stone and then carry them up incredibly steep stairs to the top of the quarry. Many prisoners died on these stairs, earning them the name 'The Stairway of Death'. Anka said, 'the shock of seeing the name [Mauthausen] provoked the onset of her labour'. She began to give birth to Eva on that coal wagon.

Anka had to climb unaided off the coal wagon and onto a cart for prisoners who were not strong enough to walk up the steep hill. Anka had people lying on her and under her, people dying and dead from typhus and typhoid fever. A Nazi officer spotted Anka giving birth to Eva and told her, 'You can carry on screaming'. Anka always told Eva that she was screaming not only because she was in labour but because she thought this was her very last minute on this earth. She thought she was about to die.

It was on this cart that Anka gave birth to Eva. At first Eva didn't move or breathe, and a doctor who was a prisoner was allowed to come to Anka. Eva tells us that this was presumably because the Germans could hear the Allied guns in the distance. The doctor cut the umbilical cord and smacked Eva to make her cry and breathe. Eva weighed around three pounds. A baby born at this kind of weight would today be put straight into an incubator. Instead, Anka just clutched baby Eva to her, wrapped in newspaper.

Eva tells us that one of the reasons she believes she survived was that on 28 April 1945, the day before she was born, the Nazis ran out of gas to operate the gas chambers. Had the train arrived any sooner, Eva and Anka would have been gassed. On 30 April, Hitler killed himself, leaving the Nazis in disarray, knowing the end of the war was upon them. Anka found that the prison guards suddenly changed their demeanour in a way that was 'cloying and horrible', offering food when the day before they might have easily killed her.[30]

The German prison guards began to disappear and the prisoners wondered if they had been left in the camps to die. On 5 May, the American army liberated the camp. Anka believes that she wouldn't have lasted much longer, surrounded by people dying untreated of typhoid.

After around three weeks, when Anka was strong enough, the Americans asked her if she wanted to be repatriated to Prague. She did, and so Anka and Eva were put on yet another train, an ordinary train. They arrived back in Prague in the dark of night. Anka says that this was the worst moment of her three-and-a-half-year incarceration in camps. This was the first moment when she allowed herself to think about what might have happened to all the other members of her family. Until then, Anka had been surviving using her Scarlett O'Hara theory—'I'll think about that tomorrow'. As they arrived at the station, there was no one there to greet them.

Anka pulled on her last reserves of optimism and decided that if any other family member had survived, there was a chance it might be her cousin, Olga. And she had. Olga and her sister, Hana, had survived Terezin and had been sent back to Prague just a few days before Anka and Eva arrived. Eva asked Anka later, 'What if she hadn't been there?' but Anka was convinced that she would be there.

Anka asked someone for some money to go on the tram to get to Olga's house, saying that people couldn't stop staring at them on the train because it was obvious where they had come from. This wasn't because people had a clear understanding about what happened in the camps. Even after the war it was a shrouded subject. However, Anka was incredibly gaunt, revealing in simplicity some of what had occurred.

Anka was a very practical woman, and when she arrived at Olga's door, she told her, 'We haven't got any lice'. Eva and Anka, however, were crawling with lice and scabies. She asked her cousin if they could stay a few days to recover. Anka and Eva actually stayed for three years.

Anka later returned with Eva to her family home. Her father's factory had been taken over by the Nazis and subsequently the Soviets. Anka, with baby Eva, was the only survivor in her family, and yet she was only 'allocated one room in her parents' house' with a shared bathroom. The rest of the house was occupied by the Soviets.

Some people were very cruel to Anka when she came back. One woman saw Anka pushing Eva in her pram and spat nastily at Anka, 'that's a German's baby'. Eva tells us, 'The irony was, of course that I was a German, but a Jewish German'. Regardless of this, the comment is layered in misogyny; if the baby had been conceived as the remark suggests, it was unlikely to be conceived with consent. Rape, as it so often is in war, was an ever present threat for Jewish women both inside and outside camps, with those women who survived such ordeals then being branded, as in this remark, as collaborators.

Eva tells me that this cruelty wasn't an isolated experience, particularly for women survivors of the camps. As property at this time often belonged to men in the family, women who returned having lost their families found it difficult to recover their possessions. A friend of Anka's came back with absolutely nothing. She went to a friend who had been given various items belonging to this woman's parents. At first, they didn't welcome her and then they offered her a cup of tea in the porcelain cups and saucers that belonged to her family. They refused to return anything to her.

However, not everyone was so cruel; perhaps while some in the patriarchal mid-century society viewed single mothers with suspicion, others may have felt a sense of duty towards a woman alone with her child. A farmer came to Anka's one room in the factory. He had a horse and cart with him, and he told Anka that her mother had given him something to look after. Anka hopped in his cart and went with baby Eva to his farm. The cart pulled up to a haystack in the barn, out of which the farmer proceeded to pull a whole twelve-piece dinner service and tea service. Anka felt absolutely mortified. The risks the farmer had taken to keep this china safe were enormous.

***

Anka and Eva's harrowing tale of endurance and survival didn't end with their return to Prague. In Prague, Anka began to piece back together her life and her family, but she also had to reclaim her identity. Though the Allies were attempting to repatriate all those displaced by the war, many didn't want to return to countries that had betrayed them so deeply. Wendy Holden suggests that 'there were between eight or nine million survivors of war to settle into Displaced Persons camps run by the army, or by voluntary agencies'.[31] The repatriation process sometimes took years for those with no documentation or way to prove their identity, or with no family to sponsor their return. Many Jews 'planned a mass exodus to the "promised land", Mandatory Palestine'.[32]

Anka always told Eva that 'the people, survivors, they just wandered around like flotsam, if they didn't have anybody, if none of their families survived. They were just floating about. It was very difficult.'

Anka had to reclaim her citizenship, but this was not a simple matter. Anka was Czech by birth, but when she married Bernd, she had become a German. Though she hadn't chosen to become a German, women are often seen by the authorities to adopt the nationality of their husbands. This is something that is still perpetuated today.

Gender discrimination in nationality law, though forbidden in the Convention on the Elimination of all Forms of Discrimination Against Women in 1981, abounds in at least twenty-six countries. In these countries, the legislation 'unevenly limits a mother's ability to confer their nationality onto their children compared to the father'.[33] In seven of these countries, women are forbidden from conferring their nationality to their children with no, or extremely limited exceptions.[34] This leads to statelessness when a father is not present or is not a national of the country in which the child is born and the mother cannot pass on her national identity to her child. Furthermore, around fifty countries 'deny women equal rights with men in their ability to acquire, change or retain their nationality, or to confer nationality on non-national spouses'.[35]

Anka was considered a German citizen when she married Bernd. A decree in November 1941 stripped all German Jews who left German territory of their nationality; this included those who were deported to camps. This left Anka stateless, a situation that was further complicated as, after the war, Czechoslovakia expelled around three million Germans.

Anka told Eva that she pushed Eva in a pram to the local government offices in Prague every day for three years to regain her Czech citizenship.

The 1948 Declaration of Human Rights, followed by the 1951 Refugee Convention, began to address issues of statelessness and displaced people more systematically. Before the war, there had never been such levels of displacement and migration. The systems implemented, such as that of identity cards, foregrounded the border controls and identification requirements seen today.

Versions of the passport have existed internationally since the early Middle Ages in the form of safe conduct documents or letters, written by a person of power, most often granted to those with wealth and standing. Such forms dipped in and out of popularity but were rolled out as an international standard after the world wars.

Crucially, the passport also served to control the movement of groups of people. While great efforts were being made to repatriate those displaced by the war, there was still a great deal of antisemitism, and many countries were unwilling to host large numbers of destitute refugees. Indeed, Jews, as a diaspora of people who have often migrated—with 'uprooting and deportation' as 'concepts deeply embedded in Jewish tradition'[36]—have often suffered from both forced migration (or expulsions) and restrictions of movement (in the form of border control).[37]

Anka knew the importance of symbolism and identity, and so gave Eva a name the brevity of which, Anka hoped, meant that it couldn't easily be changed. She also gave Eva a second birthday, on 5 May, the day that she became a free citizen, having been incarcerated from birth. Eva tells us that she has quite an elaborate birth certificate, beyond the one given to her in Mauthausen. After the war, Anka had Eva baptised by the Protestant brethren in order to 'get the Jewishness out of me'; she wanted to protect her daughter from everything that had happened to her. She realised very quickly that this wouldn't have an impact on Eva's identity.

Fairly soon after Anka returned to Prague, she was told of Bernd's death. A friend saw Bernd being shot on a death march outside Auschwitz nine days before Auschwitz was liberated by the Russian Army. Eva explained that in many ways being told this was a blessing, as 'if you don't have closure, you live in hope'.

This closure allowed Anka to move on and consider a new life. She met a family friend, Karel Bergeman, who was also Czech and Jewish. He fled to the UK in 1939 and joined the RAF, where he was made an official interpreter. After the war, he came back to Prague to pick up the pieces of his family, most of whom had been killed in Auschwitz. Anka and Karel married in February 1948, and they left for Cardiff in October. Eva tells us that they left because Prague was taken over by the communists. This further uprooting, though not directly motivated by violence, like Anka's previous deportations in cattle wagons, was precipitated by the threat of persecution; they didn't want to live under a regime that was also strongly antisemitic.

Eva emphasises that, though they came to the UK legally, 'we might have come as refugees, we might have come as asylum seekers, we might have come as migrants'. Their fates, as are the fates of many, were the result of coincidence and chance. Eva finally shows us a photo of Anka with Eva, Eva's two children and their children, reflecting on how unbelievable it is that they survived and, extraordinarily, thrived.

The mass migration that happened after the world wars of the twentieth century seems unconnected to the migration patterns caused by wars in the Middle East, Africa and beyond, which dominate the world today. Yet the twentieth-century wars in Europe and the migration patterns of today are entirely interwoven.

Anka's story reflects those of refugees stuck in misery today—not only have they been forcibly displaced by war, social unrest or persecution, but they are being hampered in their recovery from their trauma by hostile visa, citizenship and border regimes. Furthermore, her story reveals the layers of vulnerability and hardship that pregnancy, from both consensual and non-consensual sex, can add to such stories of migration.

Academic, activist and researcher Celine Cantat points out in conversation with us the threads tying the migration caused by previous wars to migration caused by the wars of today.

Celine primarily focuses on the Balkan route, which is the migratory route trekked by people fleeing from war in Syria or Iraq, through Turkey and winding through either Bulgaria or Greece. In our interview, she says:

> I looked at histories of migrants and national studies during my PhD. Politics change. They are recorded by the states and the histories change. If it had been down to the British government in the 1930s and late 1940s, they wouldn't have opened their borders to people fleeing the Germans. People on the ground forced those borders open.

Many survivors of the world wars, especially women, would have not only remained stateless if it were down to certain governments, but arguably not have survived at all. That survival and recalibration of international communities was instead because of the solidarity and humanitarianism of civilians on the ground. The people who forced borders open during the twentieth-century wars, like Anka in her reclamation of her citizenship, left a door ajar but not fully wide. As the emphasis in Europe today is solely on economically valuable, tax-paying migrants, and the right to family reunion is under ever-greater threat, we can see the same reluctance to grant rights to migrant women, or to see them as separate from their husbands.

Celine describes how there would be spaces along the Balkan route, with:

People who had activist biographies and then people who were moved by humanitarian motives. They ended up using the same spaces and influencing each other. People would approach the work in a non-political manner but then become politicised because they would see how awful the policies are and make friends with the people you interact with.

Friendship and migration have created concrete communities of displaced people around the world, but we visit one specific place where this has occurred, in Hampstead Heath, London. In this little village in a city, an elderly photographer and Jewish woman is surrounded by a community of similarly creative Jewish people in the village who all ended up there after they or their parents migrated to the city to escape persecution after World War II. It is the strength of these communities that underlies the story of Dorothy Bohm.

Creation and Migration

Dorothy Bohm, much like Eva, had a life shaped by the Second World War and the violence perpetrated against Jewish communities. Dorothy was sent to England as a child from her home country of what was then East Prussia and is now Germany. This was as tensions in Europe were escalating to what would become World War II. While she escaped, her family did not. They were not captured by the Nazis and taken to concentration camps, but were instead taken by the Russians and sent to Stalin's labour camps.

Dorothy would not see them for decades. As with Eva, although not herself being disappeared as a consequence of the war, her life was passively shaped by the disappearance of those she loved. Both Eva and Dorothy are, in their own ways, legacies of this loss. For Dorothy, this displacement and distancing from her family and her identity was something that fed into her future creative work as a life photographer. She names her move to the UK and displacement as a cause for the beauty in her photographs, her ability to see others' lives from this unique perspective, an outsider looking in.

Creativity is a theme that runs throughout *Wander Women*, a thread tying together the lives and survival of many of our interviewees despite their different backgrounds. In our chapter on Western Sahara, we discuss how the Saharawi use creativity as a form of resistance. The motto for FiSahara, the world's only film festival in a refugee camp, is 'The Sahrawi people have chosen audio-visuals as their weapons'.

Ravensbrück was a women-only concentration camp in northern Germany, where over 50,000 women were interned.[38] Over 5,000 women were murdered in gas chambers, and countless others died from lethal injections, medical experiments, disease and starvation. The SS also carried out sterilisation on the women, and made many women work in brothels.

One form of resistance from the women living there was to form underground educational classes for each nationality. Women would make small trinkets and rudimentary pieces of jewellery for themselves as a momentous act of rebellion. These small creative pursuits could cost a life and similarly save one.

For so many of the people we spoke to for this book, their journeys and identities have been defined by their creativity, reflecting their migratory experiences as well as of the world around them. Creativity is used as a tool for coping with and interpreting trauma as well as resisting and rebelling against the limits placed on people's movements and expressions. Dorothy's creative output communicates her interpretations of the world, as someone who has migrated, expressing the juxtapositions of someone who is immersed in and yet outside the societies she moves through.

***

One of our favourite, yet possibly most incompetent interviews, happened just before the UK's second coronavirus pandemic lockdown in October 2020. We made our way through Hampstead during a rainstorm to the house of photographer Dorothy Bohm. We were intimidated by the thought of interviewing someone considered to be a 'doyenne of British photography', and to make matters worse, we were also terrified of accidentally causing her death because of the risk of carrying coronavirus. In between lockdowns during the pandemic we were going against our better judgement and into the house of a ninety-six-year-old Jewish woman who had survived the Nazi occupation of her home country to document the changing world of the late twentieth century.

Dorothy did not share our concerns. When we headed upstairs with her daughter Monica we were met with the sight of a table set for tea in the most traditional sense, with doily mats, cheesecake and teapot. Dorothy was waiting upstairs, leaning over the banister, her waved white hair clipped back. Monica had already told us to remove our masks because of her mother's hearing problem, and we pulled the chairs we sat on back from the table.

Dorothy instantly asked us to come closer. When we mentioned something about being careful because of the virus, Dorothy reassured us that she hadn't been anywhere and wouldn't pass it on. It didn't seem to cross her mind that she was more at risk than ourselves. This minor moment quickly told us something about the strength of Dorothy's character—reinforced again and again throughout our conversation.

Upon our arrival, it quite quickly became obvious that her poor hearing negated our role as interviewers. We were to sit, listen and wait for her stories. Dorothy was a person who did not need prompting with questions. The good stuff emerged on its own.

Monica warned that we should be aware that Dorothy might not be able to speak for an extended period of time because of her age and frailty. She might have appeared frail, but as soon as she started speaking, an energising pleasure in conversation and reflection emanated from the photographer, who kept us entertained for a couple of hours. This ended, despite our and Monica's protest, with Dorothy ordering us to follow her from room to room. She propped up her walking stick on various tables to show us old travel photos, still-life polaroids, portraits of grandchildren and a book on Marie Nordlinger—a close friend and role model—and her correspondence with Proust.

Dorothy shared her life stories with pride and amusement, but never sadness. Considering how her family history is defined by more than a fair share of traumatising events, the absence of regret in her storytelling was striking. Dorothy was born into a wealthy Jewish family, the Israelits, in Königsberg, East Prussia in 1924. 'The town where I was born doesn't exist anymore. It's very strange to think how many things have changed,' she told us.

Her life was soon impacted by the rise of Nazism in Germany, and her family decided to relocate to Memel, now Klaipėda, in Lithuania in 1932. She had an older brother, who was, in her words, 'very good-looking and unfortunately completely ruined by it'. Her father, whose own mother was a business-owner in a time when women were rarely breadwinners, had a respect for women that enabled him to see the promise in his own daughter.

In the introduction to the retrospective book on Dorothy's photography, *A World Observed*, Colin Ford writes: 'Dorothy's final frightening memory of Königsberg is of a Hitler Youth parade outside the family home'. This tide of hatred followed the family to Memel, where Dorothy's father's success made him a target on radio and in person. According to Ford, rocks were thrown at their family home, and Dorothy was called 'Jewish toad' in the street.

By 1939, after being warned by a friend that the Nazis were on their way to the city, the Israelits moved to another city in Lithuania, Šiauliai. Only three months later, Dorothy's father organised for his daughter to follow her brother to the safety of England. As she stepped onto the train her father passed her his Leica camera, a seemingly spontaneous action. In retrospect, this appears to be laden with meaning, but at the time, it bewildered Dorothy, who never took photos and (as she does still to this day) hated having her photograph taken.

She would not see her family again for another twenty years, but the details of these difficulties and losses are glossed over as we speak. She tells us that her parents were 'saved from the Nazis, but not from Stalin. I didn't even know where they were. The Soviets deported them before the Nazis got to them'. Monica explains that before they could be taken to concentration camps, Russians arrived in Lithuania and deported the Israelit family to labour camps in Siberia.

At the school Dorothy was sent to in Ditchling, Sussex, where she was 'the first foreigner and certainly the first Jewish person', she managed to finish her school certificate in one year, having started with very limited English. Dorothy recounts this with absolute pride. The people there, she says, were 'wonderfully good' to her.

'I'll tell you how I came to be a photographer,' Dorothy settles into her narrative. 'My first cousin, a doctor, came to England. He had been present when I was born and kept an eye on me. When I got my school certificate, he knew I wanted to study medicine. This doctor, Zimmerman, came to talk to me at my school and said, "There's no money, it's all lost. We don't know where your parents are. You will have to find a profession which will bring you an income when you leave." He said, "What about photography?"'

Dorothy overcame this disruption in her life plan, from the disappearance of her family to the impact this would have on her future, with an impressive amount of self belief and resourcefulness. When Dr Zimmerman took her to visit the Baker Street studio of French-Czech photographer Germaine Kanova, Dorothy was 'enchanted'. She thought: 'If that's photography, I would love to learn'. Kanova offered to help her, and told Dorothy to return to the studio in two weeks' time.

Three days later the beginning of the Blitz meant the end of Dorothy's collaboration with Kanova, but not of her career in photography. Manchester came next. This seemed to be the start of a pattern of significant accomplishment for Dorothy; she went on to Manchester College of Technology—where her brother attended—to undertake a course in photographic technology, which took four years to complete. She finished it in two and received an award for her portraiture.

When we asked why Dorothy became a photographer, there seemed to be no clear answer beyond her relative suggesting it as a pragmatic career and her discovery that she was very good at it. Once she finished her course, she worked in a studio, quickly developed a good reputation and started up her own: Studio Alexander.

She discovered a second love in the city, too. Louis Bohm was a Polish-Jewish refugee introduced to Dorothy through a friend. Their friendship turned into a marriage proposal, which Dorothy refused 'unless he continued with his PhD. I said I would get married to you but I will be the breadwinner.'

So she was. Dorothy would take up to sixty portraits a day while working in her studio. Eventually, Louis' own career would take off, but Dorothy made it all possible in the beginning. 'I'm still proud of that to this day,' she tells us.

It was fortunate that she allowed us to stay and chat for so long, because more nuanced aspects of her career and life emerged, especially when it came to what motivated her photography. She took photos across thirty-two countries, published fourteen books with a variety of themes and focuses, but the entirety of her work consistently seems to have one thing in common: generosity. Despite the abject poverty in which some of her subjects are living or their apparent low moods, the way in which Dorothy has photographed them is empathetic rather than emphasising any visible struggles.

Instead, she creates a visual playfulness. In one black-and-white photograph, two women in Israel in 1970 are sitting on and in front of a low brick wall. They are bored and not engaging with the camera, but one woman leans in such a way that the bush behind her appears almost to be resting on her silhouette, and it seems impossible that there can't be some kind of collaboration between photographer and subject. The reality most likely has something to do with Dorothy's eye.

'I think that's why I take photographs. I can't take ugly, nasty things. There's no need,' she tells us. Dorothy mentions the photographer Martin Parr, and when she doesn't elaborate on her point, Monica adds that his photos are 'slightly cruel'.

Though Dorothy originally came to photography as a result of her family's deportations and her own refugee status, it didn't take long for her creative talent to become the driving force in her travels from one land to another. In 1947, she went to Montreux in Switzerland because of an opportunity to buy a portrait studio there, only to find out the building was going to be pulled down in a few years. This turned out to be a twist of fate—instead of extending her career in portraiture with a new studio, she ended up visiting a village called Ascona on the recommendation of a cousin. Here, she and Louis discovered a well-established artistic community.

According to Ford, Dorothy had borrowed a lightweight battered camera from her window cleaner in Manchester, and it was in Ascona that she found the confidence to photograph outside, supported by the creative residents the couple got to know. They would return regularly over the years. One of her photographs from the early 1950s shows Paul Vogt, former director of the Museum Folkwang in Essen, Germany, where he rebuilt the collection after the Nazis had purged it of 'degenerate art', according to the website Art Forum. His hands are busy with a sculpture of a large male head; a pipe rests in his mouth; a cat stares directly into the lens in the background. When Dorothy tells us that she 'fell in love completely with the place', it is easy to imagine seeing a photo like that.

Every change or decision is linked to her visiting a new city or country that inspires her to move onwards. It is tempting to read this as something to do with migration being so firmly embedded in her roots—a freedom, or ability, to adapt quickly and see things clearly.

Soon afterwards, she and Louis moved to Paris. When we ask if she liked the city, she exclaims: 'I loved it, I loved it, I loved it!' Despite the post-war shortages ('we couldn't find a restaurant'), Dorothy spent endless time exploring and photographing the city. She told Ford that this was where 'photography became an obsession'.

The next big transition in her work is again linked to a journey. She and Louis travelled frequently for his job, and in 1984 they were in Japan when Dorothy saw a man taking photographs on the street. She found out they were in colour and asked him what film he was using. 'From that time on, I turned to colour. Not both. They are an entirely different way of seeing. I am very happy there was no colour to begin with,' she says.

Each progression in her technique and work is final and decisive, without a backwards glance. One of the first photographs she took in colour on that trip is of a Japanese woman on a boat, taut wires criss-crossing behind her as she looks down at the ground. It is a breathtaking photo, marking a timely transition in her photography.

After an hour or so of talking, where Dorothy punctuates each chapter of her life by pausing and saying 'It's been an interesting life', she tells us what we have been wondering from the outset. How did her initial experiences as a refugee impact her life? Consistent as ever, she considers herself lucky. 'I think it's been an advantage both being a woman and not quite belonging. You notice things somebody might take completely for granted.'

In 1994, Dorothy and Louis went on their last trip together, to Ireland, where Louis passed away at the age of seventy-four. After this, she almost completely stopped taking photographs before realising that this wouldn't have been what Louis would have wanted. Telling this story, she again didn't linger on how difficult it was to lose her life partner. Instead, she spoke of the generosity she encountered from the Irish people during that trip. 'The Irish way. Incredibly kind and good. That's important,' she says. More than anything, this seems to be the Dorothy Bohm way—kindness above all else.

Dorothy is an acclaimed artist, yet it is the otherness she describes feeling that makes her photographs so extraordinary. Her daughter Monica, an art historian, has written extensively on the Jewish women creatives living in London after World War II and how they moulded so much of the creative landscape in Britain. In an interview included as part of the Insiders Outsiders Festival in 2020, she says:

> A good place to start, I think, is to consider how many iconic markers of British life (from the London bus stop sign through *The Tiger Who Came to Tea* to the Festival Hall or Glyndebourne Opera) were wholly or in large part the creation of refugees from Nazi-dominated Europe. By doing so, we not only acknowledge the pervasive influence of so many of these refugees but are forced to interrogate the very notion of Britishness.[39]

Here, she not only links the identity of a country with the identity of the migrants living there, but she also makes an important connection between the country's identity—'the iconic markers of British life'—and creativity.

If creative output holds so much significance in a country's identity, then the people behind this output and their personal, individual identities are quite literally woven into how a place is seen. Hearing and retelling a person's life story, making sure their context is recorded and understood, can help us understand the aesthetic of the world around us. This is significantly more important when that person comes from another country, interweaving cultures in ways that can be both obvious and more nuanced.

Their identity isn't made visible in their creation here; only those who know about the life of that migrant will see a bus stop sign and link it to Jewish migration. But, Monica writes in an article entitled 'Contemporary Anglo' as part of the Jewish Women's Archive, for many Jewish women who relocated to London because of the Holocaust, art was a way of exploring and expressing their identities.

> Aware of their complex 'otherness' as women, Jews, and artists, they put that awareness to good creative use, and in so doing, proved that art has a crucial role to play in exploring—and perhaps crystalizing—issues of identity.[40]

She gives the example of Marlene Rolfe, a Jewish painter living in London. When her mother was alive, she knew little about her past in Germany, and it was only when her mother reached old age, unable to speak or communicate, that Rolfe desperately wanted to know more. 'Rolfe belatedly realised that her mother's inexpressible experience had marked her whole life and particularly her old age. She always felt herself to be in exile, "torn up by the roots from her family, her *Heimat,* her language",' Monica writes.

Rolfe's mother, Ilse, according to Monica, was part of the German Communist Party in Berlin before being interned in concentration camps for several years. She was freed in 1938, moving to the UK and eventually marrying a non-Jew. Marlene decided to travel to Berlin to learn more about her mother's past. 'I found some clues on a tiny scale, such as miniature subversive leaflets in false covers, or illicit embroideries and playthings made by the women at Ravensbrück,' she says.

In these stories the women's actions, which may seem small, carry so much importance. As many borders are sometimes invisible, so too is the importance of some people's actions and choices. The great strength of these actions are revealed once they are retold beside one another; in Anka's secret pregnancy in spite of the Nazis; the manner in which Dorothy has utilised being an outsider for her photography; in the staff who turned up to work every day at the first private abortion clinic in Northern Ireland despite the presence of protestors. The intersections of women, trans people and migrants come together, with the bold individual choices creating momentous changes that rewrite the tapestries of their environments. From the British bus stop sign to Irish legislative changes, the legacy of movement, creativity and resistance shapes our present and will reverberate into our future.

Aminatou

MATRIARCHS IN THE DESERT

I was kidnapped and disappeared for almost four years and
kept in a secret location and blindfolded, without any trial.
They took away my future as a young woman.

The person that tortured me in 1987 is the same person
that tortured me in 2005. I see them every day.

The backdrop of a photograph in Lanzarote airport shows a queue of tourists: a hot-pink suitcase, baby prams and blurry, reddened faces. In the forefront, three men are slouching on a row of chairs as if guarding Aminatou Haidar, who is swaddled in a pile of blankets and looks away from the camera.

Aminatou Haidar is from Western Sahara, the last remaining colony in Africa. She has dedicated her whole life to the Saharawi fight for self-determination and campaigning against Morocco's continued colonisation of Western Sahara.

'In 2009, again, I was the victim of atrocities of the Moroccan government,' she says during a conversation with us in London over a decade later.

When, after receiving the Train Foundation Civil Courage Award, Aminatou returned from New York to her homeland of Western Sahara, she was required to fill out a form to get back into her home country. Aminatou wrote that she was a citizen of 'Western Sahara' instead of 'Morocco', and Moroccan officials refused to let her in and instead deported her to Spain.

In response to this, she began a hunger strike in Lanzarote airport that lasted thirty-two days and received support from the Kennedy family as well as filmmaker Pablo Almodóvar. Her protest also highlighted the complicity of the Spanish government with the Moroccan occupation of Western Sahara, in that specific moment and also historically. Since Morocco occupied most of Western Sahara after Spain's withdrawal in the late twentieth century, many Moroccan people, from the government downwards, have persecuted Saharawi citizens, including restricting their freedom of movement, alongside reports of physical, verbal and sexual violence.

Aminatou said, 'It was a lesson in dignity to governments who have no principles. My children can live as orphans, but they cannot live without dignity.'[1] Her efforts, including this protest, have won her a Robert F. Kennedy Human Rights Award, as well as a nomination for a Nobel Peace Prize.

Aminatou was born in a town called Laayoune in Western Sahara in 1966. Laayoune is the largest settlement in Western Sahara, filled with dusty pink squat buildings and not far from the North Atlantic sea. The Canary Islands, a popular package-holiday destination for many budget travellers, sit in a cluster not far from the coast of Western Sahara.

At the same time as Tenerife and its neighbours developed a reputation as party islands through the 1990s, Laayoune was the site of guerrilla warfare between the indigenous Saharawi population and Moroccan occupiers. This was followed by failed UN-orchestrated peace talks and continued protests and violent clashes between the two sides.[2]

In 1975, when Aminatou was nine years old, Western Sahara, supported by the International Courts of Justice and the United Nations, was on the brink of self-determination. However, King Hassan II of Morocco took advantage of the process of decolonisation and marched between 200,000 to 350,000 unarmed civilian Moroccans, with some 20,000 soldiers, into Western Sahara (then Spanish Sahara). 'The Green March', as this has come to be known, allowed for a casualty-free annexation of Western Sahara, pressuring Spain to sign the Madrid Accords, which ceded the northern two-thirds of Western Sahara to Morocco and the southern third to Mauritania.

Between 40,000 and 80,000 Saharawi civilians fled from the Moroccan and Mauritanian armies to refugee camps in Tindouf, Algeria, pursued by napalm bombs. Aminatou and her family remained in what then became known as the occupied territories.[3]

Our meeting with Aminatou Haidar was scheduled in a Travelodge not far from King's Cross Station in London. The contrast between the enormity of Aminatou's reputation and the plastic mundanity of the Travelodge was stark. Amidst the vinyl tables and slightly-too-loud pop music, Aminatou seemed an oasis of calm and tranquillity, which belied the iron determination that has defined her work as a human rights activist claiming space for her stateless people, tens of thousands of whom still live in refugee camps today.

Aminatou is very still and poised as she talks about her experiences with the Moroccan government in 1987, with Meriem, her translator. She describes how she was blindfolded and kidnapped at a peaceful demonstration and disappeared for almost four years in a secret location, without any trial.

> My family didn't know where I was. I was tortured. Physical and psychological torture. I was kidnapped at the age of twenty, which meant they took away my academic study. They took away my future as a young woman.

The conflict between Moroccans and Saharawi citizens led to the birth of the Polisario Front: a liberation movement that is currently recognised by the United Nations as the legitimate representation of the Saharawi people. In its infancy in 1975, the Polisario Front resisted what the Saharawi people saw as an invasion with guerrilla-style attacks on Moroccan- and Mauritanian-controlled cities. This war continued for sixteen years until the ceasefire in 1991.

Aminatou was liberated from jail, along with many other political prisoners in the UN-negotiated 1991 ceasefire between the Polisario Front and the Moroccan government. Mauritania had signed a peace agreement with the Polisario many years earlier, in 1979. This ceasefire was agreed with the promise that there would be a referendum for self-determination the next year. Attempts to hold this referendum have stalled repeatedly over the thirty years and counting since the promise was made, due to debates over who is able to claim Saharawi ethnicity and, therefore, who is able to vote.

Up until recently, the Polisario upheld that (so long as Morocco abided by the ceasefire) their only means of furthering their cause would be peaceful, leaning heavily on international diplomacy and advocacy. Today, the Polisario has political representatives in most countries and, for the past couple of decades, these representatives have spent their time building networks and communities across the world in order to raise awareness and support for what they see as their right to self-determination. With the people of Western Sahara unable to gain freedom, leaders have no choice but to move abroad to make their case. At least a third of these elected representatives are usually Saharawi women. One such woman is Omaima Abdeslam, who we call for an interview in the spring of 2021.

When Omaima first became a representative of the Polisario Front in Finland, she tells us she was far from welcomed by representatives of the Moroccan government. During meetings and in front of political representatives from Finland, the Moroccan men would say to her: 'you are a slut, you are a bitch, we will rape you, we will kill you'.

They would hurl this abuse at her in Arabic, assuming the Finnish representatives wouldn't understand or notice. But Omaima says, 'the Finnish people could understand their anger'. She was followed home by these Moroccan men, who would continue to verbally abuse her. Despite this, after being assigned her role as Polisario Front representative in Finland in 2010, she set up an office and opened an association for helping Saharawi people in the country and increasing advocacy and awareness of the cause. To do so, she had reluctantly left behind her three children in Western Sahara, the youngest being only a year and six months old.

> It is a terrible thing for a mother to leave her children. But I wanted to find a way where I can work for myself and my family, and I can also take care of my people.

At the beginning of our interview, before we even have a chance to ask her a question, Omaima tells us: 'My name is Omaima Abdeslam. I consider myself a militant of the Polisario Front. I consider myself a Bedouin in a modern war. I am a mother of three.' This remains a constant pattern throughout the conversation. She defines the boundaries as we speak and we respond to that, rather than the other way around. This determination and knowledge of herself is perhaps what has made it possible for her to be both a political representative and a mother.

For Omaima, it is important to do both. There is another reason for Saharawi women to take up the mantle when it comes to protesting and activism in the occupied territories. According to Omaima, since the violence against Saharawi men has been greater than against Saharawi women, more men are silenced, leaving the women in the occupied territory to take up the torch.

> We have lost so many militants because Moroccans have taken them from the streets, to the desert, beaten them and told them 'next time you speak up, I will kill you. I will make a hamburger from your body'. So we have lost those Saharawis, a thousand of them. Especially men have been taken this way.

Omaima explains that this has left many women to adopt the role of protester and activist.

While there is still brutal violence enacted against Saharawi women by Moroccan people, their own culture's respect for women, which our interviewees tell us translates to domestic violence being a rare experience, is a point of pride for Saharawi civilians. The Saharawi principles of communal care, responsibility and peace clearly have a sustainable positive impact on gender-based relations. Omaima tells us this also creates a marked difference between Saharawi treatment of women and the extreme violence that Moroccan policemen use against Saharawi women.

> The violence against women doesn't exist. No man dares put his hand on a woman. So seeing these occupiers beating our women, raping them, and the men cannot do anything because they are afraid. They have destroyed our population and they have changed it.

Aminatou Haidar furthers the comparison, telling us about the gender-based violence experienced by Moroccan women— revealing this issue to be pervasive within Moroccan society.

> A lot of Moroccan women have told me that they hope and wish to marry a Saharawi man to be well-treated. My answer was that the real struggle is to fight for your rights as Moroccan women to be treated properly by Moroccan men.

Aminatou explains that they are starting to protest against their husbands and male family members. She tells us that it has become a joke among Moroccan men in the occupied territories that Moroccan women are being poisoned by Saharawi women.

The focus on gender equality is prevalent within every conversation we have with the women we interview. Aminatou tells us that 'women have a primary role in Saharawi society' and 'are at the forefront of the struggle in Western Sahara'. Aminatou believes that there is little domestic abuse in their communities, and that the autonomy of Saharawi women is an innate part of their culture, but she also sees the work to maintain and improve gender equality in Saharawi culture as a parallel struggle to that of self-determination.

When asked whether she would prefer to live in the refugee camps in Algeria or in the Moroccan-occupied territories of Western Sahara, Aminatou said: 'Even if there is modern infrastructure in the occupied territories, there is also torture, arbitrary detention and harassment. Women are particularly marginalised in the occupied territories.' She would rather live in the refugee camps.

Torture and ill-treatment, intimidation as well as a continual police presence in the occupied territories is vividly shown in *3 Stolen Cameras*, a Swedish documentary co-produced by RaFILM and Équipe Média. Shaky footage from a camera precariously peeping over the edge of a roof records the force and violence with which peaceful demonstrations are met by security forces in occupied Western Sahara.

This documentation is vital because of the lack of investigation and documentation of such human rights abuses by the security forces and Moroccan justice systems. Use of violence and torture is particularly prevalent in police custody as a means of obtaining confessions to secure convictions.

A report by Amnesty International[4] notes that 'these abuses persist due to the failure to implement existing safeguards, including investigating alleged torture'.[5] The report details 173 reports of abuse between 2010 and 2014. Such a large number of people willing to come forward and speak should be evidence enough of the depth of this problem.

Many individuals told prosecutors and investigating judges 'of the violence to which they had been subjected':

> In a few cases, courts ordered medical examinations, but no investigations were opened in spite of the availability of witnesses, including co-detainees and students who saw the reportedly violent arrests on campus. Perpetrators were not disciplined, prosecuted, or held to account.[6] ... Further, individuals seeking medical examinations in public hospitals said that doctors refused to provide medical certificates when told that injuries were inflicted by security forces.[7]

The international community's satisfaction with Morocco's lip service paid to human rights declarations, while these are persistently contradicted by the actions of security services in the occupied territories, according to testimonies, suggests there is something else at play.

Conversations with Omaima and the Amnesty report both suggest that the international community are ignoring these abuses of human rights to 'counter terrorism or control borders'.[8] She tells us that the silence of international bodies and governments gives the impression that they are considered unimportant.

Aminatou has witnessed this impunity first-hand. In 2005, she was again arrested after a peaceful demonstration. She was arbitrarily detained for seven months.

> The same person that kidnapped me in 1987 was the same person that arrested me in 2005. He was governor then. The person that tortured me in 1987 was the same person that tortured me in 2005. How can Morocco talk about compensation when the people that performed torture on me are still free?

When she was let out of prison, she refused to sign a document from the Moroccan authorities that asked her to renounce her struggle and to say that she was at peace with Morocco and wouldn't pursue her human rights action.

Aminatou received €45,000 in compensation for her mistreatment during her 2005 imprisonment, showing Moroccan acknowledgement of their actions, but she tells us that 'Even a billion euros wouldn't compensate for one night spent in jail under torture'.

Despite her ordeals and the dangers of her activism, Aminatou persists. Due to the presence of security forces in the occupied territories, most of Aminatou's work continues inside the home.

During our interview, Aminatou says:

> I really, really suffered as a mother as well. That gave me more determination to give a voice to all other mothers who left their children behind in the occupied territories and had to flee and stay in the refugee camps in the Algerian territory.
>
> I am a mother and I am a housewife so I do day-to-day tasks as a mother and a housewife but I also receive victims of violations of human rights in my house. I go to visit their families, the families of political prisoners, when they're trying to prepare a demonstration. I meet the people in charge of organising them and talk them into remaining non-violent and giving them advice, but always in houses.

bell hooks writes that, 'despite the brutal reality... of domination, one's homeplace was the one site where one could freely construct the issue of humanization, where one could resist'.[9] While Polisario envoys network around the world, the best way Aminatou and others like her can advocate for their freedom is from within their own societies and within their homes. Aminatou tells us that 'the Saharawi woman in her house is the boss'. For the Saharawi, a metaphor for their home and resistance is their tent. Mohamed Sulaiman speaks about the symbolism of the Saharawi tent: 'We have four doors. The range of welcome is spread from the north to the south, from the west to the east. Come from any direction and you are welcome.'[10]

In October 2010, Saharawi protesters explicitly politicised the concept of the Saharawi tent, starting a traditional tent camp at Gdeim Izik in the occupied territories; within a month, it had swelled to 5,000 residents. It was swiftly destroyed, and tents were banned from being set up in the occupied territories.[11]

The traditional nomadic tents, or *khaimas*, represent the Saharawi's cultural history and now symbolise resistance. Saharawi in the occupied territories persist in building their tents to resist but also to guard against Moroccan assimilation and to protect such symbols of their identity.

The protection of cultural roots is an incredibly important part of life for both Saharawi refugees and those in the occupied territories. The documentary *Life is Waiting: Referendum and Resistance in Western Sahara*, made by Cultures of Resistance Films, captures the painful beauty of this culture. Until more recently, Saharawis had been doggedly pursuing non-violent means of protest such as creative resistance. In *Life is Waiting*, Yslem Hijo Del Desierto, a rapper in exile, says:

> Creative resistance is a non-violent weapon but it hits hard. Music, theatre, painting. You can express yourself without shooting a single bullet, without causing any deaths, you just target people's consciousness.

The peaceful resistance inherent within these creative actions is echoed by oppressed communities around the world, most notably reminiscent of the women at Ravensbrück, whose minor rebellions of jewellery-making and crafting held the greatest penalty.

The Saharawi camps in Algeria are characterised by the colour of sand. Clustered in the rolling dunes are sand-coloured buildings and a number of traditional tents, an improbability in this huge desert. Even the cloudless sky looks dusty. Inside the tents, however, colour erupts from the draped walls and the clothes of the Saharawi people. Their cultural identity too is a burst of intensity in the featureless landscape.

The Saharawi are elegant and fierce in their love of creativity, responding to the invasion of their homeland with a determined assertion of their attachment to those roots; we refuse to be moved, they seem to say. This is the case even among those who have been forced to flee over the Algerian border; they even host the world's only film festival in a refugee camp, FiSahara. Its creed is simple and on brand: 'The Sahrawi people have chosen audio-visuals as their weapons'.[12]

***

Almost fifty years after the Moroccan invasion of Western Sahara, between 45,000 and 90,000 Saharawi still live in refugee camps in Tindouf, Algeria.[13] This figure varies hugely between pro-Saharawi or pro-Moroccan perspectives. It also excludes refugees living elsewhere in Algeria, in Mauritania (around 26,000)[14], Spain and elsewhere in the world. Because of the harsh desert conditions, they are completely dependent on humanitarian aid for food, water and other basic necessities, like building materials and clothing. Sidi Breika, UK representative of the Polisario Front, tells us that, 'The UN is still dealing with Sahrawi refugees as if they were an emergency case but they got there forty-five years ago'.

Algeria, Mauritania and Spain have opened their doors and given refuge to the Saharawi diaspora, but it does raise some questions. For how long will the Saharawis bear the label of refugee? For how long will they be dependent on humanitarian aid?

Sidi tells us:

There is always a shortage in every kind of supply, food and health services. There are serious diseases amongst the refugees: anaemia, malnutrition in children, asthma because of the dust—fortunately not epidemics. Diseases that are caused by the poor quality of the food that is given to us by humanitarian assistance, and the variety.

Imagine forty-five years in the middle of the desert and all the circumstances that make diseases flourish among the refugees. Sometimes you're given rice, sugar and oil—it ends in less than a week when it's meant for a month. You have to find other ways to manage.

The people living in the refugee camp are becoming more impatient because of the lack of a solution, more desperate. That's not a secret.

When recounting the situation of the Saharawi to a friend, we were asked why they are still waiting in camps after almost fifty years—why don't they move and start lives elsewhere? While many Saharawi have moved abroad, particularly for educational needs, the Saharawi remain almost as a matter of principle: 'We're here to show we want to liberate our land'.[15] The camp has been divided into different districts that are named after occupied cities in Western Sahara; they are creating a Sahara state in exile, a hub for Saharawi identity and culture.

When we speak to Minetu Larabas Sueidat, the youngest Secretary-General of the National Union of Saharawi Women in its history, about her work in the camps, it seems like she could almost be a fifth member of 'the Squad'. At the time of writing, the complacency of some senior Democrats in the USA has been disrupted by 'the Squad', started initially as a group of four young female politicians elected in 2018. They are known for all being under the age of fifty, championing progressive political issues and a more diverse version of party politics.

Wearing large round glasses, not dissimilar to US representative Alexandria Ocasio-Cortez's own, and speaking with great enthusiasm about the social issues affecting the younger generations in the Saharawi refugee camps in Tindouf, Minetu fits the mould.

'I feel very supported and when I speak, people listen. My voice matters,' she tells us during our interview in the summer of 2019. This is happening over video call because one of our press visas was denied the day before our scheduled trip to the camps in Tindouf. Perhaps this was because at the time, there was ongoing civilian unrest and protests in Algeria, which became known as the 'Revolution of Smiles' and eventually led to the resignation of the president, Abdelaziz Bouteflika.

Minetu had planned for us both to stay in several different homes across the camps, with women leading very different lives. This, she explained to us, would educate us not just about Saharawi culture and politics, but also the issues connected to gender equity in the camps. Instead she outlines these issues during our interview, speaking so rapidly that it is sometimes difficult to keep up. 'I talk a lot!', she comments.

Headed up by Minetu and led by a national committee, the work achieved by the National Union of Saharawi Women is spread across seven departments, which focus on everything from international relations, culture, education and health. But the principles that govern Minetu's own work were founded long before she began her political career.

This started as early as thirteen years old, when she had to leave the camps and attend an Algerian secondary school, where she would be separated from her family for nine months at a time. 'For almost nine months, you don't hear the voice of your parents and you don't know the details of what is happening to your family. It's very difficult,' she says.

Despite these difficulties, she created a family away from her own. She and other young Saharawi women who were also attending the school would form small groups and call each other 'sister'. If the sisters were sent different amounts of money from their families, they would pool all of their funds and equally divide it so nobody was left without.

> That was very good for us. With the other girls at the school, it was a family away from your own family. From a very young age, we learned to defend ourselves using only a very small budget.

After finishing her education, Minetu worked as a programme officer for the Norwegian People's Aid Humanitarian Disarmament Programme, where Minetu worked towards clearing the approximately seven million unexploded landmines that litter Western Sahara as a result of the historic conflict between Morocco and the Polisario Front. At the same time, she also became increasingly active within the Saharawi Youth Union.

Minetu identifies a split between the generations in the camp. Older women active within Saharawi politics, who were the ones to migrate away from the conflict and created the refugee camps in Algeria, primarily focus on the Saharawi right to a referendum and self-determination. In contrast, Minetu and her peers, who have only known life in the camps, also want to advocate for improved quality of life within that infrastructure, creating more opportunities for women and tackling problems such as skin bleaching and unhealthy weight gain in order to achieve a beauty ideal.

Before becoming a representative for the Polisario Front, Omaima Abdeslam also spent twelve years constructing a school for women in the refugee camps, which prioritised teaching subjects that would enable the students' financial independence. 'This is the most important thing I have done in my life. Some women, because of their social roles, have not had the same chances as me,' Omaima tells us.

She and seven other women who graduated from university in Cuba would teach students on subjects like agriculture, how to make solar panels and how to make carpets. 'This small school made a big impact. For the first time, Saharawi women had confidence in other women,' Omaima adds.

However, while many of the female political representatives and activists across generations have focused on the empowerment of women in the camp, the issue of self-determination and displacement has remained a priority—especially for the older generation of women.

When we speak about self-determination with Omaima in early 2021, she vehemently states that 'Morocco does not have legal sovereignty without the consent of the Saharawi people. Only the people can give legality to the presence of Morocco in Western Sahara. And no one has asked them.'

While the referendum for self-determination seems a clear and simple request from the Polisario, it grows more complicated with each passing year. The Saharawi diaspora is scattered through Algeria, Spain and Mauritania, as well as those that remain in the occupied territories. Meanwhile, the Moroccan settlers encouraged to establish lives in Western Sahara have now lived there for generations, and significantly outnumber the Saharawi.

Within this context, it seems less clear who should have a voice in the referendum. Is it right that someone who was born and lives in the refugee camps in Algeria to Saharawi parents should have a greater say over the determination of Western Sahara than a Moroccan who was born and lives in Western Sahara? It is rightfully the land and home of the Saharawi, but the possibility of displacing Moroccan settlers is also ethically questionable.

How and when do you belong to a place and it to you? And what determines your right to stay? If your ancestors occupied or took ownership of a land by force, can it never be yours?

The apathy and paralysis of the international community is not only political but also extends to the media. Mohamed Laabeid says, 'it's a media war. Without media there is nothing. When they forbid Saudi women the right to drive, it's a scandal, but when 100 women are dragged on the streets of Laayoune, nothing happens. And this hurts, it really hurts.'[16]

This feeling of abandonment pervades. Omaima says, 'We thought that with our good behaviour, that they were going to reward us with our right of self-determination. Now, we can see that we were very naïve.'[17] For almost fifty years, this community has protested and resisted the Moroccan occupation in face of persecution, torture and oppression using non-violent strategies. But, despite these efforts, little progress has been made.

Carne Ross, a diplomatic advisor, describes a conversation that he witnessed between a Saharawi representative and a South Sudanese leader of the Sudan People's Liberation Movement 'shortly before South Sudan's independence referendum'. The Saharawi representative asked: 'Why did you get your independence referendum and we didn't?' The Sudan People's Liberation Movement leader did not hesitate before replying: 'Because we told everyone, very clearly, that if we didn't get it, we would go back to war the next day'.[18]

The generational gap in the camp extends to the topic of conflict, with those who had experienced the war pushing for peaceful methods of resistance and those who grew up in the ceasefire becoming increasingly restless. But without the support of the international political or media communities, it seemed that going back to war was inevitable, if, at the very least, for the purpose of bringing the lens of the world to witness the Saharawi plight.[19]

As Omaima speaks to us from Switzerland, there comes a point in the conversation where she begins to falter. After half an hour of discussing both her personal journeys and political motivations, the conversation moves towards the recent war between Morocco and the Polisario Front. This commenced in October 2020, when Morocco invaded the demilitarised zone in response to a peaceful protest, and in so doing ended the thirty-year ceasefire. Our interview happens in April 2021, around six months after this, and the first Saharawi civilian deaths have occurred as a result of Moroccan missiles the day before we speak.

The violence on the frontlines, which runs along the 2,700 km wall separating Morocco and Western Sahara, is linked closely with the violence against Saharawi female activists. Omaima explains that the Polisario's military activity on the frontlines is being responded to by Moroccan police forces against civilians in the occupied territories. In towns across Western Sahara, women Saharawi activists have been subjected to physical, verbal and sexual violence from Moroccan forces for decades—and since the war commenced in November 2020, this violence only escalated, according to Omaima. In March 2021, Spanish Communist politician Manu Pineda asked the European Parliament:

> Over the last few weeks there has been another crackdown against activists and human rights defenders in Western Sahara ... When does the Commission intend to condemn this escalation of repression in Western Sahara?[20]

She tells us about another woman, Sultana Khaya, who lives in the town of Boujdor, and has been kept under house arrest since November 2020 because of her activism. Inside and around their home, Sultana, her sister and her eighty-three-year-old mother have been brutally beaten and had urine and other substances poured into the rooms of their house by Moroccan troops.

Photos show them looking shaken with purplish-black eyes and faces that are misshapen, swollen, bloodied and bruised.

Sultana, after having lost her first eye to Moroccan violence during a student protest many years ago, almost had permanent damage done to her other eye recently by the policemen who are guarding and imprisoning her in her own home.

'All these threats and all this repression is because of what's happening on the other side of the wall,' Omaima says.

Around this point in our conversation, Omaima stops speaking and begins to cry. Speaking about the war that is now happening, despite years of efforts on the behalf of the Polisario Front to participate in peace talks with Morocco, she says: 'There is no Plan B'. The decades of abuse and injustice, as well as the complicity and inaction of the international community, has taken its toll.

'It's a mess. It's a failure of the United Nations and of all the countries in the world. We are a beautiful people who have been pushed by the international community to take up arms again,' Omaima says, later adding: 'So it's okay to lose thousands more lives, like in Syria and Iraq, because it's just another Arab who has died.'

A year after we spoke to Maima Abdeslam and she told us 'we have paid a big price', the situation for Western Sahara worsens again. Spain, Morocco's long-term ally, in March 2022 acknowledged the plans drawn up by the Moroccan government to govern Western Sahara. This plan would enable Saharawis to have their own administration but this would exist under Moroccan sovereignty.

The Saharawi people are long overdue a reprieve from the human rights abuses that they have suffered for decades. A solution might not be clear (muddied by the long stalemate and shifting population demographics) but one thing: Saharawi women who have dedicated their lives to working towards a better future—whether by campaigning abroad, fleeing to safer places for organisation, or stubbornly staying put and building networks within Saharawi homes—are a part of the solution. The last UN-organised peace talks, which happened in 2018, led nowhere. Perhaps the outcome might have been different if one of these women had had a seat at the table.

Lubna

4

WOMEN OF SYRIA

REFUGE, RESILIENCE AND RESISTANCE

ash-shaʻb yurīd isqāṭ an-niẓām!
('the people want to bring down the regime')

In Tunisia on 17 December 2010, a street vendor called Mohamed Bouazizi set fire to himself.

He had been selling fruit and vegetable produce from a cart when the authorities began to harass him on the premise of needing a vendor's permit.[1] Bouazizi's family claim that he was slapped, spat on and had his electric scales confiscated by an officer. Interestingly, the officer who allegedly assaulted Bouazizi was a woman. Her gender played a definitive role in Bouazizi's reaction.

His sister 'acknowledged that the blow from an official, especially a woman, had undoubtedly shamed her brother'.[2, 3] However, Bouazizi also had a history of violent restrictions on his freedom to peddle, and had had his cart confiscated a number of times. He went to the governor to report this harassment and warned the governor that if he didn't see him, he would burn himself. He was refused an audience.

Bouazizi returned to the governor's office with a can of petrol and cried, 'How do you expect me to make a living?', before setting fire to himself.

Bouazizi's actions and what they represented—the struggle with poverty and employment compounded with an autocratic and corrupt regime—sparked the beginning of a series of uprisings, from protests to armed conflict, that spread through the Arab world, and became known as the Arab Spring. Citizens from many countries took to the streets and held elongated protests. These often began as peaceful protests against high levels of unemployment and corruption. In countries such as Yemen, Libya, Egypt and Syria, these protests were escalated into conflict by violent military responses from governments.

The peaceful pro-democracy protests in Syria were enflamed by an event in late February 2011, in which 'Syrian children were arrested, detained and tortured in Deraa by the Syrian regime for writing graffiti critical of President Bashar Al-Assad on city walls'.[4] Beyond sparking greater protests, this event symbolised crucially that this wasn't going to be a war that just concerned men; this was going to be a war that encompassed the whole of Syrian society, men, women and children. Women particularly have played a critical role in holding Syrian society together, both in Syria and abroad.

Celine Cantat, who holds a PhD in Refugee Studies at the Centre for Research on Migration, Refugees and Belonging, at the University of East London, was living in Syria as these demonstrations were travelling through the Arab world. As an academic who has dedicated her work to researching migration, humanitarianism and solidarity mobilisation, and who has watched the shifts in attitudes towards migrants closely from

2010, she provides a nuanced and different perspective, one that is simultaneously professional, political and personal.

When we speak to her, she is sitting in her living room in Paris. After spending years living in different unstable regions around the world and conducting work as both an academic and an activist, she has shifted her path in life somewhat. During our conversation, she shares her experiences of building a life in Syria when the country was at the cusp of the civil war. She describes living under a dictator as 'complicated', not knowing 'where the red lines were'.

> To me, the boiling over of the country was obvious. There was this moment of total opening up. Syrians spoke about it for many years. But it's ten years on now, things are so bad. It's almost painful to remember that moment.

It is an often touted line that 'rape is always a weapon of war'. Indeed, headlines surrounding the Russia-Ukraine war read 'Rape as a Weapon';[5] 'The world can't ignore Russia's use of rape as a weapon';[6] 'Russian troops "using rape as a weapon..."';[7] the list goes on. One article quotes a conversation between a Ukrainian, Antonina, and her mother after Antonina began to arm herself against rape between bombing raids.

> My mother tried to reassure me: 'This is not a war like that, they don't exist anymore, they are from old movies.' I have been a feminist for eight years, and I cried in silence, because all wars are like this.[8]

Despite this, rape was only defined as a war crime by the UN court in 1996, when charges were brought against eight Bosnian Serb officers. In fact, astonishingly, marital rape in the UK has been illegal for four years longer than rape has been considered a war crime. While other prior cases have included rape charges as a secondary offence, the Bosnian trial was the first that focused solely on sexual assault offences, marking 'organized rape and other sexual offences' as 'crimes against humanity'.[9]

In the Bosnian war, much as in the Syrian civil war and the Russia-Ukraine war, rape was used as a 'strategy to terrorize people'.[10] Rape is not a by-product of war; it is a decision. Commanders can choose 'to order, tolerate or prohibit rape'.[11]

The protests in Syria did not prevent the use of violence against children as a weapon of the Syrian regime. Indeed, the use of violence and sexual violence against children has reportedly been encouraged by Assad's government. Bassam Al Aloulou and Abdelharim Mihbat, before they deserted, used to work for Assad's regime. Al Aloulou was a prison director in Aleppo and Deraa, and Mihbat was a military intelligence officer. They both corroborated that they had been ordered by Assad's government, around spring 2011, not to differentiate between minors and adults in the prison system.

'Because they are at protests with the adults, we will treat them in the same manner.'[12]

This lack of differentiation of treatment extends to torture, according to Mihbat, and it was a calculated decision. He said, 'To say that there would be no difference in the treatment of men, women and children was a way to terrorize the population so much that they would stop protesting.'[13]

Celine tells us:

Even when the images came out of children being tortured, I wondered is this really happening, in the same territory? The escalation of violence, it's not as simple as becoming desensitised. We just don't know what to do with it. We felt the responsibility to bear witness, to watch the videos that came out.

One such video was of Hamza al-Khateeb's body. Hamza was thirteen when he attended a protest on 29 April 2011 outside Daraa. His body was returned to his family on 24 May, bearing signs of horrific torture and mutilation.[14] His body was filmed so the world could see how he died.[15]

Hamza's death signified an escalation of the uprising. On 20 April, the protests had spread to twenty cities across Syria. On 25 April, Bashar al-Assad's brother, Maher al-Assad, launched a ten-day military assault on the city of Daraa known as the Siege of Daraa. This vicious attack, against what Assad called 'extremist and terrorist groups', forced opposition supporters to take up arms in self-defence.

By 15 July 2011, the International Committee of the Red Cross declared the fighting so widespread that it should be regarded as a civil war.

At the forefront of the civil war, feeling its fullest impact and also leading the way in opposition efforts, you can find Syrian women. Celine Cantat believes that gender 'is so central, it's something that is super crucial at every level. As a Syrian, your experience as a woman was completely shaped by gender.'

Celine points out that this was changed by the uprising, where a lot of important figures leading the resistance were women. For example, she points out, the actress Fadwa Souleimane played a key role in resisting the Assad regime, and she became one of the recognisable faces of the opposition, including sharing the podium at a rally with soccer player Abdel Basset Al-Sarout and other prominent Syrians.

Her presence in the resistance was notable because Fadwa was from the Alawite community, which makes up around 10 per cent of the Syrian population and which Assad also belongs to. By adding her voice to the opposition alongside the majority Sunni population, she was showing that not all Alawites stood with Assad. Her activism carried an enormous amount of weight and power. Peter Harling, an analyst from the International Crisis Group, believed that 'sectarian violence in Homs would be worse if it weren't for Fadwa Souleimane'. She died from cancer in 2017, in exile in Paris.

But, as Celine points out, the gender inequality that existed before the war was in so many ways only amplified by the conflict. Women often relied on family structures for mobility: 'it was how you were organised by the state. Husbands go first and depending on rules around family reunification, you follow.' She talks about how humanitarian work that focuses on supporting women refugees often requires them to present themselves in a certain way:

> If you speak to [Syrian] women, they often say that with the European women NGO workers they speak to, they often try to act like them. They need to perform their womanness to be understandable. The moral economies of good and bad refugees are very gendered. Are you a good mother? A good partner? As we know from research, people instinctively understand what's expected from them to be eligible for certain things.

For Sama, the documentary made by Syrian journalist Waad al-Kateab, charts five years of the female filmmaker falling in love, making a family and living through the uprising in the Syrian city of Aleppo, one of the oldest cities in the world, which was heavily bombed during the civil war. An estimated 51,000 people were killed in the city during the government attacks.[16]

At the beginning of the documentary, which is filmed by Waad, there are photos of her at eighteen, when she started university in Aleppo. She looks very young, beautiful and confident. She describes how she was headstrong to the point of being reckless, and her parents warned her to be careful. She didn't truly understand what they meant by this until she had her own daughter.

For Sama is distinctly a woman's perspective, not because of how Waad sees the war and violence around her, but instead because of how this war shapes her experiences of motherhood and her concerns for her infant daughter's safety moving through a city under attack. The documentary cuts from Waad at university to her filming her baby daughter, who is smiling and trying to eat her own foot. In a split second you can hear a crashing, the camera begins to shake and people flood into the room. Waad yells 'someone take Sama!' as they all rush to the safety of the hospital.

This hospital too is hit; you see a flash of orange flame and the corridor is filled with smoke. Waad is rushed to a shelter with her husband and some friends. You can hear her saying to her partner, 'ever since you said they wouldn't bomb the hospital, it hasn't stopped being bombed'. She is reunited with Sama, to whom a woman is feeding milk. She seems calm, but there are tear tracks across the baby's cheeks. Sama throws her bottle on the floor, people laugh and a man says, 'Sama says, Mum, why did you give birth to me? It's been nothing but war since the day I was born!'

Waad's voice speaks over the footage, saying, 'Sama, you are the most beautiful thing in our life. But what a life I've brought you into. You didn't choose this. Will you ever forgive me?'

For Sama received more nominations than any other documentary in the history of the BAFTA awards.[17] Off the back of the documentary's success, Waad created, in exile, a campaign organisation called 'Action for Sama' to raise awareness about the state violence and call for those in power to push back against Assad's regime and for accountability of the war crimes he has committed. She said in an interview with Info Migrants:

> Many people came to me crying and said they are so sorry that they let that happen... It shows you how many people care. But on the level of decision makers... We have tried so hard to push for action, do something, to make sure these things don't continue to happen... If you are in a position where you can change something, I don't want your tears, I want you to do something. You can make a difference.[18]

'Action for Sama' became somewhat of a celebrity cause outside of Syria. Waad, who had fled to the UK, was interviewed in a podcast by Carey Mulligan. She and her husband are featured in a promotional Choose Love video alongside celebrities Harry Styles, Michael Palin, Dua Lipa, Olivia Coleman and Rupert Grint, among others. There is a photo of Waad alongside her husband and filmmaker Edward Watts holding up signs at the BAFTAs that read 'STOP BOMBING HOSPITALS'. Her voice has been consistently loud and—strangely for a woman forced far from her home from a war-torn place—quite consistently heard.

The silencing of women who have lived through and fled wars is and has always been egregious—but most particularly for women from ethnic minorities. In a UNHCR video from March 2022, Australian actress Cate Blanchett addresses the gendered violence migrant women experience. In the video, Cate says:

> Wherever they are in the world, from Ukraine to Syria, from Iraq to Afghanistan, women fleeing conflict are at far greater risk of experiencing violence or abuse. The truth is that forced displacement is a root cause of gender inequality and gender inequality is a root cause of forced displacement. All refugees and displaced women deserve equal opportunity and equal treatment.[19]

A lot is being said between the lines in this video. When Cate states that all women refugees deserve equal treatment, there is an implicit acknowledgement that this is not currently the state of affairs. Since the war in Ukraine, many news reporters, presenters and prominent officials have been called out for their racist commentary. In an interview with the BBC, Ukraine's former deputy general prosecutor David Sakvarelidze stated, 'It is really emotional for me because I see European people with blue eyes and blond hair being killed, children being killed every day with Putin's missiles'.[20]

Many people in Europe have commented that the war in Ukraine has impacted them emotionally because it's 'so much closer to home'. The implication here is that the conflicts that aren't happening on our doorstep are not our responsibility and do not elicit the same emotional response. This makes a farce of the so-called international 'community' and the international bodies governing it.

Waad al-Kateab transcended these boundaries of caring that have been so starkly revealed in the past few months—a Syrian woman speaking about a conflict that was forgotten then and is forgotten now. She utilised the universal aspects of humanity to make powerful people care about something very specific. She may have fled Syria, but she made a powerful impact as a refugee; she made watchers care about her, her child and her mother country.

Even once they have left Syria, Syrian women often continue to be limited by their gender, and by the way their gender and nationality is seen by the world. Syrian women have been particularly affected in their journeys as refugees, and the ways they have fought to overcome those challenges, finding ways to define and protect themselves and fighting to overcome challenges, even as their homes and their world as they know it disintegrates.

We will also learn how difficult and constrained life was for many women in Syria even before the war, and how the war has exacerbated and exposed some of these challenges. First we speak with Lubna, a women's rights organiser who has continued her work amid the physical and social disruption wrought by the war; then, we meet Guli—who fled Syria partly because of ethnic boundaries between Arabs and Kurds—and Najat, both of whom found that their time in refugee camps was profoundly shaped by their experiences as women.

'One moment I had ownership of my life, then I had no control'

It's 2018 and we're on the phone with Lubna Alkanawati, country director for Syrian civil rights organisation Women Now For Development. In between conversations about the suppression of women's rights and the devastating conflict that had ravaged much of Syria, Lubna is moving around her home, making the distinct noises of someone tidying and sorting their house while the children are at school.

She is living in Turkey, where she was forced to move when her home of Eastern Ghouta in Syria came under siege by President Bashar Al-Assad's regime in 2013. She transformed from school teacher and women's centre manager to refugee, the subject of her activism and her own life blurring into one. Despite these difficulties, she continued her work and became the country manager of Turkey for Women Now, helping with Syrian women's self-empowerment and improvement from a distance.

When we catch up with Lubna four years later, she is again multitasking—halfway through the interview her phone rings and she has to drop off briefly to take another phone call. But this time she is speaking to us from France, where she was forced to relocate recently because she and her family were not safe in Turkey. In January 2022, a nineteen-year-old Syrian man called Nail al-Naif was sleeping in his room in Istanbul when a group of men broke in and stabbed him in the chest. He died later that night.

This followed months of escalating violence and hatred perpetrated against some of the three million Syrian refugees living in Turkey, including an eighteen-year-old Syrian man being stabbed as he walked through a park and several young Syrian construction workers dying after a Turkish man set them on fire.[21] Lubna tells us:

The situation in Turkey became very critical and unstable for Syrians and for human rights. It's hard because you feel like you are comfortable somewhere, and then you figure out that it's not safe and you have to start all over again. The French laws are very strict and they're not flexible for activists. The procedures that refugees have to go through here...

When the French authorities finally found a home for Lubna, her child and her ex-husband, it was very difficult for them to live in. Lubna tells us that she is calling from a friend's house in France, where they are temporarily staying because she, her ex-husband and her five-year-old son were provided with only a room to live in, which didn't have Wi-Fi so she couldn't conduct work meetings. 'It was very small for three people, it's not a proper place to raise a child.'

Commenting on the procedures of the French government, she says that 'they don't really care about what you are doing, they deal with you in a very basic way. One moment I had ownership of my life, then I had no control.'

Lubna has had to battle for control over her own life for a long time now. When we spoke to her in 2018, she described the success of Women Now. They had created several community centres across Syria in the cities of Idlib and in Eastern Ghouta, and one in neighbouring Lebanon. The services provided in these centres were so popular that there were waiting lists for the literacy courses and other training courses and projects. Setting up these women's centres took much perseverance in the face of constant questioning.

This would usually come from military groups, who would ask them, 'What are you doing here? Why are you opening a centre?' because there was no such pre-existing place. Outside of the safe spaces of the centre, Syrian women were facing unprecedented challenges. Lubna told us that 'women's rights have vanished from the area. They already didn't exist, but it is very serious that women don't have space to talk to each other, or to think about their futures.'[22] These obstacles existed because of the negative attitudes towards women's rights in the area, but they would be quickly overshadowed by the impending destruction that would be caused by the continuation of the conflict.

A lot changed in the few years between our two conversations, and Women Now very nearly ceased to exist because of the forced displacements that the women faced, Lubna tells us. When Eastern Ghouta fell to the regime in 2018—putting Assad in the most secure position he had been since the start of the then seven-year conflict[23]—the community centres fell within the city as the women who worked to provide the services in the centres were themselves displaced. 'Our team had to spread all over the world,' Lubna says. 'After this, we faced more displacement in Idlib too after the offensive committed by the Syrian regime and the Russians. We lost our centre in Idlib in 2019.'

The combined impact of the war, with the international community moving on and taking its funding too, meant that Women Now floundered. However, after five months of struggle, they reopened their centres in January 2020. When they reopened, the Women Now team ensured that they worked to support each other in their recoveries after going through so much as well as working to support other Syrian women through their projects. 'We delivered services to other women but we ourselves were inside this chaos. We are activists and we need help and support for that,' she tells us.

A crucial part of that recovery included expanding their focus to finding justice for women, specifically focusing on raising awareness about gender-based violence and sexual violence. She and her colleagues worked to raise awareness about a variety of largely ignored human rights abuses, including women who were being sexually assaulted in Assad's prisons, the prevalence of child marriage in Syria and the thousands of Syrian women who have been forcibly displaced inside the country since 2014.[24] 'You can't talk about peace and justice without including women,' says Lubna.

On top of the impact of the war and the displacement of staff, the coronavirus pandemic created further physical restrictions. Their centres were closed for three months, during which time all of their courses and services were moved online. However, for many women this meant they could no longer continue their studies.

'We lost access to specific groups. We lost access to helping Syrian girls because they would come to the centre with their mothers but they don't have access to smartphones or direct access to internet,' Lubna explains. But as with all the challenges that came before the pandemic, the women of Women Now managed to adapt and create positive change from this.

They eventually developed a mixture of in-person and online training, which meant that women and girls who didn't have internet could still go to the centres, but women who couldn't access the centres because they lived far away or in villages where they weren't allowed to freely move could use the online services. 'A lot of women aren't allowed to use transportation, so now we can reach them. Everything has a good and a bad side. It's not causing any harm doing [some work online] and now we're getting the maximum benefit.'

By the time we speak to Lubna in the autumn of 2021, the number of women using their services in person has dropped to between a third and one half of their usual intake. But, she adds, the economic difficulties created by the pandemic for many families also means that it's better for many women to be able to access as much support from their own homes.

The list of initiatives Lubna and her team are developing is endless, and they only continue to move forward, reaching more women in more crucial ways as the years pass despite the continuing disruptions and difficulties in their own lives. As the Syrian war has continued for so many years, many activists, NGOs and support organisations have left the country or turned their attention to other crises in the world. But Lubna continues to fight for the rights of her fellow Syrians, no matter what the cost. And this cost cannot be underestimated.

Finding herself living in a too-small and disconnected house in France, between raising her son and her advocacy work at Women Now, Lubna tells us that:

> It's exhausting to balance activism with motherhood. We're currently having a workshop about feminist economics and one of the topics is about motherhood and work. It's about how it's double the work without getting paid for the first one. It's exhausting and it sucks all your stamina. I'm working all the time, from 6am to 8 or 9pm and then I just sleep or do nothing.

Lubna's relocation to France makes it even harder to cope with her work and parenthood. She finds herself without the tools she needs 'to comfort myself or to support myself and my family. But I'm figuring out how to manage this.'

Doubtless, she will figure out how to thrive in France in the same way she has figured out how to cope with every stage of displacement she has lived through so far. Regardless of where Lubna ends up, she will continue to make it impossible for the international community to completely forget the women of Syria as they fight for their rights to justice, equality and freedom, under and apart from Assad's regime.

***

Both Najat and Guli migrated to the UK via the Syrian Vulnerable Persons Resettlement Scheme. This programme began in 2014 and ended in 2021, and around 20,000 people were resettled within this time period.[25] It aimed to help vulnerable people, such as those with medical conditions, those who were survivors of torture, those at risk due to their sexuality or gender identity, as well as women and children. It was the largest formal resettlement scheme the UK had undertaken in modern times, and it also was one of the only safe and legal routes to the UK for Syrians fleeing the war. But to give context to this figure of 20,000, just one camp of Syrian refugees in Jordan currently numbers over 78,000.[26]

The UK has yet to announce any further plans for helping Syrian refugees currently in camps, but they have announced a 2022 Afghan Citizens Resettlement Scheme, modelled on the Syrian scheme, opened to resettle Afghan refugees, where another 20,000 refugees are to be resettled.

However, this scheme has been critiqued due to the way it presents the language of resettlement and evacuation. 'Evacuation' refers to the removal of people directly from the country, whereas 'resettlement' requires the person to have crossed the border of the country they are fleeing, which is what the UK is currently doing.[27] While there are many dispersed peoples in Afghanistan—around 300,000 newly displaced in August 2021, bringing the current total to 3.5 million[28]—far fewer have crossed borders into neighbouring countries, rendering the UK scheme somewhat unhelpful.

The response of the British public to the Afghan refugees has also been noted in comparison with the response to the Ukrainian refugees. The Homes for Ukraine scheme, a programme in which Ukrainian refugees can be sponsored by members of the British public, was met by overwhelming support. More than 150,000 homes were offered to Ukrainians in the month following Russia's February 2022 invasion in comparison with the 1,822 rooms offered to Afghans in the month after the fall of Kabul, August 2021, only a couple of months before.[29] At the time the Homes for Ukraine scheme was launched, more than 12,000 Afghan refugees were yet to be housed, and were still in hotels across the country, unable to fully begin living their new lives in British society.[30]

This prioritisation can be seen also in Germany, where Afghan refugees are being 'evicted' from their homes to be replaced by Ukrainian refugees. Ukrainians are also offered a 'quick residence permit valid for up to three years, thanks to the previously unused paragraph 24 of the German residence act', unlike Syrian refugees, who had to apply for asylum.[31]

Further evidence of clear legal discrimination is that, unlike asylum seekers in the UK and unlike the Syrians and Afghans in Germany, Ukrainian refugees in Germany have freedom of movement and residence, despite Ukraine not being in the EU. This is compounded with the actions on Ukrainian borders, where the UN admits discrimination against non-European refugees, which followed accounts of Black, south Asian and Mediterranean refugees being 'blocked at borders... while white Ukrainians have been prioritised'.[32]

It is difficult to write this without sounding resentful. The changing of attitudes towards refugees, no longer being seen as a 'crisis', is something to be celebrated, and the plight of Ukrainian refugees must be empathised with. However, it has to be asked whether this change in attitude has something to do with skin colour or refugees' 'European-ness'. These factors themselves seem a version of border control as much as policy or physical borders. These are borders of racism, at the Ukrainian border and internally, in the housing available to Afghan refugees.

People who qualified for the UK's Syrian resettlement scheme were identified by the UN, screened by the Home Office (including a full medical screening) before being resettled all over the UK. This is known as the UK's dispersal policy, where asylum seekers and refugees are placed in locations across the country, so that 'no one area would be overburdened by the obligation of supporting asylum seekers'.[33] Generally, this policy prefers a ratio of one refugee or asylum seeker to 200 residents.[34]

However, the dispersal of refugees and asylum seekers has many flaws, including isolating people from existing social networks, particularly in remote and rural areas. This in turn can lead to prejudice and racial harassment. Human geography professor Jonathan Darling, in his book on dispersal and asylum, suggests that 'Dispersal represents a form of *distributed violence*', positioning 'asylum seekers and refugees within hierarchies of worth and location that sustain inequality and produce harm'.[35]

Reports suggest that, because local authorities have to agree to participate in the scheme, it is most often Labour-led councils that are participating. This means that asylum seekers are predominantly being sent to the very poorest areas of the UK, putting strain on the health care and education systems.[36] This policy has encountered problems with Afghan refugees in Dorset, where some of those offered asylum accommodation other than hotels have refused, instead holding out for accommodation in places like London, where they have family.

Guli and her family came to the UK five years ago from a camp in Iraq as part of the Syrian resettlement scheme, having been identified for resettlement by the UN. Guli and her family are Kurdish.

There is a huge amount of discrimination against Kurdish people in Syria. Growing up, Guli says that she 'had to speak Arabic at school, by government mandate'. She was allowed to speak Kurdish at home and with her friends, but not at school. From 1963 to 2014, teaching Kurdish in Syrian schools was banned, with teachers at risk of arrest.[37] Similar bans on Kurdish language and culture were extended throughout Turkey.[38]

Around the same time, in 1963, a population census was conducted by the Syrian government, the result of which stripped as many as 300,000 Kurds of their citizenship.[39] Guli tells us that 'they were considered immigrants in these countries'. Their new classification as 'foreigners' or 'unregistered' dispossessed many of their land and prevented many from getting jobs or education, and from participating in politics.

Guli believes that the discrimination against Kurdish people has spread to all areas of life. She gives the example of jobs, saying they 'always prefer the Arab person to the Kurdish person', even if the Kurdish person is more qualified. Kurdish people were not allowed to wear traditional Kurdish dress or to celebrate Kurdish festivals. Guli mentions Newroz—a celebration of the new year around the Spring Equinox—that was banned by the Syrian government in 1986 after Kurds in Kurdish dress gathered to celebrate it. Guli tells us that the festival, because of its proximity to mother's day, was replaced by a celebration of mothers. These slow erasures are designed to eat away at Kurdish culture and identity.

Najat says that the Kurds and Syrians don't mix together socially, still to this day. Guli says 'it's very very difficult for Kurdish in Syria. They don't like Kurdish there'. Guli tells us that this is because Kurdistan was an undivided cultural and linguistic territory that was then divided because of French and British occupation. When Guli tells us this, both her and our translator, Mona, laugh, rolling their eyes.

Historically, Greater Syria included parts of Turkey, Lebanon, Israel/Palestine and Jordan. The Great War from 1914 to 1918 brought British and French forces to Greater Syria, and during this conflict, the British and French met secretly to form an agreement called the Sykes–Picot Agreement.

This self-serving plan established French and British post-war control over the area, dividing the area without any consideration for pre-existing borders or cultural ties; Kurdistan, the land of the Kurds, was divided into four countries. The subsequent

Treaties of Sèvres (1920) and Lausanne (1924) divided Kurdistan between the new republic of Turkey, the new British protectorate of Iraq, and the new French protectorate of Syria, eliminating any chance at self-determination.

Guli mentions an incident at Qamishli that reveals the extent of conflict between Arab Syrians and Kurdish people. A football match descended into violence as Arab Syrians taunted Kurdish fans with pictures of Saddam Hussein (who ordered the Anfal genocide of Iraqi Kurds[40]), and both sides began to throw stones. Long-held grievances escalated the clash, and security forces intervened, with lethal action: thirty-six people (mostly Kurds) were killed, many more were injured and thousands of Kurds fled to Iraq.[41]

Guli believes that the discrimination against Kurdish people, and the way they were made to feel like they didn't belong to Syria, hugely impacted their actions in the war. Guli tells us that the 'Kurdish people didn't want to join any protests. Syrian and Iraqi people were for and against Assad and Saddam Hussein. But the Kurdish people decided to remain impartial, to not interfere.'

Indeed, it is suggested that 'Syria's Kurds, who want the right of self-government but have not fought Mr Assad's forces, have added another dimension to the conflict'.[42] Since 2003, Syrian Kurds in the north of the country have been represented by a force known as the Democratic Union Party, who say their main aim is 'regional autonomy within a decentralised Syria, not independence'.[43] Their commander suggested in 2017, amid the fight against ISIS, that 'it would have no problem with the Assad government if Kurdish rights are guaranteed in Syria'.[44] Between 30 and 40 per cent of the fighters in this force are women.[45]

Guli grew up on a farm twelve hours away from Damascus with her seven sisters and one brother. She describes the houses there as made from 'mud from the river and cow dung. They make very good houses. Better than bricks and mortar. They keep the heat out.' Guli went to school from when she was six until she was about twelve, when she began to work on other people's farms. She did this for about ten years before she met her husband, Shiar.

Shiar's sister and one of Guli's sisters were neighbours. Guli giggles girlishly when she tells us this. After she got married, Guli stopped working to raise her children. She now has four children: two girls and two boys.

When the conflict in Syria began, Guli and Shiar lived in Damascus. She describes the city during the war, saying, 'There were bombs everywhere, bombing everywhere'. When the violence became too much, they moved back to the village where Guli grew up. From there, they decided to travel to Iraq.

Guli tells us that the discrimination against Kurdish people was actually a massive factor in her family leaving Syria, as well as the war. She says, 'the government wanted to get rid of the Kurdish people, they were glad to get rid of the Kurdish people' because of the conflicts between Syrian people and Kurdish people, like at the 2004 football match. She says that although they were born in Syria, 'we feel deep down as though we were Kurdish people, not Arab. It was easier for us to leave and go somewhere else because this is what the government wanted. They encouraged us to leave.'

They left around two years after people first began fleeing from Syria. 'So,' Guli says, 'it was more organised than when people first began fleeing. There were documents you had to provide, and checkpoints.' Despite being so close to Iraq, 'it took a whole day,' Guli tells us, 'from 8 in the morning to 8.30 at night. The children were so cold and starved'—just to get to a boat that would take them to the other side of the River Tigris. 'The boat journey only took twenty minutes. It was a safe journey. Nobody died.'

Guli and her family spent three years in camps in Iraq. Guli, who is friends with another of our interviewees, Najat, and has discussed her journey with Najat, says that when she got to the camps, around 2014, they were better than when Najat and her family were there, at the beginning of the war. She says, 'after two years of the war, things were a lot more organised than when Najat and Mustafa went. The camp used to be a fire hazard, but by [the time we arrived] they had built purposeful camps.'

The UN provided them with food every month, such as sugar, pasta and pulses, and they would use their ration books, which would get stamped. As it was more organised, there were shops inside the camps, so they could supplement their food supplies. Guli says that 'we brought money with us to buy food'. There was electricity available, although it was more cut off than on. There were also public toilets and kitchens that they could use, but they went back to their tents every night.

Although the fire risks were lower than when Najat was in the camps, Guli says that 'the tent was always a hazard with electric wiring for the children to touch or cause fire. A lot of people liked smoking a lot. And if anyone threw their cigarettes, within minutes this would cause a massive blaze.' Guli tells me that the tents were treated to make them waterproof to prevent the rain coming through. However, this treatment was highly flammable, making the risk of fires very dangerous as they spread so easily.

Fires are a very real concern for refugees in camps across the world. Around six million refugees, 22 per cent of the world's population of refugees, are living in camps.[46] The Anadolu suggests that:

> The fire in Bosnia's Lipa camp destroyed the lives of nearly 1,400 people in December 2020. In September 2020, the shelters of 12,000 refugees became unusable after the fire in the Moria

camp on the Greek island of Lesbos, which is known as the largest camp in Europe.

The fire that broke out in March 2021 in the Cox's Bazar refugee camp in Bangladesh, where Rohingya refugees fleeing the Myanmar regime took shelter, left 45,000 people homeless and 11 people dead. It was one of 84 fires in the first quarter of 2021.[47]

These are the result of overcrowding, materials used for building, poor wiring, open fires for cooking, candles for lighting as well as arson and carelessness. There were other risks; Najat was very worried about scorpions when she lived in the camps, while Guli was worried about foxes.

This life would be stressful and perilous for anyone, but it is particularly challenging for refugees caring for small children—the majority of whom are women, as couples are often separated in times of upheaval due to death and injury but also because men will often stay behind to fight or travel ahead to earn money in a new country. The Zaatari refugee camp in Jordan is home to 78,169 Syrian refugees, of which nearly 55 per cent are children and nearly 20 per cent are under five years old; 30 per cent of households are female-headed.[48] Women and children comprise more than two thirds of those displaced by the Syrian conflict.[49]

Guli says that 'the tents were very tiny'. They had a small tent for six people: her, Shiar, an uncle and aunt and two of her children. (Her other two children were born in the UK.) Guli brought some curtains from around the camp, quite thick ones. They used them as a barrier between themselves and the ground. At the beginning, the only blankets they had, they decided to put underneath them because the weather was okay at the time. Later, as more donations came, they were given other blankets.

Guli says that it was either 'too hot inside the camp or too cold in the winter'. Guli laughs as she tells me about when it was scalding weather in the camp. She says that they would go 'outside the camp and get water and pour it over them and the children'.

After three years in the camps, they were selected by the UN for the initial screenings that would bring them to the UK. 'How did they make that decision?' the translator, Mona, asks incredulously. If there are 5.6 million displaced Syrian refugees outside Syria and the UK accepted 20,000 refugees through their scheme, only around 0.3 per cent will have been accepted. Guli tells Mona that her 'husband has disabilities because of his ears and his back', and the UN were choosing people who were vulnerable, as well as those with young families. It took around four months of meetings and screenings, including a medical examination, for Guli and Shiar to come to England. The flight took two days, with three stopovers.

Guli and Shiar and their family have been in England for nearly five years now. Guli tells us that, while they have taken a while to find their feet, moving between a few houses, they have had some great support from groups that help with everything, such as doctors and schools.

Guli and her family's ability to adapt is remarkable, but perhaps leaving Syria itself was inevitable. In many ways, it seems that Guli and her family made the decision to move primarily based on their outsider-status as Kurdish people in Syria, with the war precipitating the speed with which this happened. The manner in which they were excluded from society in Syria might explain the way Guli has managed to find ways to belong in the UK, building a strong support system of women to support her and her family. Motherhood is central to Guli's story, and her thriving children are testament to Guli's love and courage as she guided them through life, from refugee camps to the small streets of Dorset.

***

Najat is a fiercely welcoming, strong-willed, tiny Syrian woman, around whom the whirlpool of her family eddies. We met because of Najat's passion for learning. She has two young boys and is determined that they will succeed; Alex B tutors them. Najat firmly believes that education will provide a path for a good life. This belief system was inherited from Najat's father. He believed that women should be educated and ensured that Najat received her higher education. Najat has six siblings, and all of them finished university.

Najat lived in Aleppo but spent all her weekends on her grandfather's farm in Idlib. She tells us that for weekends and holidays, they would go to the farm, but that Aleppo is better for schools and universities. It has a lot more opportunities to offer than the countryside, but she says she knows everything about the countryside. She says that Syria is a beautiful country. All the seasons are special to Syrian people; it is very hot in summer and very cold in winter.

In Syria, Najat taught in schools before the war, in the countryside and later Aleppo. She tells us that 'everything was good in Syria' before the war. Najat was known for her teaching because of the way she would adjust her teaching style for Kurdish pupils. Not only was the Kurdish language forbidden from being taught, it was also forbidden to teach in Kurdish, or for students to talk to each other in Kurdish.[50] However, many Kurdish people didn't speak Arabic. When they went to school, they were severely limited by the language barrier.

Najat would begin by teaching her Kurdish students Arabic by using pictures. She points out that these pupils would otherwise have fallen behind, not because they weren't clever but because they simply didn't speak the language. This has a massive impact on the education of Kurdish people. For the first two years of school, many Kurdish children don't understand the lessons in Arabic.

Najat is an Arab Syrian who was living in the Kurdish quarters of Aleppo. She would often take on Kurdish students after school who couldn't afford to pay in money but would find ways to pay in kind. One day when she was meeting the mother of some children that she taught, there was a man in the house watching football. This was Mustafa. He didn't come up and say hello after Najat said 'Hi'. He just watched football, and Najat tells us pointedly that she hates football.

A couple days later, Najat's neighbour told her that Mustafa would like to marry her. They hadn't spoken a word to each other. Najat replied, 'No thank you', because he hadn't spoken to her and because he was a Kurd. Najat says she knew the rules between Kurds and Arabs.

Najat next met Mustafa at a festival for Kurdish New Year, where he was singing. Najat told her friends, 'I don't like this man but I like his singing'. Mustafa, however, told everyone at the party that he loved Najat. After that, Najat's colleague invited Najat for coffee in the park. Her colleague said she had to go to the toilet. When she left, Mustafa appeared. They spoke. Najat said that she knows people, and she saw that Mustafa was honest and 'spoke the truth'. They became friends for a couple of months.

Mustafa won Najat's heart through a series of good deeds, helping Najat's friends to get a taxi and singing to them. All of her friends told her that he was a good man. One day, Najat was locked out of her school because she had left her key at home. She went home to get a key, but she knew that her sister, who was a doctor, was asleep inside. If she woke her sister up, it would cause an argument.

Mustafa climbed up onto the balcony, which was very high, and broke in through the doors to get her key. While Najat was teaching, he spent all the money he had on a lock to fix the doors. Najat's neighbour told her that Mustafa would sleep hungry that night because he had spent all his money on the lock. So the neighbour and Najat cooked a meal for Mustafa. A few months later, Najat says, 'we were in love'.

Najat's family had a very strong prejudice against the Kurds, as many Syrians do, believing that Kurds were like their impression of the decadent West: drinking alcohol, not respecting women, living without rules. They believed the Arabs and Kurds could work together and study together, but they could not marry each other.

Eventually, Najat's family began to accept Mustafa, including Najat's brother, who, it turned out, was best friends with Mustafa's brother. Still, Najat's father said no. For five years, many men asked Najat to marry them and still she said no. Mustafa was asked by his family every olive harvest to marry, and he also said no.

Najat helped Mustafa to set up his own shop with her savings from teaching, allowing Mustafa and Najat to gain some independence from their families. After one year, Mustafa earned enough to pay Najat back, but Najat invested it back into the shop. The shop was successful and Mustafa gave his mother money to buy two sheep and two goats for their farm. This financial independence was part of convincing Najat's father that their marriage could work. Mustafa's brother told Najat's father that 'from my heart I love your daughter because she makes my brother a good man'. Najat's father asked that they spend two months with him in the village to show that they are still good Muslims, praying and obeying the rules. After that, Najat's family finally consented.

She married Mustafa when she was thirty-six, which is seen as quite late for Syrians. Najat and Mustafa had a big big party, because all their friends were so happy that their love had been successful. They celebrated until three in the morning, dancing, laughing and being happy.

They lived in a house in Aleppo. She describes her house as the same as all the houses in the city, with three rooms. In Syria, nearest the door is a living room for visitors. Najat emphasises this because of the importance of visitors, friends and welcoming to her life.

The boys were born almost as the war began. They were born in quick succession, first Mohammed and then Ismail. When Ismail was born, they moved to Mustafa's house in the countryside, because Aleppo was too dangerous. However, the area in which Mustafa lived was recruiting a Kurdish militia. This was very dangerous for Mustafa, because he has very poor eyesight. Najat had also had a big operation and had two very young children and needed help. Mustafa's mother told the militia that they can take all her children but not Mustafa. She would go instead of Mustafa if they insisted.

Najat and Mustafa fled to Najat's family farm in Idlib, where they stayed for one month. Najat was told that Mustafa might be targeted, perhaps by Arab neighbours in this area because of fighting between Syrians and Kurds. Najat's father gave her some money for them to flee to Iraq. They went to Aleppo, where they spent two nights.

It was dangerous again in Aleppo and, on the advice of a friend, Najat and her family stayed in a house underground for a whole night because of bombs being dropped. After that, they decided to leave for Iraqi Kurdistan. They thought they might only stay there for a little bit, to see what happened, and then they would go back to Idlib.

They went to Iraq by bus and by foot. Najat tells us that:

> If it was dangerous and there were bombs, the driver said it's too dangerous to drive, you needed to walk. And then we would take another bus.

Najat and the children stayed the night in the hotel, but they were woken at around four in the morning. A man told Najat that, 'some people are coming, you need to all empty this place'. Najat said that, 'All the women went onto one bus and all the men stayed for one hour more. But I was afraid that it was dangerous for my husband and I was afraid for my two children.' Fortunately, nobody was captured and the family was able to reunite and complete their flight.

It took two days and around eight separate buses. Najat's boys were very young, two and three years old. When they arrived at a hotel, Najat asked for some milk and the man replied that, in Syria, there was no milk for children now. Najat made tea and soaked bread in it for the children to eat.

When Najat and her family arrived in Iraq, in March 2012, they stayed in a hotel using the money her father had given them. After eighteen days, the money ran out and they prepared to head back to Syria, but the UN stopped them, saying it was too dangerous, and instead took them to the camps.

Najat and her family were only planning on staying in Iraq for a month or so. They ended up staying in camps for nearly five years. Najat says that the camps were like a desert with tents and insects. As we heard from Guli, Najat and her family were amongst the first refugees at these camps, which meant that for the first two months, the water was bad and there was no electricity.

Najat said that she was afraid all the time because it was dangerous. She heard stories about people taking other people, taking women from the camps. It is difficult to find figures to corroborate the levels of abduction, as it is a necessarily underground practice and indeed, many statistics that do abound are based on assumptions and 'extreme gymnastics'.[51]

Female refugees, particularly, face not only the risk of abduction but, more prevalently, the threat of sexual and physical violence. Caritas Lebanon report that 'More than 50% of women seeking aid from Caritas Lebanon have told social workers they have been sexually abused [as refugees].'[52] Furthermore, according to refugees in Jordan, young boys are being targeted in refugee camps for sexual violence, because their 'virginity is not an issue, and because boys' movement are not as restricted as girls'.[53]

Najat told us that, when she first came to the camps, she cried every day. She says it was like 'in the past, when people lived in caves. In Aleppo, everything is done by machines and with electricity.'

After one week, she realised she needed to wash her children's clothes. She brought water to her tent but didn't know how to wash clothes by hand. An old lady in a nearby tent saw Najat crying over the washing that she couldn't get right. She asked Najat if this was the first time she had washed clothes by hand, and Najat told her yes. The lady told Najat that she could teach her how. She went on to teach Najat everything—cooking, washing.

Najat told us about a tree that she planted near her cleaning water. It grew large quickly, and children would play in its shade. This simple action, of planting the tree that grew out of Najat's domestic actions, seemed so symbolic. The tree's growth represented the time that Najat and her family had spent in the camp, but it simultaneously gave back to those children. Najat's son, Ismail, remembers this tree.

After two months, Najat was told that there was some kind of police system set up, and the camps were safer. She said that, more than this, they got to know everyone in the tents around them, which made them feel much safer and more confident. This community was a huge support system for Najat.

A man from the UN asked Najat if she could help him provide services to other refugees. The older lady told Najat that she could look after her children while she went to help this man, making sure people knew where to find water, milk for children and so on. He spoke Arabic, but with a different accent. He knew that Najat was a teacher, and he asked if she could help him. She worked with him for one year as a volunteer, and the second year, she was paid to help.

Najat never forgot this man. All her life, Najat had spent her life in school, with children and with books. She felt like she didn't know anything about life with adults, how you can speak with people, how you can help them. This man taught Najat everything about life in a community, about how you can be kind and, Najat uses the word, 'gentlemanly'.

The man left the camp after two years, moving to another camp. After two years of working, the camp was built and functioning, with food, water and electricity. Najat said, 'everything was okay'. The man told Najat that he was worried about her. Najat felt that she needed to go back to Syria to find her family. The war hadn't gone away, and she said that 'if my family is die, I am die. No need to stay here'. She also told the man that it would be difficult for her to stay in the camps with no work once he had left.

The man spoke with a friend of his to get a job for Najat. They worked building a market outside the refugee camp. She told us that she worked with people, helping to build, to clean, to farm—everything. In order to get the market ready, she sometimes worked for twenty-four hours, with the same salary. 'This was not good,' she said, but they were working for money and for their children.

The work became easier after the market opened around 2014. Najat was working in the office on the first floor above the shops. There were companies from all over the world in this office. Najat worked as a receptionist to bring people in, make them comfortable, make sure they had water and cakes.

Najat spent two years doing this and she said it was easier, working from 9 to 4. It took an hour to get there, but because the bus stopped at many villages, she had to leave at 6am, getting back at 6pm. This was hard. She could only spend time with her children on the weekends during the winter, because they were asleep when she left and when she came back.

She was always worried about her children. She tells a story about once when Ismail was playing with what looked to be a worm that he found in the sand. One of Najat's neighbours noticed and cried out because it wasn't a worm. It was a dangerous snake. Najat thanked her god that this didn't lead to more serious consequences. The camps were dangerous for children.

After two years in the camp, they made a school for the children. A doctor from France whose daughter died made a place for the children to play from her own salary. The doctor said that now all the children in the camp were her children. Many of the workers in the camp and at this school spoke Kurdish. The children picked up the language quickly.

Najat's work with the UN in her first two years in the camps meant that she was able to apply more easily to come to not only the UK but many countries. The man doing the applications said that their chances of getting accepted were four million to one. Najat said however that she needed to go back to Syria. She didn't want to plan to go elsewhere because she wanted to get back to her family and her job.

After four years in the camps, the UN told her about the resettlement program for coming to the UK. Najat and her family agreed.

After around three months, the details were sorted. They were booked into a hotel for three days, and after that they headed to the airport. They had a stopover in Germany before they arrived in Bristol in June 2017. They were met by someone from the Home Office, who picked them up and took them to Dorset.

When Najat was in the car, she was upset because she only saw 'jungles' and no houses from Bristol to Dorset. However, when she arrived in her town and saw buildings, she realised that it was the same as Aleppo. The streets and shopping were the same, the museums. She said that 'people were nice and friendly'.

Najat's now been here for five years and she can't believe how quickly the time has gone. She says it's 'like a dream'. She's learned how to cook with English food during coronavirus, mentioning jacket potatoes, chicken soup and fish and chips. She says that people have been very kind to the children; in the camps it was different, without rules for the children. Najat has built a community in England, just as she did in Syria and later in the camps—one with women at its centre.

Najat has made lots of friends in England. She was alone at first in the UK, but she has got to know many other Syrian families in Dorset. During coronavirus, Najat talked with a group of Syrian women on the phone every night after the children were asleep, discussing being in England, the language, cooking and Syria, among other subjects.

Najat says that she got very frustrated while learning English, but again she found help in the company of a woman. Alex B's mother was her first English teacher. Najat says that she was always smiling and understood Najat's frustration. She listened and made Najat feel more confident with English. She says that if a teacher is friendly, it helps you to like a language.

Before she came to England, she was told that England is a difficult country for Muslims, because everyone drinks wine and takes drugs. She was told that 'no one will speak to you and you will be isolated'. She thought this would be hard for the children, but she saw this was different when she came here. She says that she loves the rules, with no one breaking the law. 'People are very kind here'. She said that in Syria, 'some people look like Muslims but are not Muslims inside'. She says that here, 'people are not Muslims, but inside, they look like Muslims'.

We spoke with a Syrian man who has been integral to aiding the resettlement process in Dorset, helping translate and providing housing and furniture. He talked about the tenets of Islam, saying that the beliefs are of kindness and giving. He asks that we judge the concept of Islam rather than the people. In this, he tells us volumes about the Islamophobia in the West, that people judge Muslims by the extremists and their actions. Instead, he would rather we look to the core of Islam and see people like Najat who believe in kindness and giving.

Najat says she wants to be able to give back to the people in England who have been so kind to her. We told her that she doesn't owe anyone anything. But Najat replies, 'I want to say thank you'.

Ranjan

5

THE MARRIAGE CONTRACT

FREEDOM BOUND

For many women, marriage has led to certain freedoms—increased finances, leaving a difficult family, an increased opportunity to make their own decisions—but for many more, it has only limited their freedom. In 1871, Mary Ann Evans, under the pen name George Eliot, wrote, in a novel about a small English town—most likely with a touch of irony—'a woman dictates before marriage in order that she may have an appetite for submission afterwards'. Some 146 years later, author Min Jin Lee writes, in her novel *Pachinko*, about an intergenerational Korean family set in twentieth-century Japan, 'for a woman, the man you marry will determine the quality of your life completely. A good man is a decent life, and a bad man is a cursed life—but no matter what, always expect suffering, and just keep working hard.'

Both women were writing about normative heterosexual marriages across centuries and the world. Despite these contrasting settings, the limitations of traditional marriage on women's lives is palpable in their writings. Similarly, in the stories presented in this chapter, women make life-changing journeys because of their marriages and, particularly for Ari, Patrice and Elizabeth, suffer because of their husbands. Their freedom to make these journeys is set against an absence of freedom to choose. But beyond the restrictions of their marriages, all four stories are marked by distinct moments of pushback and resistance, of women defining their own lives.

***

Ari's journey began in war.[1] Her seeking of asylum was precipitated by domestic abuse, but her endurance and strength of self belong entirely to her. She extends the discussion of the vulnerability of women whose visa is dependent on a man, and she makes us ask the question, how can a woman be free from an abuser if her country doesn't want her to be?

We met Ari through the film *Migrant Voices in London*, in which four migrants living in the UK were given video cameras and asked to document their experiences.[2] Ari's words in particular captivated us. She describes with simplicity and unwavering clarity the sky while filming scudding clouds on blue:

> The sky is available. No matter where you are, it's the same sky, whatever country you are living in.[3]

Now we are meeting over Zoom, separated by a pandemic but joined by the same sky, and she tells us about her childhood. Both of Ari's parents are ethnic Armenians, born in Georgia. Ari grew up in Tbilisi, the capital of Georgia, a small country bordering the Black Sea, sandwiched between Russia and Turkey. Ari's childhood coincided with the Georgian Civil War (1991–3).

This bloody war erupted shortly after Georgia declared independence from the Soviet Union. In May 1991, Zviad

Gamsakhurdia was elected as the first president of an independent Georgia. His militant reactions to ethnic separatist tensions, primarily those of the autonomous oblast, South Ossetia, and the Abkhazians, led to his deposition not long after his election.

Conflict erupted between pro- and anti-government factions of the National Guard and paramilitary groups. Conflict and unrest continued in Georgia until 1995. South Ossetia and Abkhazia formed *de facto* states, but tensions still persist.[4] This was not the end to violence in Georgia.

Ari recalls growing up in this conflict:

> I grew up with candles all the time. We had no electricity, and we had no hot water. And, of course, my mum would not allow us to go outside to play with other friends. So we would be all the time at home. The worst bit was around 1994, they were just shooting people around so we would sleep in a bathroom because it was very dangerous just to walk around when through the windows you could catch [a bullet].

Without anything to occupy her during these long days, Ari would draw with her mother, initiating a lifelong fascination.

It was not the war, however, that led to Ari's family's migration from Georgia to Russia in 1994, but rather one particular incident. One evening, when Ari was around ten, they were robbed:

> Four people came into our flat, because my dad, he was a jewellery maker. And I remember that they tied me and my mom together. But my brother was under the bed. He was so little, he was maybe around six.
>
> When they left, my mom was so happy. My dad was holding his head while he was bleeding.
>
> 'What are you laughing at?', I remember he said.
>
> She said, 'Because we're alive.'
>
> We stayed alive. She was so happy. Imagine! She was truly happy. And we left straightaway.

Ari's family moved to Russia to stay with her father's sister, in one room, sharing a bathroom with other families from Georgia. Ari found it difficult to adapt to the strangeness of this new country. Neighbours would often call the police and point the finger at the Georgian families. Ari remembers the feelings of danger that came from having police checks at all times. 'They would bang on the door at five in the morning, making you feel guilty, like you'd done something wrong, just for being there in Russia.'

This sense of not belonging has followed Ari. 'Who am I?', she asks us. 'I don't speak Armenian, I don't speak Georgian. I speak Russian but I'm not Russian and I live in the UK. If somebody asks me where I'm from, I answer, "Everywhere".'

Despite this, Ari's family acquired the right to live in Russia and Ari prospered, studying at school, where she met a boy, Boris,[5] who would later become her husband, and then studying Environmental Design at university. After Ari had given birth to her first child, Ari and Boris moved to the UK, following Boris's prestigious job in finance, him on a Tier 2 Intra-Company Transfer Visa, her on a dependent visa. They had two more children in London before settling in Bournemouth, a quiet place by the sea.

Things seemed ideal. They lived in a beautiful place and had three wonderful children and were financially solvent. But Ari didn't speak a word of English. She was isolated from the support systems available—even speaking to her GP was a struggle, and her husband was abroad a lot. Ari was lonely:

> I was so unconfident, and it was just something that was slipping inside, over this time. When I was looking at reality, it was always like looking at it through a window. It's not something that you can touch. I had no opportunities to do things myself. I was dependent on his opinion, on where we were supposed to live, or how. But I had to trust that he knew better because he

was in that life which I was trying to look at through glass, like again, a border.

Alarm bells first rang for Ari when her mother became seriously ill with cancer. Ari hadn't seen her for the five years that she had been in the UK, and it began to dawn on her that she couldn't help her mother. Health care and medication in Russia require money, and all Ari's money was being controlled by her husband. She had no money of her own. She realised that without money of her own, she couldn't buy plane tickets to go and see her mother to give her a hug.

Ari began to draw flowers and still lifes to earn money to send to her mother. There was something missing from her work, but she managed to exhibit it in street fairs while pregnant:

> I started to sense this independence, this sense of freedom. How was I living without it? What belongs to me? Everything is not yours. You rent a flat but the space is not yours. I used to feel really lost.

Ari opened a bank account for the first time and got her own contact number. She started using social media and discovered other artists. She describes watching a musician playing:

> It's not like watching TV and seeing artists, it was something different; it was like something open. And it's real and someone can express themselves with such freedom and it's not a star in front of me, it's just a creative soul. And it inspired me so badly. I started to draw completely different things, wild things. My mum—she's a teacher at university—would always say, 'Add more colour, work on your shading'. When she saw this, suddenly she said, 'Oh wow, Ari, what's that?!' And I understood that this was it, that was it!

As she describes this surge of creativity that finding some freedom gave her, Ari is glowing, her voice full and musical. Her enthusiasm and joy are infectious, but then her voice takes on an edge.

'He started to feel like he was losing me from his control.'

Ari wasn't aware of how this sort of coercive control was a form of domestic abuse. 'It was mental, psychological and financial at first,' she tells us. Before, Ari's husband would use punishments like making her sleep in a separate room, something that would really upset her. But as Ari was regaining her sense of self, these punishments affected her less and less.

'I started to come alive basically, and this is when the physical abuse started to happen.'

At first he took her computer, not liking the independence it gave her, and he would abuse her verbally, calling her vicious, dirty words. Ari had the sensation that her reality, this glass world of windows, was starting to crash and fall around her. She explains the paradox of fear and freedom that she felt as her numbness receded:

> It was so scary. It was horrible, but at the same time, it was something new. I would never be able to live the life which I lived before.

One day at a children's centre, a member of staff asked about a bruise on Ari's wrist. For Ari, the children's centre was one of her only connections to people outside her family, and she regularly took her kids there for activities. When this staff member began questioning Ari about potential abuse, Ari was so surprised that her story began to pour out of her.

She told the staff member about everything, about the abuse but also about her visa that needed renewing, dependent as it was on her husband's job, and that her husband was threatening to send her back to Russia and keep their kids with him in England. The staff member called social services and a new nightmare began.

THE MARRIAGE CONTRACT

Ari had no idea of her rights or how the system operated. She was told that, unless she collaborated, her children could be taken away from her. Ari still spoke very little English, and could only partially understand the social workers, magnifying her fear exponentially. Social services found her a refuge to which she could flee and Ari packed her bags, trying to obey the instructions of the social workers. Ari was filled with fear and trepidation, not knowing what would be waiting for her in the refuge. She desperately tried to believe the promises of the social workers, who told her that everything would be alright and that they would support her with the visa and help her with her children.

Finally, the day came for Ari to leave for the refuge. She was crying, looking around her at her flat and the remnants of her life and she found herself stuck, unable to leave. Ari told her husband about what she had been planning on doing. He was furious, and took it out on her physically, berating her for bringing social services into their lives. He found the social worker's number on Ari's phone and called the social worker, spewing another vitriolic tirade, before breaking Ari's phone. From that day onwards, Boris stayed at home constantly, watching Ari's every move. In addition to her phone he had broken her computer, leaving her completely isolated, tiptoeing around the flat:

> Once I saw a pigeon, white pigeon on the balcony. The pigeon was stuck by his one leg in a net, alive. I'm telling Boris, 'There is a pigeon, let's rescue him'. We tried. Then I went upstairs and knocked on the neighbour's door. I think the neighbour put the net there on purpose so that birds won't come onto his balcony. He ignored it and I was watching this pigeon dying and I couldn't rescue it because it was quite high. And when I saw this pigeon basically dead, that was how I was feeling, unable to change anything. This is me.

Six months into this new torture, Ari's mother's cancer was progressing, and she was due to undergo an operation that she might not survive. Ari begged Boris for tickets to Russia to see her mother, and he agreed to let her go for three days. Ari couldn't believe that she would be able to see her mother again, after all this time. When they were reunited in Russia, Ari was overwhelmed with how good it was to see her mother, to touch her and smell her, to see those familiar hands that she had missed so much. Ari's mother survived the operation, and Ari told us very simply: 'I came back because of the kids'.

When Ari returned, she was filled with a sense of optimism. Boris had let her go to Russia and hadn't left her there. He even met her at the airport. But things became so much worse. It was constant. Ari might be sitting quietly, trying to obey and then suddenly he would hit her, when she least expected it. Every moment became fraught with danger. Every time Ari looked at her kids, she thought it might be the last, whether he would do it or whether she would do it to herself.

Social services closed their case because Ari was sending them reassuring texts, dictated by her husband. He couldn't seem to understand why they would even need to be involved. One thing Ari was allowed to do was to volunteer at church, running an art class for kids. This position needed a DBS check and so Boris, who had possession of all Ari's documents, sent the church her physical ID.

Soon after, Ari experienced a day from hell, with constant abuse, from morning to evening. Ari's face was bleeding and the walls were spinning in front of her eyes. Her hair was ragged and she was covered in bruises. The next day, her husband had to travel abroad for work. Grateful for the respite that his absence promised, Ari was looking through the post when suddenly, she came across a letter addressed to her. All their letters, council tax, bank statements, everything, were always addressed to Boris. As Ari opened the letter, a small photo of Jesus fell out.

Ari points to the wall behind her. 'This photo, here,' she says. 'I take it with me everywhere.'

Inside the envelope was her ID. Ari acted immediately: 'I said, "That's it, kids. Let's go." I dressed them up and we just ran away.'

Ari went back to the children's centre, where a member of staff called the police, who in turn involved social services and the immigration police. The police determined her case as an extremely high level of domestic violence, removed her and her children to a B&B and gave them access to a food bank. But Ari was told that, because she had left her husband, she no longer had access to her dependent visa; she no longer had any rights in the UK. Ari was told by social services to go to the Russian embassy, but she didn't because, at that time, domestic abuse was not illegal in Russia.

A UK government Corporate Report on Russia in 2015 published these figures: 12,000 women are killed annually in Russia as a result of domestic violence, which is one woman every forty minutes.[6] In 2017, Russia amended their laws on domestic violence, decriminalising 'a first offence of family violence that does not cause serious harm requiring hospital treatment. Only violence that leads to serious injuries like broken bones or a concussion would remain criminalised. The law would apply to violence against any family member, including women and children. Abusers, if found guilty, would face a minimal fine, up to 15 days' administrative arrest, or compulsory community service.'[7] These amendments were passed after a campaign to relax the law, in the name of 'traditional family values'.

Indeed, Ari's own family were also of the opinion that Ari was in the wrong, and selfish for leaving her husband. 'In our culture,' she said, 'women have to obey'; domestic abuse is also still legal in Armenia, her parents' national culture. The one person in her family from whom Ari received support was her mother.

> My poor mummy. She knew. She knew because my dad was really abusive, very, very. When I was looking at my husband, some things were normal to me but some things, I would say, 'at least he's not as bad as my dad'.

These plaintive words are reflective of domestic abuse statistics around the world. WHO suggests that 'globally about 1 in 3 (30 per cent) of women worldwide have been subjected to either physical and/or sexual intimate partner violence or non-partner sexual violence in their lifetime'.[8] These figures were based on reports across 161 different countries and areas from 2000 to 2018. In the US, it is suggested that, 'on average, 20 people per minute are physically abused by an intimate partner'.[9] These figures seem astronomical, despite the fact that domestic abuse is widely underreported.

Yet domestic abuse figures surged across the globe during the coronavirus pandemic. In the UK, reports of domestic abuse increased by 18 per cent in the period affected by the pandemic.[10] From March to April 2020, 'incidents of domestic violence in the Greek Cypriot community increased by 58%'.[11] The UN suggests that:

> In Australia, 40 per cent of frontline workers in New South Wales reported more requests for help with violence. In France, domestic violence cases increased by 30 per cent since the lockdown on March 17. In Argentina, emergency calls for domestic violence have increased by 25 per cent since the lockdown on March 20.[12]

This was due to the increase in time spent at home and lack of access to outside support systems, but it is also due to a failure of protective systems. Only a small minority of domestic abuse cases reported to police are prosecuted.

Ari's precarious situation—as an immigrant on a dependent visa, suffering in her new country—is not the only way that domestic abuse and migration law can combine to leave women extremely vulnerable. The UNHCR Convention and Protocol relating to the Status of Refugees defines a refugee as 'someone who is unable or unwilling to return to their country of origin owing to a well-founded fear of being persecuted for reasons of race, religion, nationality, membership of a particular social group, or political opinion'.[13] For a woman to receive the protection of this label from gender-based violence, she must first be outside her country of origin, which in and of itself presents a host of difficulties, such as finding money to travel and the dangers of travel itself.

Another key difficulty for a person seeking international protection from gender-based violence is faced by women everywhere: how to prove and provide evidence for your abuse. Beyond physical evidence, women must rely on their testimony in the face of trauma and cultural and language barriers. And despite this, often decision-makers decree that domestic abuse is a private matter, and not one that sits under the five reasons for persecution.

In this regard, Ari was lucky. She was moved to a refuge in London. She describes being like a blind kitten, naïve and vulnerable.

> It wasn't the best experience... but I said to myself, 'At least this is a real reality, without glass'. I would look at the sky and I would say to my friends, 'Guys, you can't imagine, the sky is open!'

Ari was in a refuge for three and a half years, after applying for humanitarian protection and refugee status, negotiating legal and financial aid. To live in the refuge, you need governmental funding. Ari didn't want to claim support from the National Asylum Support Service, a section of the Home Office responsible for supporting and accommodating people seeking asylum, because they wished to send her to Liverpool. Ari was suffering with PTSD and struggling to support her children, and didn't wish to start all over again in a new city. After Ari and her children had left her husband, the child protection services found that there were no further dangers to the children, and so were unwilling to support them financially.

However, Ari was able to find support through social services who supported her in London and paid for her accommodation, though she had to fight fiercely for this support. Ari describes the difficulty of having to prove her vulnerability without seeming so vulnerable that they might deem her unsafe for her children. She was advised to just be herself. Ari tidied away the children's toys and made herself look presentable, to make herself look less broken in order to protect her kids. But as she began to speak to her visitor, the truth of her situation began to spill out, and they agreed to support her.

The Home Office was very keen to move Ari to a different city and a car once came for them, but Ari refused. It felt like victory, but Ari had to fight for every little thing. She had solicitors for social services and for immigration, as well as a police case for prosecuting her husband. The police were worried that if she was deported they would lose their witness.

Ari remembers the pain of having to speak against her husband and feeling unable to breathe as his solicitor asked her questions in court. Her husband was found guilty but appealed, and so Ari had to speak again in court. She talks about the merry-go-round of interviews, from court to the Home Office to National Asylum Support Service while trying to support and raise her children on a tiny budget. She couldn't access school meals and sometimes she didn't have enough money for her Oyster travel card to take her children to school.

It was the little things that were most difficult through this whirlwind. A car like her husband's would pass her on the street and she would freeze, unable to move. It felt like her body was protecting her from the pain. But she was also trapped in the refuge. There were cameras everywhere, and the levels of control and restriction felt like another kind of abuse. Though the restrictions were understandable for the protection of the people in the refuge, Ari found this level of containment and observation very difficult.

Ari began volunteering as soon as she could, to get out of the refuge and to feel like she was worth something to the country, to feel like she was useful. But her status continued to limit her ability to act or travel the city freely:

> At my age, at thirty, these are the most energetic years for any human being when you already have some life experience; you've studied, you have some knowledge and now, it's time for you to apply it in order to improve your life, especially when you have children. And suddenly, your hands are tied. You can't do anything. I wanted to study, 'No, you can't study'. I found some courses for asylum seekers but I struggled to attend because of the Oyster cards and things like that. And through all of this, you're thinking, 'When will I receive these rights?' So my way out was to draw, just to switch it off and go to these worlds. I was drawing wildly.

Ari began to feel like she was stuck in a labyrinth, coming up against barrier after barrier. And at each barrier she berated the Home Office and the people who kept closing doors in her face: 'I will do anything if you just give me this air to breathe.'

Out of the blue, the refuge took Ari and her children on a trip to Littlehampton, in Sussex. There Ari saw a sculpture. Against a gloomy sky, the sculpture seems like swoops of caterpillar tracks, diving backwards and forwards, with some of the spokes replaced by dashes of colour. Through the whirls of the sculpture, you can see the line of the horizon. Ari was frozen on the spot. It was like the sculpture had stepped out of one of her paintings, these circles. And finally, here in Littlehampton, Ari was able to walk through the sculpture, through to the other side, to where she could see the horizon, unguarded.

> When I saw this horizon, I said to myself, there is no one who can say that I am free and no legal thing can tell me who I am. I understood that I, Ari, am free. Within one month, I received my rights.

A stomach bug and lice had hit Ari's refuge the day that she received the letter granting her refugee status. The house was upside down when Ari came flying downstairs, joyfully crying, screaming, 'We are free, we are free!' Ari's kids replied, 'What do you mean, Mum, we are free?' And Ari realised that her kids had been free the whole time—'kids don't see the world with these sorts of boundaries':

> Those kids are my wings. No matter what, you have to stand up, you have to take them to school, you have to find a place and you have to make home. They kept me going. They were my wings.

Today, Ari paints abstract watercolour landscapes and provides therapeutic artistic activities, using her experiences and understanding to draw expression and feeling out of others.

> Asylum seekers mostly feel that they are stuck, that there is no air, that they don't have rights. They can't work. There're so many talented people who are willing to work. But I realised that I had never been stuck. I always moved. I was looking through my drawings and I remembered every period which

I passed through, some of them really dark. But I was always moving. I was always looking forward.

'He had sent for me'

Britain's history with migration is intrinsically entwined with colonialism, and looking at Britain's expansive and exclusionary borders means looking at the British empire. At its peak, Britain's empire spanned across 23 per cent of the world's population, and though many people mark its breakdown as the end of World War II, the reach of its legacies are still insidiously impacting people who move.

The end of imperial Britain could be firmly placed with its reconstruction as the Commonwealth around the end of World War II and the introduction of the British Nationality Act of 1948, but the transition to post-imperial Britain was far from a clear break. The Commonwealth is a voluntary association of countries recognising the British monarch as their head of state, most of which are former British colonies. The British Nationality Act of 1948 was a legal structure that extended a single form of 'British citizenship', and therefore the rights of entry and residency, to citizens of British colonies and newly independent Commonwealth countries. Together, these served to create a continuity and unity that, Ian Sanjay Patel suggests, 'was a conscious effort to keep Britain's post-war imperial ambitions intact'.[14]

This conscious effort, however, had a very different result than that imagined. Patel continues, telling us that 'Britain's politicians in 1948 never expected large numbers of non-white British and Commonwealth citizens to exercise their right to migrate from one part of the Commonwealth empire to another'.[15] Indeed, the act did encourage migration in order to supplement domestic labour shortages; it has often been described as Britain asking for help 'rebuilding post-war Britain'. But crucially, they were expecting temporary migration, a workforce that maintained the structure of the motherland and that could be returned after its use was spent.

This warped thinking resulted in a double standard that can still be felt in every 'But where are you really from?' asked. Though the 1948 Act granted legal entry to British shores to British citizens, the citizens moving to Britain were not seen as citizens, but rather immigrants and labour. As many of these citizens were migrating from the Caribbean and South Asia, this created the perpetuating fallacy that non-white British passport holders do not belong to British society. James Trafford describes these 'colonial strategies and techniques deployed "at home"' as '*internal* colonialism'.[16] This was exacerbated by the 1962 Commonwealth Act that restricted the right of entry to the UK to those born in the UK, creating a hierarchy of citizenship, with some British citizens paradoxically *not* granted the right to enter the UK.

Despite the gradual introduction of restrictions on Commonwealth nationals moving to or even visiting the UK, Patrice's journey to England was akin to that of many other people in her community. This diaspora is often termed the 'Windrush generation', named after the HMS *Empire Windrush*, a ship that was commissioned in 1948 to carry passengers from the Caribbean to Britain. Over 300,000 people migrated from the West Indian islands in the years surrounding the sailing of the *Windrush*, settling in the UK in the post-war years. While many women arrived from former colonies to work—for instance, as nurses—many others followed their new or future husbands, as Ari would decades later. And, like Ari, many would suffer for it.

In many of the discussions with Ranjan and Patrice—and Elizabeth to follow—their families mentioned how important this interview was in recording the oral history of their family.

A number of these people asked to have a copy of the recordings we made in order to pass on to their children, to continue the oral history that they started. Amy, Elizabeth's daughter-in-law, referenced the Yoruba word 'ireki', which translates to explain an oral form of storyteller. Indeed, Leah Cowan, in *Border Nation*, explains how borders and immigration controls can often 'attempt to stem the flow of ideas, stories and histories', and to counteract this attempt, we must document these experiences. This book is, in part, an attempt to reclaim these stories from colonisation and borders.

Patrice[17] grew up in St Lucia. Her mother died giving birth to her. When Patrice was born, she was so small that they placed her in a shoebox. Her father couldn't cope with his children without their mother, so Patrice and her brother were given to the nurse who had birthed her; the rest of the children were split up. Patrice refers to the nurse only as 'the Barbadian lady'. She, in turn, handed the children to her own mother, who raised them.

This new circumstance was difficult. Patrice's new family were very strict, and beat her and her brother for the smallest misdemeanours, like being late home from school. Patrice worked hard on the farm with the horses and cattle, and life for her was very hard. She recalls a night when the son of the family had a knife and was on the verge of storming into the house to kill his father. Patrice urged him not to, and begged him to run away instead. He fled to America. He and Patrice have had very little contact since.

Patrice found a way to escape this through marriage. Patrice was fifteen and her husband was around thirty. Mary,[18] Patrice's daughter, explains that her mother was so young, it was almost paedophilia, but it was an escape nonetheless.

Patrice moved to the UK in many ways to get away from the people who raised her. However, the decision to move was her husband's. He set himself up in England in the 1950s and he sent for her and their child in 1960. We asked her if she wanted to go. After a silence, Patrice replied, 'He had sent for me.' Patrice's wishes didn't matter. He was her husband and he had sent for her. So Patrice took the boat to Southampton with her child; it took ten days.

Mary asks, 'What did you do on the boat?'

Patrice replies, 'Nothing. I just looked at the sea.'

'Wasn't it scary?'

'Not really.'

Patrice landed in Southampton, where she was meant to meet her husband, but she didn't see him. So she took the train to Waterloo.

Mary asks incredulously, 'How did you know to come to Waterloo? You hadn't been to England before! Had you been on a train before?'

Patrice replies, 'No, but I see'd a sign for Waterloo. Anyhow I asked someone.'

She waited for her husband in Waterloo and he came. She describes England: 'It was horrible, dark, cold and cloudy. I didn't like it at all. I wanted to go back right away.' Their flat was cold and had just one bedroom. It wasn't big. Different families from different rooms in the house shared one cooker. They would all race for the cooker before Patrice, so Patrice always got the cooker last.

She got a job in a laundrette but it was hard work. When the clothes were finished, she would take them out and put them in a big dryer, and when they were dry, she would take them out and fold them and put them away.

'Your wages, I bet Daddy took it,' said Mary.

'Oh yes, he always took it,' Patrice replied, laughing her creaking laugh.

She didn't work there long because they said she was too slow.

Shortly after coming to England, her husband decided that it was too expensive to have Patrice and her child living in England with him. So he sent them back to St Lucia, where she stayed for three years. Her husband would come and visit, and Patrice soon had another child.

He then sent for her a second time. This time she came on a plane with her two children, and, knowing what England was going to be like, she was very reluctant to come:

> He sent up for me and so I came. I didn't want to come. But my friends tell me I should go so I came back. It was cold and wet but I didn't feel I had any choice because my husband had asked me to come.

Despite forcing her to join him in England against her will, Patrice's husband spent much of his time back in St Lucia, and didn't really help to support the children financially. Although she didn't divorce her husband until her thirties, by the age of twenty-four Patrice was a single mum with five children living in a strange country. Mary tells us that Patrice's relationship with her ex-husband was very difficult:

> I think he tried to kill her once. It's true. I remember it. It was really horrible. I think he didn't want a divorce or didn't want to pay money. He was so mean.

Patrice raised her five children on a cleaning job at the university at Elephant and Castle in London. At times, Patrice worked two cleaning jobs, one at night and the other during the day.

Patrice describes her routine at the time:

> I used to work at night cleaning, 10pm to 5am, and then went straight to the morning job at Elephant and Castle. I used to leave the kids, make sure you had eaten and put on your nightie and everything and then see that you had all gone to bed.

She would then come back after working all night, get them all dressed for school. Those who could go on their own went on their own and then she would drop off those who were too young. After dropping the kids at school, Patrice had to be careful about sleeping so that she didn't sleep through picking up her youngest children from school again. Then she had to cook and go back to the afternoon job.

Patrice tells us that, 'After a time, I couldn't manage it'.

Mary says, 'I remember those days. I thought it was normal!'

We asked Patrice when she slept. She told us, 'not much, not much. I didn't keep it for long because it was too much.'

For Patrice, the church has played a huge role in her life. It was a 'nice warm place full of people that love you'. Mary tells us that the church had many women in similar situations to Patrice, often raising children alone in this foreign country. Like Guli and Najat finding female solidarity and community, both in the refugee camp and after arriving in Britain, the women in Patrice's church came together to help each other with the challenges of motherhood. Patrice was part of the choir and went on many trips to the seaside with her children. Her fried fish was the envy of many churchgoers. The support of these women transformed life in Britain for Patrice, and made it a home.

Patrice tells us that 'There was a time when I wanted to go back and then I got used to it and then when I had children, I couldn't go back. This is now my home.'

Mary says to Patrice, 'All your friends are from church.' Patrice demurs at first, but then when trying to list friends not part of the church, she reveals how important the church is to her socially. For her, this has been one of the greatest challenges of the pandemic. Patrice's diabetes made going to church an impossibility. However, one upside to Covid-19 has been the way in which it has changed accessibility.

Many places of worship that went online during lockdown have continued to livestream services for the benefit of vulnerable members, even after the lifting of restrictions on gatherings. Patrice can now join in her church services by watching it on the TV, which means a great deal to her. Finding this 'chosen' community was of great importance to Patrice, as it was for many other immigrants like her, who faced immense hostility from wider British society.

Patrice was a cleaner at a university in Elephant and Castle for more than thirty years. Initially, Patrice told us that the people she interacted with were 'alright' until Mary protested.

'That's not the story you told me. You told me some of them were racist,' said Mary.

Patrice conceded. 'It was only one woman that was racist to me. She didn't do nothing horrible. When I washed her cup, she didn't like it, so she used to hide the cup, even if it was dirty. Even sometimes when she hid it and I saw it, I would take it and wash it.' Patrice laughs her creaking laugh again.

There are many different ways of showing hatred, and many different ways of fighting back.

Mary told us that they had neighbours in the late 1970s at the end of the street who were part of the National Front. She told us this was normal, that people from the National Front would be at their local street market handing out pamphlets. Patrice and Mary's neighbours would throw abuse at them when they would walk past. Mary tells us again, 'This was normal. We didn't take any notice of them.'

However, one day when Patrice was at church, a friend came rushing in to tell her that her house was on fire. The neighbours from the National Front had set fire to Patrice's wardrobe in her room with her cats, Sandy, Dandy and Andy, in it. By the time Patrice arrived home, the fire was out.

'It was alright,' Patrice tells us in a way that hints it was definitely not alright.

We asked about any form of justice or punishment, as they seemed to know very clearly who had set the fire. There was a silence as Patrice looked at us, baffled. Mary explained, 'In those days, even now, it was just normal. There was no complaining to the police because the police were racist and they weren't interested. It was just normal. Nobody had lost their life.'

'They wasn't interested. They didn't do nothing about it. They didn't do anything about it,' says Patrice. 'I felt disgusted. Anyhow, after that, those people moved. And then everything was alright after they moved.'

Unfortunately, the legal framework implicitly questioning or limiting the 'Britishness' and belonging of these postcolonial citizens has persisted and expanded through to the present day—and with it, race-based tension and aggression. The legitimacy of many West Indian people's presence in the UK was actively called into question by the British government, as part of the hostile environment created by Theresa May as Home Secretary.

The 2014 and 2016 Immigration Acts, in trying to crack down on 'illegal' immigration, accidentally demanded that these British citizens who sailed to Britain, amongst many others, *prove* they had a right to be here. There were no records held by the government of their arrival or status, and in fact, in 2010, the Home Office destroyed, in the name of data protection, many landing cards (known as registry slips) that might have been integral to proving the status of many of the Windrush generation.

Cowan suggests that '164 members of the Windrush generation are known (and many more likely unreported) to have been detained or deported as part of the British government's soulless pursuit of deportation targets'.[19] While this hasn't affected Patrice, talking to her is a stark reminder of all the people who have been affected, and how vulnerable they are.

Patrice is potentially younger than some of those deported, and yet, with her struggles with diabetes and dementia, it is possible to see how being deported to a country she hasn't lived in since she was sixteen would debilitate her.

The hostile environment (still in place but now rebranded) has been enacted by both policies and propaganda. The 2014 Immigration Act altered Britain's external borders, making them a pervasive presence throughout society, turning teachers, landlords, doctors and nurses into our border police. This legal action was compounded with a campaign to encourage those in the UK without papers to leave voluntarily.

Vans that featured billboards reading 'Go home or face arrest' circulated in areas of London. This use of language, perpetuated and endorsed by the government, overtly supports a rhetoric of racism. 'Go home' became a commonly heard racist refrain in the 1970s and 1980s, and it is still a term that is parroted and causes hurt. Beyond those wrongfully deported or penalised, this broader climate of suspicion and animosity fostered by the hostile environment has had real-world effects on all those in Britain deemed to be outsiders, and on their ability to thrive in their communities.

One afternoon, Alex B was with Najat's and Guli's families, playing and picnicking in the park.

We had all been playing football, hammering out a hot game of loose passes and lousy footwork with a deflated ball, when two local boys arrived. Charlie and Michael, somewhere between eight and ten years old, the same ages as Mohammed and Ismail, sheepishly approached the fence.

'Can us two take on you lot?', they asked with shy arrogance.

'What, all of us?'

The boys smiled and pulled out their ball.

After a vigorous game, the adults flopped in the shade of a climbing frame. We were pinching sunflower seeds from their salty shells, bathing in the sunshine. Arabic flowed around, when one of Najat's sons approached Alex.

'Can I talk to you in private?'

Alex, thinking they probably wanted another game, agreed.

'Those boys are not letting me play. They're asking if I'm from Africa, telling me to go home and they're kicking the ball really hard at me,' Mohammed told Alex.

Alex marched to the fence, trailed by Mohammed, Ismail and Guli's three oldest children. Charlie and Michael curtailed their game sullenly when she called them over. The crowd behind her was strangely silent; this was ceremonial.

'So, what's been happening? Have you not been letting Mohammed play with you?'

'No.'

Like a dam bursting, tirades streamed from both sides.

'...he swore at me...'

'...you swore at us...'

'...you did it first...'

'...that's because you were kicking the ball at me so hard...'

'...no, we wasn't...'

'...you said he was from Africa. You told him to go home...'

'...we were just playing...'

The 'Go home' van campaign was halted after a month but this rhetoric, as a reflection of the governmental attitude, has devastating impacts on people living in Britain, like Mohammed and Ismail. Theresa May stated that this was 'too much of a blunt instrument', but this was far from the end of the hostile environment.[20]

Life beyond the contract

Hearing Patrice's story, from her traumatic childhood to her downplaying of the racists' cruelty in Britain, made us admire her resilience, but also left us with broken hearts. For some women, it was a little easier to put the difficult beginnings as a wife who has moved with her husband behind them, and, eventually, to enjoy a new identity in the UK.

Ranjan was born in Kenya, but moved to India when she was very young. Her father died when she was around three. Ranjan's childhood was filled with wealth. She describes growing up with cars, servants and big houses. This wealth was built by her father, who moved from Gujarat to Kenya when he was fourteen.

In Gujarat, life was very difficult. Ranjan tells us, 'They only had a small piece of land, where they will grow things, so whenever there is a drought or rain or a flood or anything, there is nothing to eat and [her father] wasn't educated'. In Kenya, he had nothing, but he began working, sewing buttons on shirts, and eventually built his own very successful business. He used to clean his boss's chair and, within a few years, he was occupying that same chair. He moved his family back to India because the education for girls wasn't very good in Kenya, but also because, as Ranjan suggests, 'he basically wanted all the children to get married in India'.

Ranjan grew up with a lot of money, in a big house in a quiet area where, she says, 'we were not exposed to any evils', with even their friends chosen for them. When the time came for her to marry, the funds had run out, the wealth had gone. The dowry that Ranjan's family were expected to give to her husband didn't exist, so Ranjan had to work hard.

Ranjan studied Philosophy, Politics and Economics at university in India, before nursing for a little while and then training to be a teacher. Ranjan taught infants and juniors for five years before changing to the civil service, where she worked for twenty-three years. She told us that the teachers' wages were very poor, and that 'you just don't work for the love of work, it's money as well'. The environment in the civil service was quite different to teaching, where you have control of the class, but Ranjan said that once she tuned her mind into it, she adjusted quite well.

Education is something that is very important to Ranjan. She says, 'Education is a big instrument for ladies, for girls, boys. Everyone.'

She tells us that, 'When I went to university, the girls didn't go to university in those days.' Ranjan went to university because she was the tenth child out of eleven. Some of her older siblings had moved to America and had seen that girls were getting educated. They argued that she could bring her children up better if she was educated.

Indeed, education is so important to Ranjan that when we ask her about her mother, the first thing she tells us about her is that 'she never went to school', describing her as a 'very ordinary person'. Ranjan's mother was thirteen when she was married. Her mother used to tell her that 'all you are going to do is get married, have children and cook all your life. Don't worry, you don't have to study'.

Ranjan has taken a different approach with her children. She tells us that 'giving birth to a child is one thing, but to put them in the right track is, it's just tiring. Giving birth and feeding them is one thing, but the rest of the thing is hard work.'

She tells us about raising her children in Britain, their education and their current occupations, all of which seem very impressive. This started with Ranjan teaching them reading, writing and maths before they even began school. Ranjan tells us that, 'because we are coloured people, we have to do better than the best. Work hard at home so no one can say that you don't know anything. It's best to start early.' Ranjan says that this was rewarding, and that it made her happy to be in full control of these parts of their education.

We asked Mo, Ranjan's daughter, whether she felt a lot of pressure as a child. She told us that it was 'made quite clear to us that you've got to work hard, you've got to get a degree, you've got to get a good job. You can't not do those things. Pressure isn't quite the right word. But certainly like, this is just what you do. And so you do that.'

Education was championed in their household, and Ranjan points out that 'degrees don't make a person' but the confidence and boost and voice they give are invaluable. Ranjan says, 'In India, parents like to own their children'. Ranjan believes instead that you only 'have children, you don't own them. Let them be themselves.'

Ranjan's marriage was organised by her family. We asked whether it was strange to marry someone she didn't know, but Ranjan told us that 'it wasn't that bad'. Ranjan said she was lucky, as she was engaged to her husband for eleven and a half months, and he also came to stay in Bombay for a month, which meant she had a 'nice chunk of time' to get to know her fiancé before their marriage.

When we ask Ranjan about how her relationship with her husband developed over time, she replies, 'Keep busy'. She tells us that marriages are very different now, but in her own marriage, 'Whether I give him a hard time or he gives me a hard time, we stayed married irrespective'. When we ask whether Ranjan's husband was very present in Ranjan and Mo's lives, Ranjan laughs and tells me, 'He had his moments'.

Ranjan explains: 'To marry, it's not just to fit into a family but to bring subtle changes to improve the images in a family'. When Ranjan came to the UK, it was 'sink or swim'. Her father-in-law, who was very strict, said, 'Do not ask us to send you money. You will go into foreign land. You don't know anybody there. And if you lose your job or if you become ill, don't come back. We are not here for you.'

Ranjan remembers being very scared of her father-in-law, having grown up without a father and with only women making decisions in her household. But Ranjan knew that she and her husband were on their own, and so she applied her attitude to the situation: 'fix your mind and your body will follow'.

Ranjan came to the UK with her husband in 1964 when she was twenty-three, with one child. Her husband was a doctor and he had come to the UK for studies. Ranjan tells us that, because her husband was a doctor, their move was in many ways made easier. Ranjan describes how the hospital provided for most of their needs, telling us that they just needed a suitcase of clothes and that was it. This was particularly useful, as to finish his training, Ranjan's husband had to get experience from multiple hospitals, and this required them to move regularly.

They came on a work visa, and after six years, they got their citizenship. Ranjan tells us that they did try moving back to India after her children—they had four together—had grown up, but she says they did it half-heartedly, and told us that, 'when you do things half-heartedly, it never works'. This half-heartedness, Ranjan tells us, comes from moving away and coming back. Ranjan gets ill when she goes to India now. 'The food doesn't suit me, the weather doesn't suit me. People in India are very hardy. They have lots of infections and diseases going around and they survive. But here we don't have those things, do we?'

Ranjan's adjustment to the UK was also helped by her brother, who was also a doctor, moving to the UK a couple of years after Ranjan. Ranjan tells us they were 'closely bonded'. 'You cling onto something you call your own'. The adjustment to England included changes in fashion. In India, Ranjan wore saris everyday, but England was in the middle of the Swinging Sixties, complete with flares and miniskirts. Ranjan laughs girlishly when she tells us that 'when you are young, you grow with the flowers'. She learned to swim, learned English, learned to drive and 'changed all the dresses and all the outlooks'.

She tells us that in India, 'when you are a girl, you listen to your parents. When you are married, you listen to your in-laws and husband. When you grow older, you still listen to your children. So you are never yourself. But here it is quite different.'

She tells us, 'The women always took a second best place. The women are never leaders, they just had to be led all the time. Your opinion doesn't count. Even if you are educated. Women in India never challenge things.' This attitude had a big impact on her marriage, as it was difficult for her husband to break with these traditions, particularly with the influence of his father, who would ask his son why he was listening to his wife; 'keep her to her own station'. Ranjan giggles.

Ranjan knew when she got married that she was 'going to have to just listen to orders now', but she followed her attitude of subtlety. She says that she knew she wasn't going to be able to make changes overnight, but she also thought that she could make positive changes quietly without arguments. 'It's not easy', she reflects.

It was also very different not having the servants and cooks and teachers. Ranjan reflects on the fact that, in England, you have to do everything yourself. 'It's adapting to quite a different system. The value of women is so different than at home. You just make yourself here. Success is there, but you have to work at it.' She believes that 'what is inside you, nobody can see it'. Ranjan managed to assert her voice in a quiet and authoritative way despite the obstacles presented to her.

Ranjan says that her children have gained a lot of confidence from the education system in the UK. She says that they have much stronger personalities. We suggest that they have inherited this from their mother, but Ranjan demurs, saying that 'I would say no, I'm not really. It's just happened. I still think I'm not a very confident person. I haven't got courage either.'

Mo disagrees, saying, 'I think you're quite a formidable person actually, Mummy. You've got inside guts. You didn't, even when things were difficult, have the option to quit and go home. That's courage, isn't it?'

Ranjan says softly, 'Migrants, they didn't cry.' She then says, in a louder voice, 'I have cried many times and then, I just go like this', she wipes her face, 'and go, this has got no room in the house for tears. It's not going to solve anything. Just get moving, that's what I tell them.'

This kind of resilience and positive attitude will have come in handy during Ranjan's early years in Britain, when she experienced the same kind of alienation as Patrice has described. She says, 'Whenever I went out, people would think I'm a doctor, or I'm a nurse, I couldn't be anything else, you know, just take it for granted.' She said this even applied to her children, where at school it was assumed they were the children of a doctor or nurse. This assumption might originate from the formation of the National Health Service (in the same year as the 1948 British Nationality Act), whose workforce was composed largely of people from the Caribbean, India and Pakistan. She tells us that people still assume things about her, like if she is out in the city, people often assume she is lost.

Mo, Ranjan's daughter, prompts Ranjan, reminding her of 'problems' they had when they moved to East London. Ranjan laughs, perhaps nervously, before telling us that her 'children had a lot of problems in the school'. She says that one of her children 'sometimes used to get beaten up, come black and blue from school'. She giggles again before saying, 'He made it. He's a hardy person.'

Mo prompts Ranjan again: 'The garage.'

'What about the garage?' Ranjan asks Mo.

'It got burnt down,' Mo says, with a note of incredulity in her voice. Ranjan laughs again. She tells us, 'We had people sometimes writing on the walls of the house and we had a fire.'

When we ask what kinds of things got written on her garage, Ranjan tells us, 'it could be just the children. It didn't make sense. Nothing bad or insulting was written.' She tells us that since they've moved, nothing bad has happened. When we ask about the fire, Ranjan continues to tell us about it in quite a dismissive way, saying, 'Somebody kicked the door. I don't know how the fire started. But nothing was said about it. And also, we're not the argumentative type. We'd rather fit into the community than raise our voice about things.'

Ranjan looks pained when we suggested any form of justice for the words that were graffitied or the fire that was lit. That was not her way. Ranjan says in regards to family, but also outside the family, 'I have never taken a revenge on anybody. So I fit in and don't talk about things that can escalate into arguments.'

Ranjan remembers her first impression of the UK, telling us that, 'when I was in India, you read in books, "England is a city of gold, paved with gold".' This saying is one commonly heard around this time; indeed, it seems to be a narrative sold by post-imperial Britain. It is one that sits at odds with the suggestion of a broken post-war country that needs rebuilding.

Both these paradoxical narratives serve to encourage migration. Leah Cowan brilliantly describes this, saying, 'Britain's only consistent export is its own inflated sense of its own greatness, and yet outrage is meted out on anyone who wishes to cross its borders and venture in'.[21] Britain was selling a dual narrative, that of encouraging migration while not wanting migrants to stay.

The same tension exists today between only granting visas to those high-skilled workers perceived as most valuable to the country's economy, and yet reviling the idea of an economic migrant. This attitude is particularly galling in a country that professes to admire people with drive who take initiative. It appears that this country only really admires certain people with initiative, and casts other forms of initiative as 'opportunism'.

Migrants who are not shamed for their desire for work or a better life might be pushed into another box: that of the 'model minority' or the 'good immigrant'. This is a stereotype that has been applied to Asians, setting them apart from other immigrants, labelling them as well-educated, hard workers, of a higher economic bracket and 'sensible, quiet and shy'.[22] In many ways, this explains people consistently expecting Ranjan to be a doctor or nurse, as this is a white-collar profession that fits the model minority stereotype.

While these may seem like complimentary things to be labelled, Wei Ming Kam suggests that this is 'code for being on perpetual probation', never leading to 'real equality, or even acceptance'.[23] Your presence in the West is tolerated only conditionally, based on your profession and your temperament. It serves to repress the voices and individualities of Asian people, while also serving a racist agenda. Wei Ming Kam suggests that the implication of a 'model minority' is that in contrast to Asians, 'black people are apparently loud and lazy'.[24]

Ranjan has faced many oppressions on her liberty, in the form of patriarchal expectations as well as the prejudice Ranjan has faced in UK society. Despite all of this, Ranjan remains cheerful and upbeat. She tells us about the vast range of hobbies that she uses to remain so positive. 'I swim or I read or do Sudoku or knitting, painting, cross stitch, watercolour, everything, go out. I do yoga and gym and all sorts of things.' She tells us that 'enjoyment in life is not just allocated to some ages, is it? It's a continuous process.' Ranjan's determined sunniness has dismissed and broken through any borders placed on her freedom and happiness.

THE MARRIAGE CONTRACT

'I just wanted to get out'

We met with Elizabeth Afilaka, an eighty-year-old Nigerian grandmother, on a sunny spring morning at her home in Essex. We travelled from Zone 2 London, the Tube journey taking almost an hour. By the time we reached her stop, the tall crammed buildings of central London had evaporated and the railway was surrounded by fields and a few rows of houses, the view of the blue sky almost uninterrupted. We then got a bus, which pulled up almost directly outside Elizabeth's house. This she calls her door-to-door taxi service.

We walked in the door with Elizabeth's daughter-in-law and her grandson, who sat with us for a while before moving to the stairs to watch YouTube videos. He told us that it was hard to keep up with what was being said, but that was okay because Elizabeth's daughter-in-law had asked for the recording after.

She saw it as a continuation of her mother-in-law's cultural history, a tradition in Yoruba culture to develop oral histories through storytelling. Elizabeth didn't remember the Yoruba name for this, but she didn't need to. The practice came to her naturally. She settled down in her armchair, half-facing the television but often turning towards us. Naturally, she started at the very beginning—her childhood in Western Nigeria. She spoke steadily, her sentences often trailing off to a murmur. She paused often to laugh at recollections, a laugh which was full-bodied and which everyone echoed instinctively, not because we understood the joke but because her joy was infectious.

Elizabeth did not want to move to England, she started by telling us over cups of tea. Her husband had already moved over and wanted her to follow—she was encouraged to do so by her pastor, who was the nucleus that her community moved around, a person whose advice should not be ignored. At this point in the conversation, she didn't tell us the main reason she didn't want to leave, but it was clear that England itself, the bleakness of it, had something to do with it. When her husband moved over in 1962 it was the coldest winter on record. He would cry and ask her, what am I doing here?

Before Nigerian independence, many Nigerians had travelled to the UK to study and acquire qualifications. This included Elizabeth's husband, who had travelled to Birmingham to study engineering. The pre-1960 wave of migration was often temporary, as many Nigerian immigrants would often return to Nigeria once they had received their qualifications. But through the 1960s, as lifestyle and opportunities in Nigeria worsened, more and more people moved to the UK to seek better fortune. This increased significantly by the 1980s.

Elizabeth's own journey preceded both the waves of post-independence turbulence in her own country and the waves of Nigerian immigration to the UK. Elizabeth had her own deeply personal reason for not wanting to leave, which she revealed later on in the conversation.

She almost missed the boat from Nigeria to the UK; by the time she reached the port in Lagos, the ship had set sail. She only made it because someone sailed her over to it in a smaller dinghy boat. She had originally arrived on time at the port, but someone had told her she still had another day until the ship would leave.

Her infant son was at home with her family, to be left behind for the time being. Excited that she would have another opportunity to say goodbye to her baby, she made the journey all the way back to Ilesa—the roundtrip taking five hours each way. She was laughing about taking the small dinghy boat out to sea when she told us that she never saw her son again. He died less than a year after she set sail for England. Her laughter was followed by a pained silence, all of us aware that the grief of losing a son across such a distance is unfathomable. Speaking about this, Elizabeth said:

I used to cry. I used to cry. Unfortunately the child died. When he died, I realised there was no point in going back to Lagos. I used to cry and wake up and cry.

While the majority of Britain's Nigerian community moved to London upon arrival, Elizabeth instead moved to the suburbs of Birmingham, where her husband had found work. She spoke of Birmingham and its people with warmth and admiration, both feelings that were lacking when she turned to speak about her time living in London afterwards. In the suburbs where she lived when she first moved to Birmingham, her neighbours were almost all white. She and her husband were the only Black couple living there.

This wasn't something that Elizabeth felt caused difficulty for them, as she described becoming part of that community regardless of the people's roots. This was not the same for when she moved to London. Since white landlords in the capital city would often not rent their spare rooms or flats to Black people—'it was the time of no dogs, no Blacks, no Irish,' Elizabeth says—she and her husband saved up to buy their own home. They found a three-storey terraced house in Hackney that was cheaper because it came with a live-in tenant.

Elizabeth made friends and found her own rhythm in London, but the fast pace and the lack of community she often felt made her relationship with the city more fraught. When they first arrived in the borough, Elizabeth, her husband and her young son knocked on a white neighbour's door. She asked where the nearest church was for them to attend, and the neighbour replied, 'your church is over there'.

'What do you mean by "my" church?' Elizabeth asked.

The neighbour meant the church attended by Black people. Coming from her small integrated community in Birmingham, this racist segregation perpetuated by her neighbour in that moment was an unpleasant surprise.

'At least, could I get a glass of water for my son?'

The neighbour refused to let them inside the house.

Despite this sinister background of segregational attitudes in Britain, working for British rail for thirty years shaped Elizabeth's life in the UK in a remarkable and positive way. She says she is 'lucky' to have worked there. Crucially, this is because she could speak her mind and stand up for herself—which is, she tells us, something she can't help but do to this day.

Because the railway industry was nationalised and unions were strong, employees' racism had to be kept in check at a time where overt racism was commonplace. For Elizabeth, hostility towards her presence in the office as a Black woman ('most of my work life on the railway I am the only Black one there') came in more subtle and insidious forms.

One day, a male colleague asked Elizabeth why she was at work when his own wife stayed at home. To this she replied 'But I am not your wife!' Another time, in the face of hostility from another white male colleague, Elizabeth told him: 'You work for British Rail, I work for British Rail. You do your job and I'll do mine.' When people tried to push her down, she would put them back in their places with her quick wit.

She laughs throughout the interview, but when telling these stories, her cackle is particularly joyous and cheeky. If she spoke back like this at a private company at the time, she would have been sacked. 'Things have changed. Before I left, there were more Black people working in the offices than when I started. But at the time, if I hadn't been working in the nationalised industry, I would have got the sack because I speak my mind,' she explains.

Elizabeth's struggles were created not only from the outside world but also from inside her own home. When her son was thirteen years old, Elizabeth, after years of struggling within her marriage, finally left her husband. Unlike Ari, she was not left destitute by the end of the marriage, as she has the right to reside in the UK in her own right due to being Nigerian, and she is fortunate to have more secure (and probably better-paid) employment in the public sector than Patrice did. Yet still the economic improvement promised by a couple moving to the UK together, the entire reason for Elizabeth's upheaval and sorrow, was now replaced by life as a single mother.

> I just had enough. I just wanted to get out. It's not easy to get out. I couldn't find a place. I didn't realise the effect the marriage was having on me. Eventually, I went to a women's shelter, which was bad. The room was quite big. After I had been there for... not a year... they found me a place. It was only one bedroom, in Poplar. I bumped into someone I knew and they said, you look so well. What has happened? This was when I realised the effect it was having on me. I thought, I'm free.

But this also meant that Elizabeth went from a double-fronted Hackney house to a one-bedroom flat. She only had her income to support her and her son, Adi. So she found a business-minded way to make ends meet. At British rail, she had to work two weeks at a time and then would have some rest days off. A friend had shown her that in Holland there was a market where you could buy Nigerian fabrics for very little money.

As an employee for British Rail, she could ride the trains for free across the UK and into Europe, and so could her son. So when she had some rest days from work, she would get the train to Holland over Sunday night and arrive on Monday morning. On Monday she would use a credit card to buy fabric from the markets there and get the train back to the UK, where she would sell the fabrics. On Tuesday she would get back on the train to Holland and do the whole thing again, before returning to work at British Rail.

She and her son could also go on lots of trips together around the UK and Europe using the railways. While Elizabeth could get free railway travel for her son, as a woman employee she wasn't allowed to get it for her husband. 'Unfortunately, by the time he could have benefited from it, I had left him!' She chuckles. Her daughter-in-law, sitting with us during the interview, comments on how great and rare this was for the average family from London. Elizabeth's hard work afforded her not only the freedom to lead her own life, but also greater freedom of movement.

It's almost two hours into our interview by the time Elizabeth pauses and tells us, 'I've been through some challenges but I thank God that I'm here. I'm still going through challenges. But I'm lucky.' Our mugs are now empty by the sofa. Elizabeth's grandson is hiding on the stairs. She has held court for this entire time, staring out from her worn leather armchair, every part the great storyteller.

Now, she is clearly wrapping up story time. She believes she has been lucky in life and we feel we have been lucky to hear her stories. We jump on the bus, Elizabeth's personal taxi, and head off, both feeling jubilant—lifted by the joy of spending a morning with Elizabeth Afilaka.

These stories of migration, told by mothers (and their daughters), tell a different version of Britain's history. This is the version of Britain's history—told through these often unheard voices—that urgently needs to be taught in history classes. These stories are haunted by racism from the British public, supported by xenophobic policies from the British government, as well as patriarchal oppressions within the home, but there is a distinct feeling that through this, these women prevail. Though Ari, Patrice, Ranjan and Elizabeth came to the UK because of their husbands, they have all created lives that extend beyond the men who brought them there. Their sense of humour and self belief have allowed them to raise loving families with children who know their worth and know that they belong in this new Britain that we strive for, one in which everyone has a place and is valued equally.

Jessi

6

INVISIBLE BORDERS

Movement is prevented and precipitated by wars, political manoeuvring, climate change and countless other reasons. The bodies that we're in often come to influence this movement, remembering Alphare's story of transitioning making it dangerous to live in her home country of Uganda or Ari's story of domestic abuse leading her to seek asylum in Britain. Our bodies themselves and societal attitudes towards them can also alter our freedom of movement.

Nowhere is this more obvious than in our cities—power centres of the patriarchy, but also hubs for the uprooted, the resistance, and those refusing to be put in a box: inhabited by all comers, yet built for no one. In this chapter, we speak with Jessi, a non-binary creative whose ability to move freely around their hometown of London is severely restricted by the politics of ableist architecture and policy; their story shines light on all kinds of marginalised genderqueer people and women struggling to get around the city. We meet women taking to the streets of Hong Kong, putting their bodies on the line to confront authority. And we learn that even those who are physically freer to move within and between cities are still constrained, both practically and socially, by gendered expectations.

We speak to two incredible women who have lived their lives all over the world and whose own work critiques the limitations placed on women in different urban centres internationally. The book written by author Marlowe Granados and the film created by Basma Khalifa are additions to a long trajectory of women speaking out and resisting these limitations; they have added their perspectives on women's interactions with different cities, and the ways in which they can carve out their own spaces in this tradition through their works.

***

It's hard to feel welcome, never mind at home, in the world when you're constantly struggling for access. I am displaced in and disabled by even my most familiar environments.

Dr Jessi Parrott is an actor and writer, and they have a doctorate in disability and employment in the arts. Jessi uses they/them pronouns; they also have cerebral palsy and the accessibility of the world around us has been a constant conversation during our adventures. Alex B, who works as an assistant to Jessi, met them through an online group for women and non-binary people in the arts.

They first met at the BFI. Alex B was very nervous, as she invariably interviews terribly for jobs. Jessi was nervous too, despite their customary courteous and welcoming demeanour. They made their way to a seminar, where Alex scribbled notes on disability employment in film for Jessi's PhD. There were many casting directors there from big TV networks, who all seemed to agree that they were very happy to be there, that they hadn't realised how much their casting process excluded disabled people from employment and that they would strive to do and be better. Clichèd as their responses seem now, Alex was in much the same boat, with very little knowledge or awareness of disability and a hope to change that.

Conversations with Jessi fluctuate between disarmingly cerebral, from long discussions on the patriarchy (or the kyriarchy)[1] to the much more mundane but often more challenging negotiations of pavements, toilets and ramps. Jessi is fiercely intelligent, with a sense of activism that is finely nuanced and balanced. Their words are weighted heavily with sources and information, as well as a shocking sense of humour. Once, upon arriving in a large hall filled with people, Alex turned to Jessi to see where they wanted to go. Jessi responded to her look with a deadpan, 'Don't look at me to decide. I'm bi.' Another favourite joke is, 'Not even my spine is straight.'

This sense of humour extends to the physical challenges of the world around Jessi. To provide stability on steep ramps, Jessi sometimes requires someone to stand on the back of their chair as they race down the incline. Alex and Jessi enacted a particularly spectacular photoshoot at the top of one farcically steep and precarious ramp: they had travelled to Wales to see a play in the Millennium Centre. After unloading themselves from the taxi, Alex and Jessi were brought up short by a magnificent and steep set of stairs. The hotel staff hurried out with a ramp; after all, this was an accessible hotel.

However, the ramp was a practically vertical slope with two narrow treads that were unattached from any secure mooring. As Jessi says, their chair isn't small; Jessi refers to it as a 'hefty beast' in one of our conversations. Yet, by the end of our stay, Jessi was wheeling with aplomb down this frightening ramp. The photoshoot was for the benefit of Jessi's mum. Alex was lying on the ground in an attempt to frame in the ski slope ramp with Jessi perched at the top, both wailing with laughter.

You might have noticed the wording—the physical challenges of the world around Jessi—and thought it strange. There are different models for viewing disability, of which the social and the medical models are the most prevalent.

The medical model of disability has been the dominant line of thought in Western medicine in the last century. It determines that disabled people are:

> Defined by our impairments and what can be done by the medical establishment, to either rehabilitate or recover, or even cure those impairments. And it doesn't really give space for the social experience of barriers and the impact that attitudes can have and the fact that actually, not everyone necessarily wants to be cured.

The social model was developed as a response to the medical model by the disability civil rights movement. In 1974, the Union of the Physically Impaired Against Segregation was formed in the UK and defined disability as 'the disadvantage or restriction of ability caused by a contemporary social organisation which takes little or no account of people who have physical impairments and thus excludes them from participation in the mainstream of social activities'.[2]

> It's essentially the idea that disabled people are not defined by their impairments and are not disabled by their impairments, they are instead disabled by society.

The barriers might be in the built environment with physical obstacles such as steps, a lack of a dropped kerb, cobbles or the lack of tactile paving. The ways in which society can be disabling include these environmental barriers but also attitudes and laws and policies that discriminate against disabled people.

A key phrase in disability activism is 'Nothing About Us Without Us'; no laws or policies around disability and impairment should be made without the influence, advice and presence of disabled people. As such, our language will reflect Jessi's preferences but, like all groups, the community of Deaf, disabled and neurodivergent people are not a homogenous group and hold a multiplicity of opinions on these models and language. This sense of the community, of one that is vocal, multifaceted and ever-changing, is reflected by academic Mike Oliver, who first coined the term 'social model of disability' and furthered the Union of the Physically Impaired Against Segregation's definition. He wanted the model to be a means by which to improve the lives of disabled people rather than be applicable to every individual experience and situation.

Jessi prefers identity-first language over person-first language, though again these preferences can vary from person to person. They tell us:

> In the same way that I would say, 'I'm a non-binary person, or a gender fluid person, or a bisexual person'—using it as an adjective, rather than a noun—I wouldn't say, 'I'm a person with non-binaryness'. I prefer 'disabled person' because it foregrounds it as part of my identity. Rather than saying 'I'm a person with a disability', like it's something that I'm carrying around and can put down at times because it's not that. It's something that has fundamentally forged my experience of navigating through the world.

Similarly, while Jessi subscribes to the social model, they stress that applying these models on:

> a wider and particularly global scale can be problematic, because it forgets that theories are always kind of contingent on the context in which they were created. It was a very particular social movement, but also a very particular group of

people with very particular kinds of impairments, who created the social model.

The social model uses *impairment* to describe the attributes that affect a person and *disability* to describe the constraints society can place on individuals with impairments or disabled people. Jessi believes that this linguistic split isn't always helpful:

> I would highlight my own experience of chronic pain, because the pain isn't social. It's within my body. Even if I was living in a 'fully accessible society', which is a fallacy in and of itself (because there's always going to be some kind of access need that hasn't been considered), I would still experience chronic pain.

Jessi notes that the particular group of people who created the split between the terms of *impairment* and *disability* were predominately people who had acquired their impairments and perhaps might have been using this to make sense of how their lives had changed. It is not unusual for someone who has acquired an impairment to lean too heavily into pride in that new experience in order to combat the internalised ableism that might have been foisted on them by society; in other words, to come to terms with their new 'disabled' status, they separate their physical condition from the negative realities of (aptly named) 'man-made' barriers. It is a valid and understandable position but not necessarily useful to apply to all situations.

This awareness of language, particularly the language of perceiving the world, is not interrogated by a lot of people. Jessi points out the myriad of idiomatic language that can exclude Jessi from the world. One such phrase is 'people from all walks of life,' Jessi says. 'I'm not from all walks of life, I don't walk'. Or 'standing up for yourself': 'I literally cannot stand up for myself. So then does that mean I'm not autonomous?' Jessi then turns to the huge list of phrases to do with blindness: 'turning a blind eye', 'love is blind', 'blind rage'. This language, on a very base level, omits Deaf, disabled and neurodivergent people from the narrative, as well as sometimes just being plain insulting.

Jessi tells us about a conversation they had with a theatre worker in South Africa, where Jessi spent the earliest part of their life. The theatre maker said, 'It's all very well to argue about language, when you don't have to fight for basic resources. We don't really have time to think about our political identity, because we're trying to make sure that we have housing and make sure that we can get out of bed in the morning'.

Jessi notes that:

> whilst British Deaf, disabled and neurodivergent people may have had similar experiences, it is also important to acknowledge the relative privilege that we do have with the infrastructure of our society. As much as certain people might wish that we didn't, and certain political movements might be said to be pushing things back, we do technically still live in a socialist society in the UK. And so that underpinning infrastructure and political ethos creates a layer of protection for us that other countries may not have for their Deaf, disabled and neurodivergent people.

Jessi refers to a socialist society in the UK, meaning a democracy with a welfare state—a social democracy. The welfare state model, a form of governmental support for basic human needs, most popular in the West, was introduced in the late 1800s, early 1900s. Its popularity began to wane after the financial crises in the 1990s; even the Nordic countries that have adopted the most universalist welfare states—ranking them amongst the highest on the World Happiness Report—have begun to permanently dismantle some of their welfare policies since the 1990s.[3]

However, the UK's welfare state hasn't always treated Deaf, disabled and neurodivergent people well. In particular, the arrangement of benefits such as the Employment and Support

Allowance in the UK, up until very recently, left many people, whose ability to work is affected by an impairment or health condition, vulnerable.[4] This was a benefit that was means tested, which means that if the income of the household increases, i.e. if the recipient of the benefits cohabits or marries someone who works, they will lose their benefit. This left the recipient reliant on their partner for financial support.

Jessi says, 'We're not pets to be kept. And I don't mean "being kept" in a sexy-but-patriarchally-problematic, Holly Golightly kind of way.' Indeed, Ari's story shows how depending on another, financially or for a visa, can limit your freedoms. There are other benefits that aren't means tested, but not everyone qualifies for that additional assistance. Losing Employment and Support Allowance due to a partner's income has left many disabled people vulnerable to abuse or exploitation, with reduced independence.[5]

Domestic abuse is unnervingly common, but in the year ending March 2019, in England and Wales, data shows that disabled women (17.3 per cent) were more than twice as likely to have experienced domestic abuse than non-disabled women (7.0 per cent). Similarly, disabled men were more than twice as likely (9.0 per cent) to have experienced domestic abuse in the year ending March 2019 than non-disabled men (3.7 per cent).[6] This abuse may include withholding medication, food or personal care or access to aids that provide independence, as well as physical, emotional or sexual violence.

This intersection of vulnerabilities, like being a refugee, increases the likelihood of violence, and increases the barriers to reporting violence and accessing services. Just as taking away Ari's computer, money and documentation made it very difficult for her to leave her abusive husband, many disabled people may struggle to access the physical support necessary to leave, including access to assistive technologies, particularly if they have been isolated from family and friends by their abuser.

And where leaving her abusive husband opened the door to a battle about Ari's legal status for her to stay with her children in the UK, disabled people leaving an abusive partner have to negotiate care requirements and accessibility needs. For many disabled people, their abuser might be a key person providing personal care and access support.

It can take upwards of seven attempts and more than two years for people to leave abusive relationships, fraught as this time is with danger, often triggering an abuser's fear of discovery and need for control. This rises to an average of 3.3 years of abuse before a disabled person leaves an abusive relationship with these added considerations.[7] Yet many domestic abuse services internationally do not cater to access needs, most often due to lack of funding.[8]

Let us reiterate. Disabled people in England are twice as likely to experience domestic violence (which we know disproportionately affects women), and yet only 49 per cent of domestic violence services have full wheelchair access, only 38 per cent offer some form of specialist service to disabled women, only 17 per cent have services for visually impaired, and only 13 per cent of refuges can provide (or have access to) temporary personal care assistants.[9] There are very low referral rates for disabled people into domestic abuse services,[10] and in 2017, after receiving support, disabled people were 8 per cent more likely to continue to experience abuse.[11] And those who manage to leave an abusive relationship do not face a good alternative under this welfare system: almost one in five working-age disabled people meet the criteria for 'deprived', compared with one in fifteen for non-disabled people.[12]

The Covid-19 pandemic has not only worsened this likelihood of hardship among the Deaf, disabled and neurodivergent community; its profound impact on everyone's freedom of movement has also changed life for both disabled people and queer people. Jessi points out that, strangely, coronavirus has had some positive effects for disabled people, as much of life has suddenly become accessible. This includes Jessi's access into queer spaces. By the nature of having been repressed for so many years, a lot of queer spaces are literally 'underground', which often only have step-access. Jessi has found that these spaces have opened up to them as events moved more online.

Similarly, the pandemic led to many companies around the world adopting working from home schemes, as well as more flexible hours. This, combined with a lack of presenteeism made work so much easier for so many disabled people. Jessi points out that, 'suddenly, the accommodations for virtual working, that Deaf, disabled and neurodivergent people have been asking for for years, happened overnight because everyone needed them. When it becomes a global health concern, then it's amazing what things can suddenly change.'

Jessi elaborates that the online environment is not a perfect substitute, as not everyone has good access to the internet, and not every meeting has British Sign Language or captions provided. Jessi, however, has found that:

> the world has become more accessible to me over the last eighteen months, because we've all been navigating and migrating in different ways because we've had to, and so suddenly the pace of life shifted to one that I'm more familiar with, and I think a lot of people with chronic pain and fatigue and pacing issues will get that too.

At the same time, Covid-19 both exposed and exacerbated many of the challenges facing disabled people. Specifically, the UK government introduced now expired 'easements' of the Care Act, removing local councils' obligations to meet people's assessed care needs, at a time when this care was more important than ever. More generally, medically vulnerable people were disregarded when governments all over relaxed or abolished Covid restrictions before vaccination programmes were complete.

Jessi's occupational therapist and social worker have both agreed that Jessi needs twenty-four-hour assistance. This is for everything from getting out of bed and into bed to personal care to meal preparation and getting around society. Despite this, Jessi's entitlement is only 80.5 hours. As they need two people for quite a lot of personal care tasks, this covers around forty hours a week, restricting their movement outside these hours.

> This just covers my personal care support. It doesn't allow me to live my life or socialise or work. We've had to fight really hard for the benefits I have now. Having to justify your basic means and reasons for existence is weird. And it does significant damage to one's sense of self. We're all intrinsically valuable, but when you are continually having to think about your own self, in terms of how much you cost the local council, you can forget that intrinsic value.
>
> So I think that, in some ways, can make me feel quite transitory within my own life. And within my own selfhood. Never mind the movement and migration that is required, in a literal sense, to navigate society when I can't cross the road because there's not a dropped curb, or I can't enter a venue because there are stairs. There's transitoriness and migration at the heart of my very existence. I am displaced in and disabled by even my most familiar environments.

Benefits, care packages and employment support, while not the most stimulating to read about, are indescribably important. Jessi says, 'Without the care package that I get, I wouldn't be able to get out of bed.' These payments are visas, passports, mobility, allowing people to get beyond their beds and out their front doors to navigate the world. Capping or taking away payments restricts the borders of so many disabled people's lives.

183

Jessi tells us about their navigation outside their house, in the city of London, where they live, and abroad. Jessi says that, 'It is an adventure even when I leave my house for me to navigate even my local community.' People often use the excuse of London's age for accessibility, as the older parts of the city haven't been built with accessibility in mind, and the historic features make people reluctant to make adaptations.

Indeed, Leslie Kern argues that most urban places are built from a 'cluster of assumptions about the "typical" urban citizen', revealing that 'Shockingly, this citizen is a man'.[13] Crucially, this 'typical citizen' is a white, cis-gendered, heterosexual and ambulant man. However, as more technology becomes available, people have been able to create accessible adaptations in more creative ways, making the excuse of original architecture less valid.

Jessi generally uses the bus or a taxi in London. The bus is difficult, because not only is the space available for a wheelchair small and often filled with people, but chairs aren't clamped in, which means Jessi feels like they have to 'hold on for dear life'. Similarly, taxis are meant to use a clamping system but a lot of the time, taxi drivers aren't trained in using the clamps. The ramps in taxis can also have an infuriating gradient that makes them difficult to use safely. Jessi has a freedom pass and also takes advantage of a system of subsidised taxis for people that need to use them regularly.

Jessi tells us that most of the Tube is inaccessible, but they like the Overground train service. However, Jessi says that they 'have had some interesting experiences, where people seem to think it's their prerogative to strike up a conversation and be like, "Oh, was it an accident?"' This is characteristic of Jessi's day-to-day movements outside the house, whether on the street or on public transport or in a park. If Jessi is alone in public for a few minutes, people come up and ask if they can help, or otherwise have a chat. While Jessi understands how this is meant with good intentions, it is frustrating to Jessi that if they were 'an ambulant person, in London particularly, there's no way that anybody would just randomly engage'.

Travel outside London presents many new barriers. Jessi cannot fly in their wheelchair. This requires them to transfer out of their chair into the aeroplane seat. While Jessi is able to transfer at the moment, there were periods in their life when this wasn't feasible, preventing them from travelling abroad. Beyond this, Jessi describes being plagued by a constant sense of anxiety at being separated from their chair, not knowing what they would find at the end of the journey, if their chair was being stored properly or handled carefully.

> Some of my earliest memories are bursting into tears on aeroplanes when we were coming back from visiting family in either Canada or South Africa, because I watched, from the aeroplane window, my chair being thrown onto a luggage truck.
>
> And air hostesses would come up and be like, 'Why are you crying?' and my mum would say, 'Well, it's like your legs being broken. That's what's happening here.'

Jessi points out that there isn't an understanding of the importance of a chair in providing independence, and therefore how 'difficult, demeaning and demoralising' it can be to see a chair treated poorly. Jessi also notes the extraordinary cost of power chairs, telling us that their interactions with aeroplanes are 'superficial' and a sign of great privilege when many can't even get a wheelchair to get around their own house.

On one recent journey, when Jessi was travelling for work, Jessi's chair got lost after a relatively easy flight. The staff told them they couldn't bring Jessi's chair up to the door of the plane. Apparently, this was because there were stairs. So they put Jessi in a manual wheelchair with no seatbelt. Jessi and their mum were confused that the staff managed to get a manual chair to the door but couldn't get Jessi's power chair to the door. It transpired that the staff couldn't find Jessi's chair. Jessi was then in the manual chair, feeling very unsafe, for over an hour. Jessi also had to be tipped back in the wheelchair to be moved because of the placement of the footplates on the airport chair. Eventually Jessi's chair was found.

Jessi also recently travelled to Canada and they tell us about the multitude of barriers they encountered on that journey. Jessi tells us about the barriers that Covid has created for them, including vaccination barriers but also the ramifications of mandatory PCR tests. Not only are they expensive, making travel itself more costly, but they create another level of difficulty to the process of travel.

Jessi tells us about their experience of getting their PCR test. They had been assured categorically before they went to do their test that the test centre was accessible. However, when Jessi arrived, there was a step. One of the staff asked the nurses if they could do the test outside, but the nurses refused, saying that it wasn't sanitary or private or dignified.

At this point, Jessi didn't have enough time before flying to book their test at a new place. Jessi told them that, 'I've dealt with far more exposing and difficult situations than this'. The nurses eventually relented, and after a few hours, Jessi was tested. Furthermore, while Jessi was being tested, one of the nurses asked Jessi's mum to explain to Jessi that it was a mouth swab, rather than speaking to Jessi directly. Jessi says, 'And that was before even getting on the plane!'

On the other hand, the pandemic has also changed the experience of air travel in ways that make it less traumatic. Jessi noted that, because of social distancing, when they got to the airport and for the whole flight, people seemed more content than usual to let them and their mum get into the relevant places and to transfer into the chair themselves. Ordinarily, people often want to help and want to make things easier, but Jessi tells us that 'sometimes it's simpler to do things in the rhythm that you're used to, rather than explaining what we need to external people'.

***

Jessi's navigation of the world is also marked by their gender. Jessi describes being misgendered because of the nominal gender on their passport on a flight to Switzerland. A member of staff came up to Jessi and put his hand on their knee and said, 'Now, young lady, I'm afraid I have to ask, can you walk independently?' When Jessi replied 'No', he said, 'If there's an emergency, we'll find some strong young men to come and help your mum.' The gendered dynamic of that ableism made Jessi's skin crawl.

Jessi has found that coming out as non-binary has been made more complicated by disability. Jessi tells us that they are not 'out' with many of the medical professionals that they engage with, because they're 'in quite a vulnerable position when we're interacting. Literally, I'm out of my chair and being moved around or whatever.' Jessi isn't sure how some of them will respond, and whether they will find the new pronouns difficult. Jessi says that:

> It's exhausting to repeatedly remind people and perform that labour. Particularly in situations where I'm already doing quite exerting stuff, physically. I'm trying to desensitise myself to it a little bit, just so that I don't feel it every single time someone uses 'she' rather than 'they'.

The way in which Jessi is made to feel vulnerable through needing physical support has an impact on their mental health. Jessi notes how complicated their relationship with autonomy is, particularly if they are being supported by people they don't know or trust. A large portion of supporting Jessi is communication and trust so that Jessi feels safe enough to ask for things to be done differently or to explain when something is uncomfortable.

Jessi tells us that their 'mental health issues are much more disabling than all of the physical access that we've been discussing'. Their dissociation and PTSD is 'in many ways more debilitating than the fact that I really struggle with going over kerbs'. 'Actually, if I have the right support, then I can be pretty independent, physically'. Jessi points out that the evening before this conversation, they had been chopping aubergine for our evening meal and 'getting far too excited about how round my slices were'. Jessi can take part in almost every aspect of day-to-day life, given the right support and can feel 'productive and involved'.

The city is disabling for Jessi, with its kerbs and steps and escalators. The vulnerability created by the design of cities, architecturally and socially, shapes how people move through the city. Jane Darke suggests that 'Any settlement is an inscription in space of the social relations in the society that built it... *Our cities are patriarchy written in stone, brick, glass and concrete.*'[14] When people are making journeys day to day, how they experience public spaces, as well as the private spaces they can access, says a lot about their wider lives. Vulnerabilities or limitations that might be less obvious once a person reaches their destination are sometimes difficult to conceal when on the move. And, as Jessi's story proves, the more ways one is vulnerable or marginalised, the more challenging the physical environment becomes.

Streetwise: From Hong Kong to Jeddah

In October 2019, Hong Kong student Sonia Ng stood on a stage at the Chinese University of Hong Kong, where she studied, to confront the Vice-Chancellor of the university. Speaking very fast and reading from a printed speech clutched in her hands, she described how she was abused and sexually assaulted by police officers when she was arrested for protesting against civil rights issues in Hong Kong.

> Our politicians have never ever sat down to properly listen to our voices. The point is to actually do something, rather than just saying: 'OK, thank you for your opinion, but I refuse to change my attitude.'

She refers to the Vice-Chancellor calling his students 'his children' and the then Chief Executive of the Beijing-backed government in Hong Kong from 1997, Carrie Lam, telling students and citizens 'you have a mother in me'. Here, Sonia criticises their empty words and shares her experiences of police brutality by directly asking the Vice-Chancellor if he was aware of exactly how the police treat peaceful protesters in Hong Kong. Rather than asking if he condemns all violence, she goes for details. She names the methods of violence.

> Did you know that from the moment we were arrested, the police would confiscate our phones and turn them off? Did you know that they would yell at us with abusive and derogatory words? Did you know that we were forced to go wherever the police wanted us to go? If they want us to go into a dark room, we go; if they want us to take off our clothes, we do. Did you know that there are still people who have been bludgeoned so hard by the police that they have to seek medical attention to this day?
>
> Did you know that the room in San Uk Ling Detention Centre where they did searches on us was pitch black?

At this point during her speech, she breaks down crying. Two friends put their hands on her shoulders, urging her to continue.

> Did you know that I am far from the only victim of sexual violence committed by the police? Did you know that other arrestees were sexually assaulted and tortured by multiple police

officers, regardless of the arrestees' gender? ... Did you know
that, during the process of arrest and detention, we were treated
like nothing more than pieces of meat?

She then goes on to request that the Vice-Chancellor condemn
'the exercise of violence by police on arrestees, which include
students of this university'. She finishes her speech with a hasty
and deep bow. Moments later the Vice-Chancellor responds
dismissively, 'I have already said earlier that violence is wrong.'

Sonia responds by asking if he condemns the violence, would
he issue a formal statement saying so? He starts his response
with, 'I already told you', without directly answering the question.

According to an article in *The Nation*, Sonia Ng was the first
woman to speak out about experiencing sexual violence in police
custody without hiding her identity.[15] Her words were brave but
seemed to have little impact; at this stage the anti-government
protests had escalated to the point where Carrie Lam introduced
an 'Emergency Regulations Ordinance'.[16]

This allowed the leader to 'make any regulations whatsoever
which he may consider desirable in the public interest'. This law
was leftover from Britain's colonial administration of Hong Kong
which lasted from 1841 to 1997—imperial China was forced to
cede the territory to imperial Britain on a long-term lease, which
would expire in 1997. The Sino-British Joint Declaration was a
treaty signed by the UK and China that declared the terms by
which Hong Kong would be transferred from British control to
Chinese control.

While 1997 marked the end of British control, there was
a mandated fifty-year period, sanctified by the Hong Kong
constitution, in which Hong Kong would maintain its existing
governing and economic systems. These were separate from
mainland China, being referred to as 'one country, two systems'.
China has a state-controlled economy and a one-party state,

whereas Hong Kong was developed under the British into a hub of global capitalism and a limited democracy. When China replaced Britain, they inherited a city and culture shaped by a century and a half of colonisation.

However, many Hong Kongers have a complicated relationship with this colonisation. An attachment to the 'one country, two systems' rule can be explained by the open economy that came with this and led to far greater prosperity and living standards there than on the mainland.

The contradictions between a Hong Kong political culture shaped by Western colonisation and Beijing's increasing curtailment of freedoms there since 1997, erupted in 2019 into a widespread protest movement calling for the protection of Hong Kong's 'difference' from mainland China. But how did we get from there to the sexual assault of a young woman in police custody?

***

Joey Siu, civil rights activist and employee at the National Democratic Institute, has some of the answers. Joey was a student at the City University of Hong Kong, where, as a student representative, she held a position at the forefront of student activism and the pro-democracy movement in Hong Kong. Women in Hong Kong are active across the civil rights movement and have powerfully shaped much of the resistance to the introduction of the national security law. By February 2020, a third of 7,000 protestors arrested were women.[17]

Joey is one of the women who has played a crucial role, both as a protester in Hong Kong and an activist working to maintain the attention of international governments. One startling repercussion of her work in activism is the way she feels this has altered her life and future. Joey always wanted to be a teacher at secondary schools, perhaps teaching English or Liberal Studies. But in her early twenties, this dream very abruptly became impossible when she became involved in the movement combating the repression of civil rights in Hong Kong.

In *Do Not Split*, a documentary from Field of Vision, you can see Joey watching a protest in 2019. She is speaking about this non-existent future.

> After the movement broke out, I was not spending time planning my future. Having a very strong political stance and being active... I don't feel like I could be a teacher anymore. None of the schools are willing to hire such a teacher. None of the neutral or pro-Beijing companies will hire me anymore.

In October 2019, in response to the introduction of a bill that would lead to the extradition of criminal suspects to the Chinese mainland, where the courts convicted 99 per cent of criminals, young Hong Kongers began to take action. This included several young people clad in black breaking into a branch of the Bank of China and setting it alight. In *Do Not Split*, a documentary which records the protests at the time, a protestor says that 'we used to have a lot of freedom ... only democracy can save us from the disaster of colonial China'.[18]

The camera soon turns to Joey Siu, who is wearing round wire glasses and blue jeans. She is explaining the protestors' five demands of the Chinese government: 1) withdraw the extradition bill, 2) stop calling the protests 'riots', 3) release all protestors from prison, 4) commission an independent inquiry to investigate police brutality, 5) allow Hong Kongers to elect their own lawmakers and their own chief executive.

The clip after this shows protestors running into an alleyway and squatting down, heads bowed to the ground. They have been tear-gassed; one elderly man who is evidently in a lot of pain explains that he has mild asthma.

Around the same time, Carrie Lam announced at a conference: 'As a responsible government, we have a duty to use all available means in order to stop the escalating violence and restore all order in society.' We can see exactly what she means by 'all available means'. Despite Lam declaring in a TV interview, crying, that she has sacrificed a lot for Hong Kong and that she could not have 'sold out Hong Kong', she also refers to the protestors as 'stubborn children'. She claims that 'if my son was stubborn and I spoiled him and tolerated his stubborn behaviour every time, I would just be going along with him'.[19]

During one protest, a young man says 'the British handed us over to China like a bag of potatoes. They sold us to China.'

Soon, as student protests escalated, police were entering the university, arresting students and dragging them away.

Then, the pandemic happened. As with so many of the stories told in *Wander Women*, the coronavirus pandemic shifted Joey's path dramatically, alongside the path of the civil rights movement. In January 2020, the city shut down, the streets emptied. A law was implemented that only allowed groups of four to meet up. The protests had come to a halt two months before this time anyway, as protestors struggled to deal with their distrust of the Chinese and Hong Kong governments.

The sudden stillness forced Joey to acknowledge the full impact of the state violence on her well-being. Joey explains:

> The experience left me very traumatised, and I believe that is also the feeling of many Hong Kong protestors. I'm not getting enough sleep. I'm not eating on time. I did not allow myself space for the negative emotions. I was too busy with other stuff. Every day you've got new stuff that makes you depressed.

But she didn't have long to rest in that stillness. In May 2020, Beijing declared plans to announce the national security law in Hong Kong. Joey quickly kicked back into action alongside her peers: handing out pamphlets, protesting, working towards getting more legislative officials elected who supported the civil rights of Hong Kong citizens. 'I believe I am in danger from the law, which could be causing us 20–30 years of imprisonment. We could even be sent to mainland China,' she says to the camera in *Do Not Split*. And, as we know, even those who remain in Hong Kong custody are not safe, especially women.

She describes how the main reaction from protestors and students to the introduction of the national security law is fear. As soon as the law is implemented, Joey posts on Twitter announcing that she will step down as student representative, ending her tweet by saying 'We will never surrender.' In July 2020, at a protest, 370 people were arrested. Ten of these arrests were under suspicion of breaching the newly introduced national security law—including a fifteen-year-old girl who was waving a Hong Kong independence flag.[20]

In *Do Not Split*, Joey records herself speaking on her phone, wearing her glasses with a cap pulled down. She has just come from the police station because her sixteen-year-old friend had been arrested. Joey went to find her with the girl's mother. 'I feel very stressed and panicked right now,' Joey says into her phone. 'I think they will arrest more politicians, activists and randomers over the next few days. We will try to hang in there.'[21]

Since the introduction of the law, arrests and imprisonments of Hong Kongers have been widespread. According to a six-monthly report from the UK government published in March 2022, since the introduction of the national security law, from June 2020 to the end of December 2021, 155 people were arrested under it.

The control of this law has spread across jurisdictions to have an almost total power over Hong Kongers. This document published by the UK government condemns the introduction and application of this law by the Chinese government:

In less than two years, China's National Security Law in Hong Kong has seen opposition stifled and dissent criminalised. Alternative voices in Hong Kong's executive, legislature, civil society and media have been all but extinguished.[22]

As a result of these extreme crackdowns, many Hong Kongers are fleeing the country. This same UK government report claims that, by the end of 2021, there were a total of 103,900 applications to the 'bespoke visa route for Hong Kongers with British Nationals (overseas) status'.

Joey is among the number of Hong Kong civilians forced to leave their homeland. She now lives in the US. Since leaving Hong Kong, she has focused on her advocacy work with the international community, including most recently to the time of writing, speaking at the Geneva Summit for Human Rights and Democracy,[23] and testifying at the Senate Foreign Relations Subcommittee on threats to freedom of expression in Asia.[24]

Joey reflects on her position in the movement in an interview with Community Democracies. Women have been at the forefront of the civil rights movement in Hong Kong, but she is aware that she is sometimes treated differently as a young woman in the pro-democracy movement. She says:

These biases and micro-discriminations as a young woman allow me to reflect on myself and be in others' shoes... who understands how it feels to be discriminated against because of your gender and your age. Having this experience when organizing campaigns, I try my best to make sure that every co-worker has equal opportunity and expectations, and no one will be looked down on because of gender, age, race or background ... I pay extra attention to women victims of the crisis or incidents... As a female leader, I can understand these experiences better.[25]

Women have been and still are at the forefront of the pro-democracy movement, and the effort is intergenerational—from the young female students like Sonia Ng protesting at their universities to the much older legislators and activists who have been incarcerated. At the time of writing, the below women political activists have been arrested, prosecuted and jailed, according to Hong Kong Watch. They are only a handful of the thousands of women who have made great personal sacrifices for their democratic rights.[26]

Cyd Ho Sau-Lan, aged 66. Sentencing: 14 months imprisonment

Margaret Ng Ngoi-Yee, 73. Sentencing: Handed 12 months imprisonment, suspended for 24 months

Claudia Mo Man-Ching, 64. Detained in February 2020 and bail denied in April 2021

Tiffany Yeun Ka-Wai, 27. Arrested in July 2020, no details on bail or release

Prince Wong Ji-Yuet, 24. Arrested in July 2020, released on bail

Helena Wong Pik-Wan, 61. Arrested in May 2020, granted bail in March 2021

Clarisse Yeung Suet-Ying, 34. Last arrested January 2021

Carol Ng Man-Yee, 50. Arrested in July 2021 and denied bail

Winnie Yu Wai-Ming, 33. Arrested in March 2022 on suspicion of violating bail conditions

Gwyneth Ho Kwai-Lam, 30. Arrested in January 2021

Agnes Chow Ting, 24. Arrested in June 2020 and sentenced to 10 months imprisonment

Chan Pui Man, 51. Arrested June 2021, next hearing February 2022 where she faces a sentence of life behind bars

Chow Hang-Tung, 36. Last arrested October 2021, sentenced to 22 months imprisonment

The feelings of many women from Hong Kong towards the complexity of their home's history might be further complicated by being displaced by recent events. The various levels of this displacement—firstly due to the transformation of the city to a place of conflict and surveillance and secondly, the possible displacement to another place in the world as a result of this conflict—is felt by many women, although for differing reasons. While some Hong Kongers might leave the city because of the specific recent threats to freedom of speech and democracy, similar feelings of displacement can come from shifts within women's personal lives. The layers in each woman's identity can come from the different places they live in and that shape them.

Where Joey Siu movingly describes how her imagined life as a teacher in Hong Kong crumbled in the face of her activism, and caused her consequent move to the US, filmmaker Basma Khalifa similarly describes the difference between her imagined futures and the ones she actually lived as a result of her parents moving her and her brothers between Sudan and Saudi Arabia, then to Northern Ireland and, finally, to Scotland. Basma and Joey's stories are examples of how places and cities shape women's identities and, in turn, how those women can shape these places too.

Women's spaces in cities built for men

When we meet Basma Khalifa at The Wing, the women-only private members' club on Great Portland Street in London, it is in its prime: lauded as a unique safe space for professional women with strained schedules and nowhere to relax in between meetings located across the city, without the risk of uninvited attention from men. Many women seem to have found the marketing and interiors of The Wing offensive from the start—a quick Google search reveals multiple articles describing the Instagrammable pastels of The Wing as nothing more than a one-dimensional bent towards social media marketability.[27]

Sophie Elmhirst, writing in *Tortoise* magazine in December 2020, visited The Wing to interview a member and sat on what she describes as 'the kind of sofas that you'd save up for and then regret, because in colour and effect the sofa would be so specifically tied to the autumn of 2019 that a year later it would be like sitting on nothing but a faded trend'.

The critique of the decor of a women's space must also itself be critiqued. In the same way that it is reductive for feminists to criticise women for wearing too much make-up or wearing clothing that defines them as overtly femme, it is similarly diminishing to critique a space for being too pink. The idea of 'feminine' decor is in itself reductive, but there is a sense that The Wing's decor was being criticised *because of* its femininity.

It didn't take long for The Wing to go from being an expensive but somewhat practical solution for women who wanted to find somewhere to relax in a discordant and exhausting city, to a failure. The combination of the coronavirus pandemic and a *New York Times* article where 26 employees complained of classist and racist mistreatment fed into its demise.

The rise and fall of The Wing is just another chapter in a long history of women trying and failing to carve out fully inclusive safe spaces in cities across the world. Specifically in London, another chapter in this history was located only fifteen minutes' walk away, in Gordon Square, almost a century ago.

The Bloomsbury Set were a group of young intellectuals—with most of the privileged young men coming from the University of Cambridge—who met in their homes in Gordon Square in London to talk, create and occasionally have affairs or marry. There were only two constant female members of the set: the sisters Virginia Woolf and Vanessa Bell. Having experienced difficult childhoods and restrained teenage years and, for Virginia, allegedly sexual abuse as a young girl, becoming part of the Bloomsbury Set must have been freeing.

In Virginia Woolf's famous feminist polemic, *A Room of One's Own*, she describes how many of the great artistic and intellectual achievements of the past have been accomplished by men, because women haven't had the means to complete the work. She sets out in quite literal terms the money and space someone needs to create.

A woman needs a room to herself and enough money to spend her time writing and working in that room to create in the same way as a man. Her sister's home is in some ways an example of that. Vanessa Bell, alongside her fellow artist and one-time lover Duncan Grant, bought a farmhouse in East Sussex, UK. Every surface of the house has been used as a canvas for their art. Vanessa's own creative expression is at the heart of Charleston House, and can still be seen all over its walls and doors for the admission price of £16.

Within these spaces Virginia and Vanessa found a freedom that wasn't possible in public spaces in early twentieth-century England. At one point in *A Room of One's Own*, Virginia describes trying to access university resources at 'Oxbridge'. She describes how: 'Instantly a man's figure rose to intercept me... His face expressed horror and indignation. This was the turf; there was the path. Only the Fellows and Scholars are allowed here; the gravel is the place for me.' Limited to the gravel path as a woman, she also wasn't allowed to access the library as a non-member of a university that women weren't allowed to receive degrees from until 1920.[28] Here, Woolf is describing the rules—still in place today at Oxford and Cambridge—about where people can or cannot walk.

These sisters carved out spaces for themselves, sometimes publicly but often in private, and at the time that was considered radical. However, they were also unwittingly doing so in a way that was still highly exclusive and inaccessible for other women. By locating their creative spaces inside their own privately owned homes, and by participating in a 'club' network, Woolf and Bell used the same limited solution to women's unfreedom as The Wing today: defending an inner circle for some women.

Even her crucial polemic, *A Room of One's Own*, wouldn't necessarily have been published without the privilege afforded to her as a member of the affluent Bloomsbury Set. The book is an extended essay based on two lectures Woolf gave at Newnham College, Cambridge University. She was invited to speak due to her connection with the principal, Pernel Strachey, also a member of the set.[29]

The Pulitzer Prize-winning author Alice Walker criticises Woolf's singular thinking in *A Room of One's Own*, revealing it to be addressing problems limited to the experiences of middle-class white women. In her essay 'In Search of Her Mother's Garden',[30] Walker uses the example of poet Phillis Wheatley, a Black women sold into slavery at the age of seven or eight. Despite this, she was the first African-American author of a published book of poetry.

Walker argues that Phillis did not own her own body, let alone her own home, yet she was able to write and create. She didn't have access to the space that Virginia deems necessary to succeed as a woman writing. At the same time, in her novel *The Color Purple*, Walker suggests that to truly escape patriarchy and thrive, Black women suffering from the double discrimination of race and gender need more than a room: they need the whole house.

A century on and white women are still carving out spaces that fail to be as accessible as they first hoped. The *New York Times* exposé about The Wing details how 'members and their guests could be casually racist. One eyed a photo board of Wing employees and remarked, "There's a lot of colored girls that work here.'"

Founder Audrey Gelman's initial vision had been to create a space for women that was 'subtly radical'. Instead, she built a pastel empire where employees described feeling like 'human kitty litter', according to the *New York Times*.

'You're representing women—so show up, and show up well'

At the time we meet filmmaker and creative Basma Khalifa in the London branch of The Wing, well before the pandemic or any *New York Times* exposé, it's just a secure and quiet place to conduct an interview. For Basma, before its demise, it was somewhere she could nap between meetings, relax and feel comfortable during an interview. We speak for well over an hour, and the comfort and safety of the club feels like a significant contributing factor to the ease of our conversation.

During our conversations in the café, Basma tells us about journeys between different spaces: from Saudi Arabia, where she was born, to living in Sudan for just under a year, to being the only Muslim girl at her school in Northern Ireland to eventually finding her feet career-wise in New York and London.

For her, a place cannot be dismissed entirely just because of failing women in some ways: it can still be made home. When it comes to how women can interact with space, they often occupy the grey area, struggling with a city or area's limitations while also celebrating the familiarities and what makes it theirs.

This grey area is communicated in the documentary Basma produced and presented for the BBC, *Inside the Real Saudi Arabia and Why I Had to Leave*.

In the film we watch Basma exploring a new life with her three aunts in Jeddah, a modern and more culturally liberal port city in Saudi Arabia. The city might be more liberal, but the film matter-of-factly portrays the limitations placed on Basma as a woman living there.

Basma tells us about what it was like to return to Saudi Arabia. Her visit there for the purpose of making the documentary was cut short after she mentioned the name of Loujain al-Hathlouf, a right-to-drive female campaigner who was imprisoned and tortured, to one of her government minders.

But, she says, this was to be expected. The team she and filmmaker Jessica Kelly were working with 'hated us from the beginning. They would always have found a reason to trip us up. They found their way and their reason to kick us out.'

When the journalist and Saudi critic Jamal Khashoggi was killed just before their trip in October 2018, the documentary became more political. 'It was never meant to be a current affairs programme,' says Basma. By the time she arrived back in London, she had post-traumatic stress disorder.

In the film, we see Basma reading out news updates about Khashoggi. The journalist, who used to be an advisor for the government in Saudi Arabia, fell out of favour and moved to the US, where he wrote a column for the *Washington Post*. In this, he often criticised the new crown prince—who Basma describes as being 'like Voldemort, listening in the walls'.

When Khashoggi visited the Saudi consulate in Istanbul, he never came out to meet his wife, who waited outside the building for ten hours. It later transpired that he had been injected with a drug that killed him. His body was cut into pieces and passed outside in a suitcase.[31]

This is a version of Saudi Arabia that Basma did not want to represent. Rather, she wanted to understand how women in the country experienced life:

> The women in my family are the enforcers. It looks like a man's world and the Western world makes [Saudi Arabia] seem more

like a man's world. It's the women who tell you that, as a woman, you shouldn't expose your body. Because you are representing women—so show up, and show up well.

At one point, she asks her aunt if she can go on a date with a man from Tinder, and her aunt's response is: 'no way'. But the power to choose this is coming from women themselves and, according to Basma, this is what matters. Those outside Saudi Arabia might believe all women are forced by men to wear abayas[32]; Basma contradicts this, and calls it out as being a simplistic and problematic external viewpoint.

'They're really excited about where the country is going and they're proud of it. Who are we to say that isn't enough? They're just chilling. That was the whole point of getting into TV, I didn't want the patronising narrative,' Basma adds.

This is the important reality on the ground for women in Saudi Arabia. But how do the decisions made by those in leadership impact women's experience of living and moving inside the country? Saudi Arabia has been ruled by an absolute monarchy since 1932, and can be defined as a hereditary dictatorship.

The reality is that Saudi Arabia sits at 42 out of 189 countries on the Gender Inequality Index, which rates the improvement of gender equality in countries based on maternal mortality rate, adolescent birth rates, female parliamentarian seats, the amount of female population with at least some secondary education and labour force participation.[33] Saudi Arabia comes just below Hungary, Slovakia and Portugal. The situation for women really has improved—but the journey has been far from smooth.

Women's rights in Saudi Arabia have been covered frequently in international media, from positive steps forward, such as the lift of the fatwa banning women from driving in 2018, to further human rights abuses such as the imprisonment of vocal female Saudi activists in the past few years, such as Loujain al-Hathlouf, mentioned earlier.

The system behind this, which labels women as 'legal minors', is the male guardianship system. Up until recently, women were not even allowed to access their own passports without the permission of their male guardian, who would traditionally be their father or husband but sometimes their brother or even son. Without this permission, a woman would not legally be allowed to work.

A government-run app called Absher, downloadable from the Apple and Google app stores, has the primary function of allowing citizens in Saudi Arabia to access up to 279 government services. It has over twenty million users.[34]

But Absher has another function. It enables male guardians to track the movements of women. If a woman is in an airport, their male guardian can block their right to travel. After an investigation into this by the magazine *Business Insider* in 2019, Apple and Google claimed they would investigate the application, which they have both continued to host. Google concluded that Absher did not violate their terms and conditions, and so they would not be removing it from their app shop. In 2019, the Saudi government did make further reforms, enabling Saudi women over the age of eighteen to travel without their male guardians. It isn't clear whether guardians are able to still track women's movements on Absher, despite the progress made with law reforms.

The restrictions placed on women's movement and access in Saudi Arabia have been loosened. In 2017, King Salman ordered that women would be allowed to access services from government agencies without their guardian's consent. In August 2019, major reforms were made that now allow Saudi women to register births and deaths, make medical decisions about their own body when it comes to pregnancy and birth, and travel abroad without their guardian.

It is difficult to reconcile this version of Saudi Arabia, revolving around the decisions made by the government, tracking slow legal reforms and often seen from and distorted by the lens of Western media, with Basma's version. But the perspective that is most valid and does tell us the most about Saudi women's lives—at least in Jeddah—is Basma's own and that of the women in her family. The truth sits again in a grey area: women *are* empowered and *are* calling the shots, despite being perceived as 'second-class citizens'.[35]

Another journalist expressing the desire not to adhere to the 'patronising narrative' so often lazily relied on in Western media is Lina Attalah. In the collection of essays *Our Women on the Ground*, where Middle Eastern female journalists write about their experiences, Attalah writes about her discomfort at being perceived as an Arab woman fighting against the outdated conservatism and patriarchy of her home country, Egypt. 'Women in Egypt, as well as in other Arab and Middle Eastern countries, are often depicted to the Western world as nothing but victims of patriarchy,' she says.

Her middle-class parents wanted her to go to a 'good school', which, according to Lina, meant a French school and an American university. She explains that because of this, 'I had direct access to the Western world. I worked in English, the lingua franca of the globe. I became an extension of the object of the typical Western gaze in that context.' She describes her discomfort when invited to speak at events: 'I didn't want to recount stories of sexism, patriarchy and oppression that would feed into commonplace Orientalist essentialism and render me a heroic survivor.'

The essay recounts how, in 2003, Attalah first saw policemen in Cairo, Egypt brutally beat protesters during a demonstration against the Iraq war. Afterwards, she resisted going back to her parents' house, where the domestic battles fought between her family members seemed 'trivial'.

'I wanted to remain outdoors, as the street and the protestors felt like a family I had chosen,' she writes. In Cairo, her movements between public and private spaces also led to a shifting between two different identities, one as a daughter and the other as a journalist and activist. 'Living two lives meant constantly guarding them from each other, safely insulated, for one risked defacing and assaulting the other. It was exhausting.'

But the shift that Attalah really emphasises in her essay as being damaging is the shift between Egypt and the English-speaking world she inhabits. This, she says, added something new and limiting to her life. The aforementioned invitations to speak, she says, made her 'feel trapped in one place, identity and body'.

This is something Basma, like Lina, has actively resisted her whole life. During our interview she tells us about how her family's movement and her own identity has shifted and transformed over the years. Basma spoke to us compellingly about how each place she lived in during her life has moulded who she has become today.

Basma spent only the first two years of her life in Saudi Arabia, but she said those memories are important to her. Both of her parents were working full-time so she and her brothers had a Filipina nanny, whom they adored. When her father got a job as a doctor in a hospital in Lisburn, Northern Ireland, Basma can still remember parting with this nanny. 'I remember leaving her at the airport when she left. It had such an impact that this woman who was like my mother just went through a barrier and left,' she describes over coffee.

When their family arrived in Northern Ireland, Basma and her brothers had to enter the school system without a word of English.

They were introduced to a woman called Mrs Featherstone, who was officially a speech therapist and unofficially 'a teacher to help us fit in'. Basma and her siblings developed a close relationship with her, and still stay in touch.

Going to school in Northern Ireland came with its own challenges for Basma. Out of a school of 700 students, she tells us they were the only students of a different ethnicity to white Irish. This was during a period in the 1990s of intermittent bouts of violence between the IRA and the loyalists. Her home was not far from the British army barracks.

She recalls doing her homework with her mum when a bomb exploded and the windows started to shake. 'Neither of us were fazed. What's that? Oh, just a bomb.' The family did not feel as though they were a part of the constitutional and physical turmoil shaking the country. According to Basma, 'For people around me, I was a bit like an alien, but not one they had to deal with. The political strife was so big that it was people's priority.'

Basma describes how tactical she was at school. She didn't want to get bullied, and she saw that, if she was friends with the people who were more likely to do the bullying, she wouldn't be a target. She struggled with this: 'I was an underdog, so I wanted to be friends with the underdogs, but I also wanted to be safe.' Her ability to adapt is shown by an early school anecdote. A couple of boys asked where she was from and she told them she was Sudanese. They then asked if she was Protestant or Catholic, to which she said she was neither.

'They said I had to be one or the other. It was a Protestant school, so I said I would be Protestant,' Basma said. But some of her classmates were Catholic, too: she describes thirteen-year-olds boasting about their dad being in the IRA without really understanding why they were fighting.

Being friends with the popular girls in this school made Basma feel worse in different ways than if they had bullied her.

They were all 'skinny and blonde'; they were the girls all the boys fancied. One day, Basma was walking along with one of the boys. When she asked him if he fancied another student called Catherine, he said he would never date a girl called Catherine 'because it was a "pikey" name and too Catholic'. Basma realised that if he wouldn't go out with someone called Catherine, what chance did Basma Khalifa, the Muslim girl from Sudan have? 'I was always going to be this weird girl who didn't fit in,' she told us.

She was only in this high school for two years before the Khalifa family moved on again. Her father found a job in the smaller town of Dumfries, Scotland. Despite the difficulties in Northern Ireland, this was heart-breaking for Basma, who, after ten years of living in Ireland, had 'figured it out and made friends who accepted me for who I was. I was miserable.' She describes crying for the whole summer when they first made the move.

Eventually she moved to London to work in the fashion industry. This was another space that she struggled to comprehend and fit into. She was living in Putney and sharing a room with her brother on an intern's non-existent wage. She describes how the fashion industry at the time worsened the status of immigrants.

> The fashion industry is only different now because of social media. They were forced into caring. At that time, seven or eight years ago, nobody gave a shit about different women. You're Cindy Crawford or you're not. Being the only Black woman in every single team, I was always on the back foot. I was never going to get the job over Charlotte whose dad lives in Barbados, or Matilda who goes to the South of France on the weekends.

At twenty-five, she left her job at *InStyle* magazine to freelance and eventually made the shift from fashion to TV. 'You have to remember that Hearst and Condé Nast are still owned by white older men. They're institutions. You can't change them overnight.'

Today, Basma has carved out her own space in the city. Alongside airing her documentary, her creative output focuses on telling people's stories across the world. Specifically, she has curated an Instagram account called 'Our Isolated World', which focuses on connecting different voices and world views from people internationally.

'Our Isolated World' shows her constant striving towards learning more about care—care for herself, her community and the communities she is learning about. In November 2021, she spoke out about the protests occurring in Sudan as a result of the Sudanese military taking control of the government. Because Basma was planning to travel to Sudan, she asked Qatar Airways for extra baggage so she could carry donations into the country.

But when the new government shut down international flights and the internet, it left Basma locked out of the country and kept apart from her family. 'My family are safe, staying indoors, running out of money because banks have been emptied and sitting tight until it's over. No one knows when that will be. But they remain hopeful,' she writes in November 2021. 'I was heading to Sudan to celebrate my little cousin's wedding. To hug my family after so many years, that seems so futile now as I think of families that have lost, friends that are mourning. Sudan is bleeding.'

Here, it is clear just how much the political is personal for Basma. She finished this post by saying 'as you are enjoying your evening... Please look around and understand your privilege. You were born not fearing death, you were born with freedom as a given. Freedom being the greatest gift of all.'

For Basma, being grateful for The Wing is part of being grateful for London—but the patchwork of her childhood migrations tells a story of making a space for oneself, as an outsider and a woman, as an opportunity in any city.

'People should be able to go where they want'

Across the pond, authoress and adventuress Marlowe Granados has carved out her own space in Toronto, Canada. But it has taken her time.

In the film adaptation of Truman Capote's 1958 novel *Breakfast at Tiffany's*, Audrey Hepburn lives in a half-empty flat with a lot of boxes, a ginger cat and a sofa that is made out of a bathtub sliced in half. The whole place seems to be only half a home. Holly Golightly arrives in New York from an impoverished background in rural America, intent on reinventing herself. She hasn't yet figured out her place in the world, but she knows what it will feel like when she does: 'If I could find a real life place that could make me feel like Tiffany's, then I would buy some furniture and give the cat a name.'

During an interview over Zoom in autumn of 2021, Marlowe tells us that, for a long time, the flat she currently resides in also remained only half a home, which she called her 'Holly Golightly apartment'.

> For the longest time, my apartment was empty because I always thought I was leaving and I never had anything here. There was a couch and nothing else. I kept it like that for a year. I was still dealing with my ex-partner at the time and trying to figure it out. When you're in the process of applying [to move to New York], you can't go to America for this particular visa so I was just stuck in Canada. That whole thing dissipated so I was like 'I guess I should decorate finally!'

But Marlowe has been in flux for a long time. Originally from Canada, she spent six years living in London and completing a university degree in creative writing before returning to live between Toronto and New York. 'My own migration patterns have been kind of stressful,' she laughs.

Her mother—who passed away young—was Filipina and her father is Salvadoran. Speaking about how her background has moulded her own movements, Marlowe says:

> Obviously my family did immigrate to Canada in the seventies and eighties and both from very harsh circumstances. It's also a funny thing because when you come from that background you also don't have that history but you have this urge to seek the kind of life you want. It's less of an urgency that makes you travel but more of a curiosity.

Marlowe has travelled a lot. She describes her time in London as mostly being too cold, and with too much time spent on public transport. But there was one crucial thing that came out of her time living in the city. She worked as a hostess in a restaurant and a hotel in Shoreditch. This mostly entailed greeting and seating the clientele of the venue, being friendly and charming. She spent hours on the same bus routes to and from the places she worked, and this is what she remembers very clearly: 'the monotony of these routes'.

But the women she met and worked with during this time also inspired her novel *Happy Hour*. Since returning to Canada, Marlowe has published this highly successful first novel about two young women's adventures over a summer in New York, and she also hosts a podcast about female-led films and romcoms called *The Mean Reds*. She describes working with a constant shifting supply of other young women who would move on after four months and would come from Ukraine, Russia, Italy, Essex—everywhere. Most of the evening would be spent chatting with these girls at the desk.

We all had the same problems. It's the girls who are club promoters or do bottle service, they are my favourite type of girl. They can diffuse a situation and we can learn together. I don't care about the literary institutions, I wrote this book for them.

Marlowe was working in hospitality with drunken men who had crawled over from their offices in the City as well as dealing with awkward questions about where she was from. In the midst of this environment, she describes something akin to a sisterhood between herself and the other hostesses.

But because her visa was only to study in the UK, Marlowe never fully settled in London, knowing that it would be impossible for her to stay. Stories about the different cities and countries she has worked and lived in often boil down to limitations of the temporary passes governments distribute to people who want to live there; she was stuck in Toronto because of her visa for New York and she couldn't put down roots in London because there was a ticking clock on her student visa. It was the very sense of shared impermanence and unpredictability, a common feature of big cities that attract workers from elsewhere, that bonded her to these women.

Happy Hour's main characters are two young women called Isa and Gala, who want to spend their summer partying in New York. They do many odd jobs, from working at a flea market to life modelling. At parties, when men ask what they do, they confidently say 'nothing at all'. The surface implication is that having fun should be enough of a goal for one summer. But the underlying truth is that, without visas, they are 'illegal aliens' who must watch what they say and where they work to avoid being found out.

Marlowe shares a line of the novel that was edited out. 'Something about both marriage and borders being institutions you don't have to respect.' She didn't want to write a novel about the illegal working conditions of people without visas but she did write one about girls who happened to have not moved over legally. 'You can have these politics without feeding it to the reader. I don't want to force someone to think a certain way,' she explains.

During our conversation she doesn't make a big fuss about what could be seen as quite a radical approach to the world. Speaking about borders, she says she 'just doesn't see the point in them. People should be able to go where they want.'

Gala and Isa have a very subtle but telling relationship with public transport in the city. There is an understanding between them that whatever the time and regardless of how broke they are, they will always get a taxi back home. This tether of safety, in lives otherwise defined by spontaneity, partying, movement and heading back to strangers' houses drunk in the middle of the night, reminds us of the spaces that are and are not available to women in the city.

In the press interviews for her book, Marlowe talks a lot about young women in general and especially young women who want to have adventures. She criticises the urge to punish young women who seek to step outside their boxes, enter spaces or undertake journeys that are considered 'risky', and claim the city (and the world) as theirs. Isa and Gala travel to a different country illegally for the summer; Isa especially is aware that as a woman of colour she is more vulnerable than Gala, who is 'a child of the Bosnian war'. The summer has ups and downs, there are limitations and obstacles—but no punishments.

They are not found out, they're not abused and they don't experience any extreme violence. No lessons are learnt. Isa and Gala are women who are limited by the regulations of citizenship as well as the fact that, as young women who are only loosely employed and have little money, they sit fairly low in society's hierarchy of power. At the same time, they are just two young women who went on an adventure and had a good time. Marlowe makes clear that they can be both; one is an act of resistance against the constraints of the other.

This reflects Marlowe's own life. She tells us that, although there is a societal pressure for women to feel ashamed of themselves or the lives they lead, she personally does not give into it.

> It's very regressive. I feel the pressure, of course. But I don't want the art I make to add to that mentality. Shamefulness about saying what's on your mind, overstepping a bit, having power in a room—even when it comes to things about your body like casual sex or abortions.

Both Marlowe's lifestyle and writing style follow in a rich literary tradition of honest tales about women who move and act freely, whether they are supposed to or not. In interviews, when asked about the writers she is inspired by, she often speaks about Anita Loos, Kay Thompson and Jean Rhys, amongst others.

The writer Jean Rhys, who penned *Wide Sargasso Sea* and imagined the true past of Bertha, the 'madwoman' in the attic from Jane Eyre, herself lived the life of an adventuress—and at a time when freedom of movement, simply for the sake of movement, was often an impossibility for women. Although she grew up on the Caribbean island of Dominica, she spent most of her time in England. Here, she became a 'demimondaine', and was the mistress of a stockbroker; she married three men; returned to Dominica with one of them briefly; met writer Ford Maddox Ford in Paris, who she had an affair with, and who also helped to shape her writing; books were written and made into films; she was forgotten and then remembered.

In her unfinished autobiography, Jean Rhys wrote:

> I would never be part of anything. I would never really belong anywhere, and I knew it, and all my life would be the same, trying to belong, and failing. Always something would go

wrong. I am a stranger and I always will be, and after all I didn't really care.[36]

Marlowe tries to draw up a twenty-first-century world where women can go where they like, when they like. Of course, it doesn't quite exist yet, but illusions of freedom can be eked out in an unfree world—freedoms that, in both life and literature, have been easier to gain in cities and often by women coming from global backgrounds, something that, as Marlowe points out, is central to her own urge to explore. *Happy Hour* is the story the young women of today deserve: rather than being a cautionary tale, it celebrates the adventuress and the women who overstep.

Marlowe

7

UNLAWFUL ACTIVISM

VOLUNTEERING ON THE EDGE

Many women who cross boundaries are stepping not over borders between countries but across lines of political acceptability and legality, in the name of helping others. The four women we speak to in this chapter—Nadezhda, Iara, Ayat and Laura—all work with and for refugees and displaced people.

These women occupy very different spaces, from legal work to humanitarian aid to filmmaking, but all with the same underlying goal of helping people. Nadezhda has gone from human rights lawyer to political refugee; Laura's activism and search-and-rescue work was motivated by her political stance on refugee rights; Ayat's humanitarian work sits apart from politics and, for her, comes down to just 'helping people'; Iara sees herself as a bit of everything: filmmaker, activist, friend to many. These labels are reductive. They do not allow for the many things these women have achieved, the many things they have forsaken to undertake their various work—or the ways that Europe's anti-refugee attitude has made aid and activism work into one more way that women are made vulnerable by government policy.

The criminalisation of empathy, care, community and help is all too common.

We discovered the scale of the persecution of migrants and just how hard the work of volunteers at refugee camps is made by various governments when we first travelled to Calais in 2018. We made two trips to Calais, where we volunteered in the warehouse and used this as an opportunity to learn more from long-term volunteers.

One volunteer we spoke to, in a temporary shelter for women refugees and their children in Dunkirk, described the extent to which the volunteers' work was being blocked. One day when she and some others were delivering food supplies in a van to the refugee camp, their vehicle was surrounded by Gilets Jaunes— part of a French protest movement at the time—who pushed and shoved the van in an attempt to intimidate the volunteers. Indeed, we were spat on and called names by the protestors when we were leaving the warehouse after one evening of volunteering. This direct experience of these tensions at the time was put into context by our research during the trip, which made it clear to us that the issue was not these workers or their protest, but rather the policy climate that has turned the culture in France—and across Europe—against migrants and refugees.

We were introduced to the field manager for charity Help Refugees in Northern France at the time, in the warehouse in Calais. Sitting in a somewhat rickety office and meeting space, with remnants of thought bubbles from past meetings left on the wall, we huddled together in our coats for an interview.

She had been in Calais since the demolition of the so-called 'Jungle' in October 2016. Before it was demolished, this was the largest refugee camp in Europe, with around 10,000 inhabitants at its peak. On the Help Refugees website, an article written by the field manager in 2019 reads: 'Today the piece of land where the Jungle camp once stood is a national sanctuary for migrating birds. Such irony.'[1]

When we visited in 2018 and 2019, she told us that at the time they were supporting a fluctuating population of approximately 1,000 refugees between Calais and Dunkirk, with around 200 of those displaced individuals being children. She emphasised to us that the population of migrants at Calais changes a lot, with the number of migrants in 2019 being more than double that of October 2018.

'Although the news cameras are very much off the situation here, the need for humanity in northern France is as great as ever,' she said. Migrants will always end up at that part of the border, she explains, because people will always be looking for safe passage to the UK. Until the government develops the policies needed for migrants to be safely and respectfully resettled, illicit Channel crossings will remain a part of their journey.

But, according to the field manager, this is not so much because 'people have this dream of getting to the UK once they get to Europe'. It is more about push factors: the state violence that migrants often experience as they travel across Europe, and which remains a dominant and disturbing part of their lives in France.

'If I tell people it's safe to claim asylum in France, they will say it doesn't feel like a safe country to live in when you're being beaten awake in the morning and tear-gassed at night,' she explains to us, conveying a life of endless and cyclical aggression and violence on the part of the French police—as much of a certainty as day turning to night.

Our trips to Calais preceded the coronavirus pandemic, and were dominated by a different zeitgeist: Brexit. Conversations across the UK and beyond were dominated by what impact the UK's withdrawal from the European Union might have or was already having, and it was no different at the French border.

Ahead of the withdrawal, both the French and the British governments were pouring funding into what they saw as 'solutions' for the migrant 'problem'. The 'real clampdown' the field manager spoke of at the time constituted tactics often used against the homeless, such as boarding up doorways, putting fencing up under bridges and cutting down trees, leaving little to no shelter. 'The living conditions are already inhumane and undignified, and then those people [who had been recently evicted from living under a bridge] will literally just walk on the streets for days after that'.

'The clampdown feels like it's because governments on both sides of the water are aware the cameras are going to be on Calais for the next few months. They want to be seen dealing with the situation, but this only moves it. The people aren't going to go anywhere, only further up or down the coast,' she tells us.

She describes a new securitisation centre that had opened not far away. This was the first time that the British and French law enforcement agencies were working out of the same building on the French side of the border. Since then, as we've seen, the criminalisation and even militarisation of the Channel has only grown worse, with the UK declaring policies including the Nationality and Borders Bill[2] and the aforementioned UK Migration and Economic Development Partnership with Rwanda, which will enable the government to 'externalise the UK's fundamental obligations to people seeking asylum in the country'.[3]

She explains exactly why this approach is so dangerous.

It's interesting because they're supposed to be clamping down on human trafficking and smuggling networks, whereas the reality of the situation is that they're as strong as they've ever been. The prices to cross the border are increasing, and without a dual parallel focus on legal routes of passage and adequate accommodation for people to be able to make clear life decisions about what they're going to do next, the states themselves are opening up huge vacuums for human exploitation.

Her frustration is palpable as she describes the cavernous gap between the government's representation of the issue and reality.

After being in Calais, we came to understand that often the best insight into the realities of migration and policing of migration can be gleaned not from speaking with 'expert' academics or researchers, but by talking to the women on the ground dedicating their lives to weaponising their own mobility for the sake of human rights work, championing migrants, refugees, the displaced and the stateless.

These interviews reveal much about the relationship between governments, migrants and migrating women; about the complete power of country leaders and the complete absence of power for the people living in those countries. More than anything, these conversations revealed the flimsiness behind the othering of migrants and refugees, the connecting threads running through the experiences of people from other sides of the world—people living different lives, with different jobs and different ideas.

The restriction of freedom caused by government policies is in tension with the determination to choose how to live one's life anyway. These women decide to sacrifice traditional ideas of home and belonging to move around the world helping others, blurring the lines between activist and migrant, volunteer and refugee. Here are the women who have chosen to live their lives for themselves, the people they know and the people they don't.

'A state inside a state'

As Russia's identity as a country morphed during the 1990s and 2000s, from Soviet Union to a breeding ground for oligarchs to what has arguably become (once again) a country run by a brutal dictator, human rights lawyer Nadezhda's own identity changed shape as many times.

Nadezhda tells us that she was 'born in the Soviet Union', but by the time she was eighteen she found herself living in a post-communist Russia that bred great economic inequality for its citizens. In December 1991, the first elected president of Russia, Boris Yeltsin, held a secret meeting with the political leaders of neighbouring countries, Belarus and Ukraine, with the intention of forming a coalition of sorts. This led to the formation of the 'Commonwealth of Independent States'. The three leaders signed a document called the 'Belavezha Agreement', which read:

> the USSR, as a subject of international law and a geopolitical reality, ceased to exist.

This was the legacy that Nadezhda was born into: a world where nations drew borders only to withdraw them, where a state could be formed and strive to be a world power, only to be signed into non-existence by a single document. National identities were spoken into existence by political leaders, with the citizens of those nations finding their own identities being shaped from a power above.

Nadezhda knew from when she was a girl that she would be the one to shape her life. Her identity wasn't just decided by the shifts of the state, but, in her own words, came from her heart. When she was eight, she attended a summer camp in the middle of a forest, miles away from her home in Ozersk. At the camp, she 'disagreed with the administration'. So she jumped a barrier, and ran all the way back to her parents' home. Her mother begged her to return to the camp. 'After that, nobody touched me, because they knew it was in my character to resist,' she tells us.

Nadezhda's working life started in her local hospital, where she worked as an emergency nurse. Doing this, she discovered 'how the body looks inside [while helping with] all types of operations and emergency surgeries'—but she also realised it was too technical. Instead, she completed a university degree in sociology. In 1988, she attended a school for fashion modelling.

Neither of these endeavours, while she was capable of pursuing this work, were the right fit. Instead, she tells us that she created her own job, during an 'environment conference'.

> I understood I wanted to be in human rights and I wanted to be an environmental defender. I won lots of cases when I still hadn't finished my law qualifications. I won my first case when I was still at university.[4]

Nadezhda created her foundation, Planet of Hopes, in the late 1990s. This fought for the rights of victims of the nuclear waste accidents in Russia's closed city, Ozersk, where Nadezhda grew up. Movement in and out of Ozersk was restricted by the Russian state due to a historic nuclear waste accident at the city's plant.

Her legal work focused on state recognition that the medical issues experienced by citizens of the closed city were caused specifically by the nuclear waste, and, following this, compensation should be paid to those who have continued to suffer physically for multiple generations. Despite the obstacles Nadezhda faced, Planet of Hopes won seventy legal cases between 2000 and 2015. In 2011, Planet of Hopes won a Nuclear Free Future Award and in 2015 *Cosmopolitan Russia* magazine named her one of the bravest women in Russia.

The obstacles were constant. During the presidency of Boris Yeltsin, Nadezhda felt that, although he was a flawed political leader, there was still a sense that there were 'many freedoms. It was lawful to fight for rights. We didn't think Putin would change it to being like Stalin times. We thought we had the right to fight.'

Nadezhda couldn't predict how her professional work could so extensively impact and shape her personal life. Planet of Hopes had been a target for the government since its inception, despite the international support for nuclear waste support work, from Germany, France, USA and the UK. Nadezhda describes what she calls the 'waves of intimidation' from the government.

In 2004, the secret service forbade sociological research looking into the lives of citizens in closed cities. Then, in 2009, her charity was accused of not paying tax on their profits. The NGO survived both of these attacks from the state. But then in 2015 she was targeted so aggressively by the Russian government that neither her personal life nor her NGO survived intact.

In the autumn of 2015, a Russian court accused Nadezhda of being a foreign agent, and the state-run TV channel Rossiya 24 aired a documentary that described Nadezhda as an agent of 'industrial espionage' who was plotting against the country's nuclear industry.[5] Nadezhda realised that the next step would be formal prosecution for supposedly working as a foreign agent—a label assigned by the Russian government to effectively criminalise NGO work that challenged their functioning.

In an interview with *The Guardian* at the time of this documentary, Nadezhda said '[In one of the programmes] the former head of the local FSB [Federal Security Service] gave an interview about me, and he had never given any interviews to anyone before. That's how I realised there was a directive to crack down on me.'

So Nadezhda made the difficult decision to escape imprisonment and her entire life, which she describes as 'the worst moment of my life'. She had to figure out not just where she should go and how to get safely out of the country, but also ensure that her three children and her cat—who intermittently appears on her lap during our interview—were able to leave the country with her. This was made more challenging by the fact that their father didn't provide support, and her parents had died because of medical issues caused by the nuclear accident. She found herself alone, facing down government attacks.

She became a political refugee in France. When the family arrived, they had no money, they couldn't speak French and she didn't have any opportunities for work.

> It was hell. One moment you lose everything. Your job, your money, a place to live. I felt like I had just been born but I was orphaned without parents. I always wonder why people don't remember their previous lives. It's extremely difficult living as a refugee. My previous life was in Russia. I understand now that it's easier to begin again with nothing when you can't remember what came before.

When she first arrived in France, Nadezhda couldn't believe that this was really her life. Her tourist visa lasted for ninety days, and she only had this time to apply to be a political refugee. But it wasn't until the last month of this time period that she finally started this painful resettlement process. 'For three months, I refused to ask for refugee status. I was sure it was a mistake. The authorities [in Russia] would find out that I was useful and that I wasn't a foreign agent.'

This moment of reconciliation from the government of her motherland never happened—there was no peace offering. Slowly and with great resilience, Nadezhda rebuilt a life for herself and her children. They lived in one French town, but the children were sent to a school far away. Every day for school Nadezhda would accompany her children on their commute to school, which took two and a half hours each way, across several modes of public transport.

Meanwhile, Nadezhda was offered therapy from the health services there. She applied to study law at the Sorbonne, the leading university in France. There was a special opportunity to study for Syrian refugees in France, but Nadezhda was allowed to apply as an exception. After one year of studying the language, Nadezhda spent another two years studying French and European law.

During this time, she created an advertisement about herself, because she was looking for a fellowship. This referred to her work in human rights and stated that she was a political refugee. For six months, she wasn't contacted by anyone while her peers successfully started work. Eventually, exasperated, she rewrote her advertisement, mentioning only that she was looking for work and that she was bilingual. She immediately found work.

Nadezhda is used to adapting who she is according to who people want her to be. She hides her work as a model from the people she has worked with in Russia; they wouldn't take her seriously if they knew. She hides her status as a political refugee to find legal work in France. The only space where she did not hide her beliefs was in her work at Planet of Hopes. The pro-nuclear attitudes in Ozersk, and the criticism towards her for challenging the status quo, has been constant.

For the local authorities in the town, Nadezhda was like 'a monster'. She tells us that she would arrive at a meeting and people would say to her 'Nadezhda! You're so thin, but you have a huge reputation, like a monster!' She laughs as she tells us this. Despite this, she persevered. 'Braveness is a personal quality,' she says.

Often, she would undertake the legal work for nuclear waste victims but wouldn't include her name because it would cause trouble for the victims. One woman with cancer wanted to receive documents proving that her cancer was linked to the radiation. Nadezhda agreed to prepare the papers and told her that she would remove her name, as usual.

'The woman said no, I would like to put your name on the paper,' Nadezhda told us. After two weeks, the woman wrote to

Nadezhda. She was very happy, because the documents had been sent to her with no explanation. 'They didn't want any scandal with this crazy woman!' Nadezhda was, of course, referring to herself, and laughing.

Now in her fifties, Nadezhda is trying to figure out what to do next. During the Covid-19 pandemic, she wrote her first book, which shared, for Russian consumption, information on the 'anatomy of closed cities'. She knows she needs to make money, not for her life in France, but to pay an advocate in Ozersk to continue her important support work for nuclear victims. The way to earn this money yet isn't clear, but will probably mean working in a field of law unrelated to her past in nuclear victim cases. In the meantime, she has started modelling again for the first time in years. She knows that the 'moment will come where I should reveal that I'm a model, a human rights lawyer and a writer':

> My first childhood memories are of leaving the closed city to visit my grandmother. My parents said: 'Nadia, you shouldn't say you're from the closed city because it's a secret. And then we will be arrested and put into Stalin's car.' So from two years old, if somebody asked me where I was from, I immediately stopped talking. I did not show that I was scared but I did not tell people anything. For this reason, I have this capacity to live two lives.

While everything else in Nadezhda's life is defined by uncertainty and complications, one thing is simple: she can never return to her homeland. Two people who connected her to Russia after she fled to Paris—Greenpeace coordinator Rashid Alomov and Gilani Dambaev, who assisted her with work in the closed city—died of Covid around the time we spoke to Nadezhda in late 2021. She describes how this made her feel further disconnected from her people and her country: 'Now I feel like everything is cutting, cutting, cutting.'

On 24 February 2022, Russia invaded Ukraine. During our interview at one point she comments, 'Russia is so divided'. As her country is fractured beyond recognition, Nadezhda will be watching from a distance, unable to be with her people or return to her beloved closed city. But still, with characteristic resilience, she cannot do nothing.

Her Instagram page shows photos of her attending anti-war protests in Paris, holding aloft a distorted photo of Putin's face and a sign reading 'AGAINST THE WAR AND PUTIN'. Several more posts show her being interviewed repeatedly on several French news programmes, speaking out against the invasion. At the time of writing, she has been invited to speak on television on the subject of Putin and Russia over fifty times in the last five months. Advocating in the past and working to collapse the borders enforced by her state has led to Nadezhda losing everything. Still, she continues to speak out.

The Hummingbird and the Forest Fire

It seems that much of our whole journey began with Iara Lee. It was her documentary in Western Sahara, bringing together women, the arts and activism, that inspired our talks with the powerful women of Western Sahara. Alex H interviewed Iara in the intersectional feminist magazine *Polyester Zine* in 2018. This interview focused on a film that Iara produced that year through her activist production company Cultures of Resistance.

The film was about life in the small landlocked country Burkina Faso in West Africa, especially how the rise and fall of the dictator Blaise Compaoré—who was president from 1987 to 2014—shaped citizens' lives. Iara made this film because she wanted to champion the people of Burkina Faso for their methods of resistance and empowerment:

People think of resistance as big political actions and marches. But it really entails the accumulation of many small actions from different areas and fields. Change happens through music, poetry, art, agriculture, architecture. I tried to show many different types of people in the film, who do different types of work to provoke change.[6]

Almost four years later, we spoke to Iara on a cold November evening. It was 9.30pm for us, and we both had paused our evening activities for the chat. It was half past midnight, however, for Iara. She leapt onto our screens with a flurry of laughter. She had just come from a financial meeting, discussing the support for the people, especially women, in Belarus ('I mean, there's so much oppression there').

She tells us, 'I almost forgot about you girls, you know!' Iara is unerringly practical, positive and enthusiastic; she believes in wringing as much money from capitalism as possible and funnelling it straight back into grassroots organisations to battle the struggles felt by invisible communities. Her energy shapes everything she participates in, from our interview with her to the films she funds and her social media. Instagram posts about various documentary works or human rights topics are peppered with videos of her pole dancing with her sister, both in their fifties. Despite the demands in her life, her joy remains undiminished.

Iara is primarily an activist filmmaker, but she has fingers in every pie. She describes herself as a hummingbird carrying droplets of water to a forest fire. She is a constantly moving force, spending her time and resources on helping so many communities. 'Life is short and there isn't much time before we die. I will keep travelling and working as hard as I can before I die. I will probably die travelling.'

This morbid statement is delivered while laughing, imbuing her words with a galvanising spirit. She describes herself as a hummingbird, but is more than anything in the business of connecting people with each other in unexpected ways. She takes footage from these tiny, unseen communities and sends it back out into the world.

At what point did Iara decide to so wholeheartedly dedicate her life to uncovering human rights abuses around the world? She tells us that she 'comes from the arts and culture world in the 1980s' in Brazil, where she produced the São Paulo Film Festival for several years. After a while she decided that she wanted to actually use arts and culture for something 'beyond arts and culture'—this is where activism came into play.

In an interview with *Quotes Magazine*, Iara specifically identifies a 'political epiphany' she had in 2000 that also motivated her complete dedication to activism. In Peshawar, Pakistan, Afghan refugees shot Kalashnikovs and threw stones at her film crew, demanding real change and screaming that 'they were fed up with journalists, photographers, and filmmakers'.

She decided to create change by using creativity to connect with 'musicians, calligraphers, dancers, poets, photographers, farmers, scientists, bird watchers' rather than just dropping into conflict-ridden parts of the world, capturing people's pain and leaving. For Iara, it is also about taking the time to understand her interviewees and sources so she can also capture their joys.

This work isn't without its dangers. Iara lists countries she has been banned or deported from, such as India, for her work with Kashmiri mothers whose sons have disappeared, and Israel, for her support of Palestine. She tells us of all the different methods and passports she used to try and steal her way back into Israel, but her name is on a Ministry of Information list. However, Iara's visible identity has always been useful to her in circumventing barriers to her movement. 'People just see me as this silly Chinese lady, not a European filmmaker or an American. I'm not very threatening. I'm quite small.'

Iara is Brazilian-Korean. These multiple passports as well as her identity as a woman have allowed her to slip into many places that should have been forbidden. 'I believe in turning weaknesses into strengths, negatives into positives.' She mentions that 'nowadays you don't even need the Secret Service'. Governments can just Google people trying to enter their country, and if they have a clear history of speaking out against 'oppressors and occupiers' they won't let you in.

Or, as Iara puts it, 'they just look at my name and they deport me, they ban me, they put me in jail, they cancel my visa'. But this doesn't always matter. When Iara was making her first film about Syrian refugees, she wasn't allowed into the refugee camps in Turkey to film. So she jumped on top of a bus that was going into the camp and shot footage from there.

But the real danger, she maintains, is from governments, not the militias. She describes being in the Niger Valley with a militia bristling with guns but only being concerned with how she was going to get her footage past governmental forces. Much of Iara's international renown comes from one particular occasion in which she smuggled out extraordinary footage after a boat raid in which nine people died.

In 2010, Iara was on a peaceful mission called the Gaza Freedom Flotilla, which consisted of six boats bringing humanitarian aid to Palestinians of the Gaza Strip in an attempt to break the Israeli-Egyptian blockade.[7] Iara's footage shows the boat travelling at night. People are sprawled all around the deck: sleeping, resting, waiting. There is an air of tension and anticipation amongst these stretched-out figures, all clothed in fluorescent life jackets. These were issued when the organisers realised that their boats were being flanked by Israeli naval vessels.

A reporter for Al Jazeera tells the camera that the flotilla has been rerouted in order to avoid any conflict. As the night wears on, people begin to assemble and mill on the open deck.

Inside the boat, activists, including Iara, are working feverishly on computers, presumably attempting to rally support and monitoring the situation. Iara looks stressed. The crew begins to pass spotlights across the roiling water behind the boat, scanning the sea. There are fewer people on deck and an uncomfortable quiet has settled over the scene.

Suddenly everyone's gaze snaps up. 'They have drones.' Iara says, almost sounding astonished. The night wears on. We see a group of men praying and Iara curled up on a bench next to them, a flowery cushion tucked under her head. It seems incongruous to the hard, utilitarian fabrics on the ship.

A man tells the camera that they have seen five ships on the radar: three were coming towards them from the western side, one was behind them and one was hanging back further away. They could see their lights but had had no verbal contact.

People begin to rush around and soon they are attacked by the Israeli military.

Nine people died. Iara had whispered to her cameraperson to switch the camera cards, as she knew it was likely that their equipment would be confiscated. It was only after they had got off the boat that Iara knew for sure that the cameraperson had remembered and had managed to smuggle the SD card in their underwear off the ship. Theirs was the only footage to have made it off the ship, but no news outlets would air it. Iara speculates that this might be due to the Israeli sway over the American government. She revealed that she was similarly censored by an internationally renowned online conference talks platform, prevented from mentioning Israel–Palestine during her talk for fear that the video would be banned from YouTube.

Iara's voice is resonant and unflinching, through her films and creative output—speaking through her social media on an array of divisive human rights issues, ranging from Palestine to the Armenian genocide. It has been over a decade since the Gaza

Freedom Flotilla, and she continues to speak out on behalf of the Palestinian people. An Instagram post in April 2022, posted to her 5,700 followers, reads:

> Elderly Palestinians sit defiant and unfazed in the face of Israeli police and settler violence at Al-Aqsa Mosque in Jerusalem. Palestinians have been resisting in various ways as Israeli forces club them with batons and fire tear gas, stun grenades, and rubber-coated steel bullets, injuring more than 300 people and arresting more than 400.
>
> The police are attempting to empty the site of Palestinians so Israeli settler mobs can invade the area, chanting genocidal slogans like 'death to Arabs'. Palestinian resistance has taken many forms, including throwing stones at the heavily armed forces or creating loud noise to disrupt settlers. For many elderly Palestinians—who have been enduring Israeli state and settler violence for most of their lives—the chosen form of resistance has been #not_budging.

In 2010, Iara went above and beyond to capture the violent persecution of Palestinians. Twelve years later, wherever she may be in the world, she continues to use the tools available to speak out about the Palestinian cause, amongst others.

Many activists often dedicate their work to singular regions and issues as a means of avoiding compassion fatigue or simply to try and make the most impact with limited resources and time.

Iara clearly doesn't see things this way; instead of restricting her focus, she has managed to expand her resources and time in a way that almost seems inexplicable—scheduling several midnight calls might explain this expanded capacity.

'How can I do this work and still live a normal life?'

Ayat Abuznade has developed a special skill. She had already trained as a dentist, working in Chicago and developing research on treating oral cancer. She has also become a dressmaker and started her own business ('they're engagement dresses, fancy dresses'). And over the past two years she has learned how to excel at arriving in a country in crisis, seeking out the people whose lives have been destroyed, figuring out what help they most urgently need and then providing it.

As the leader of the US branch of NGO Team Humanity, she has developed an approach to humanitarian aid that involves hearing about a new conflict or crisis, using her 'strong' passport to jump on a plane, and figuring out when she gets there how to help move people who are in danger but facing visa, border and travel difficulties.

In 2020, when we first spoke, the coronavirus pandemic was just shutting down the world, and it looked like lockdown was only set to last for a few weeks. Ayat invited us out to volunteer with the organisation she helps to run, Team Humanity, on the Greek island of Lesbos, where the Moria refugee camp was located. We accepted her invitation, saying that although the UK was temporarily in lockdown, we were sure it would be over soon and we would be able to travel over to Greece. Two years later, the impact and pace of the pandemic is slowing down but we haven't been able to travel to Lesbos—and Ayat is no longer there to greet us. We caught up with her one Friday morning. It has been years since we last spoke to her.

She begins the call by asking: 'Had the fire happened when we spoke?' We answer, no, we don't think so. Shortly after our call about her work in Lesbos in 2020, footage had emerged in the news of orange flames spreading across the walled camp and rumour that refugees were trapped inside. This fire changed everything for those refugees and for Ayat's work. Around 13,000 refugees fled the Moria camp.

Police blocked roads from the camp so the refugees couldn't go to nearby towns, local Greek residents of villages nearby allegedly physically fought off migrants trying to seek shelter there and many were forced to sleep in nearby fields. There were many rumours as to why the fire started, but the Lesbos project co-ordinator for Médecins Sans Frontières identified that it was 'a time bomb that finally exploded' because people had been kept in 'inhumane conditions' for so long.[8]

Eventually, the camp inhabitants were moved to a temporary camp where, according to Ayat, the conditions were worse, and they were often trapped due to strict coronavirus curfews. The refugees were then relocated to Athens, where three small camps were erected to accommodate around 1,000 to 3,000 refugees. The rest—many of whom had been stuck on Lesbos and had been waiting to resettle in Europe for years—were finally helped by the Greek authorities to resettle in Germany or other countries in Europe, while many other refugees found accommodation in Athens.

Ayat considers that, although the fire was a tragic event and in the short-term negatively disrupted the migrants' lives, in the long term it was 'the spark that ignited change', forcing the authorities to finally address the 'problem' of the migrants and support relocation rather than just creating a hostile environment.

Team Humanity had funded and built a women's shelter and children's playground in Lesbos. These facilities were provided to address the typical absence of any basic infrastructure for mothers, to support their own safety and their ability to parent in the camps. As the earlier story of Najat and her family living in a refugee camp in Iraq illustrates, the impact of living without the resources needed for parenting and women's support and safety is immense. But these facilities became redundant when the camp burned down.

Ayat explained that she hopes to eventually recreate these crucial facilities in the camp in Athens. We note that, although the fire happened two years before our follow-up call, Team

Humanity hasn't recreated their support work in the new camp yet. This isn't because of an unwillingness to do so but, as Ayat puts it, because 'so much has happened since then'.

By 'so much' she is referring to different crises to attend to, whether this is building wells in Kenya, heading to the border of Syria or focusing on evacuations in Afghanistan. When the Taliban quickly occupied the entirety of Afghanistan and the Afghan president Ashraf Ghani fled in August 2021, Ayat turned her attention to the thousands of desperate Afghan people standing at the fence of the airport.

People were begging to be allowed on a flight out of the country. The list of citizens whose lives were endangered the moment the Taliban recaptured power is endless. This included people of all genders who worked with the US military during its twenty-year occupation, but also specifically concerned women who had worked, educated themselves or entered public life since 2001. They knew their fate, as Afghan citizens who had, for a short moment, lived the lives they desired, unrestricted by an extremist regime confining women literally to the home.

As Ayat describes to us how she wants to travel to as many places as possible to provide aid to as many different people in need—'It's not about politics, I just want to help'—we are sceptical. How much difference can you actually make to a conflict or crisis when you are spreading your efforts so thin, parachuting in and out?

Iara sees herself as a hummingbird bringing droplets of water to a forest fire. Is an activist or humanitarian aid worker likely to have a more lasting impact in a place if they concentrate their efforts on a singular country, crisis, region, we wonder?

But the work of both Iara and Ayat silences these questions for us. In hearing these women speak you can sense that they operate at a different energy level to the average person; both speak fast and barely take a breath during their interviews. As

Ayat puts it, 'I guess I'm multidimensional. I have to do more than one thing to keep myself challenged.'

At the time of speaking in May 2022, Ayat tells us she is currently organising a secret evacuation of three private plane flights from Afghanistan to Portugal. 'Of course everyone on board has passports,' she adds, but she has found military sources in the US to fund the evacuation for Afghan people who are at risk of being punished by the Taliban. These individuals have been sponsored by people they know from the US, which is how she has pulled together the financial resources to make these top-secret flights happen. The evacuation may be flawed, limited as it is by outside connections to people in America, but it means everything to every person and family whose life has potentially been saved by it.

In 2022, the world watched in horror as Russia invaded Ukraine, gradually destroying the country city by city and its population family by family, wreaking more havoc and destruction than Europe has seen since the end of World War II in 1945. As of 4 May 2022, around the time we speak to Ayat, an estimated 3,280 civilians have been killed by Russian forces, including 231 children, and 3,451 Ukrainian civilians have been injured, including 328 children.[9] As of 24 July, this number has increased to 5,237 dead, including 348 children.[10]

When we speak to Ayat, she tells us she is in Odessa, the third most populous city in Ukraine. She is organising a convoy of buses to evacuate thousands of people from Mariupol's steelworks, at the time surrounded by Russian forces who were allegedly continuing to attack the buildings despite the 200 men, women and children hiding in bunkers there.[11] The bus journey would take twenty hours, because the safe route has to work around the many roads which have been closed off since the invasion.

Alongside this, Ayat mentions that she has 'some friends with private planes'. Together, they are organising to fly 1,000 people out of Ukraine. How does she choose which people can board the flight? Seven or eight of the most vulnerable people must be on each flight, she tells us, including a seventy-year-old woman with cancer. These people will have asylum when they land in Switzerland.

Ayat is always asking herself the question, 'How do I get people out and how can we help them?' We ask how she copes with it all. The first time we spoke to her in 2020, she says she likes to run and, wherever she is, that helps her cope with all the death and destruction she witnesses. But her answer has changed since. Now, she knows that she can only continue doing this work for another five or ten years before she burns out.

We exchange surprised looks when she mentions over the phone that, as a very healthy thirty-five-year-old woman, she hopes to at least live to 'fifty or sixty'. If she spends a month working in a crisis environment, she will take a week for herself afterwards, where she will do 'normal things' like writing or selling dresses. She has long-term goals in life that she knows can't just be humanitarian work; she knows she must one day be able to step away. But until then, people are lucky that, as long as she is able, Ayat will always jump on a plane and give everything she has to the people who need it the most.

'These deaths aren't real because you don't see them'

For the first two days that Laura was on board the *Iuventa 10* ship, she was horrifically seasick. 'How the hell am I going to do this?' she wondered. In the end she managed, just as every other volunteer—students, paramedics, firefighters—made it work on board the search-and-rescue vessel.

The *Iuventa 10* patrolled the channel between the Libyan and Italian coasts searching for migrants whose boats had capsized. They rescued 14,000 people between 2016 and 2017. For their efforts, their ship was seized by the Italian authorities in 2017 and the crew on board now face charges of people-smuggling and twenty years' imprisonment in Italy. Laura is one of these crew members.

'My political views on freedom aligned with the crew's. I applied and was on the ship a month later,' she told us over Zoom during the summer of 2021 from her home in the UK. Little did she know that she and the rest of the crew would be connected not only by their political views but also as defendants in a shocking and unprecedented court case.

Despite knowing her political views were similar to the principles behind *Iuventa 10*, Laura said the crew steered away from divisive subjects like politics while on board—it was imperative they remained tightly knit and alert. The job would change day to day. Missions tended to last fourteen days. The first two or three were spent sailing to the right spot, getting acquainted with the ship and going 'over and over' drills, including fire drills, search-and-rescue drills and piracy lockdown drills.

Laura describes the details of the routines at sea with precision: always someone on lookout with binoculars; always two or three people on the bridge listening to communications; the engineers on 24/7 rotation; many crew members working through the night and sleeping through the day.

She found comfort in knowing there were other ships out at sea. When the *Iuventa 10* first went out in 2016, there were twelve other search-and-rescue ships out there too, but 'it whittled down'. By mid-2017, the far-right political party in Italy was gaining momentum and launched a critical campaign of search-and-rescue boats moving between the Italian and Libyan coasts and accused them of people-smuggling. Around this time, major NGO rescue boats started to withdraw under the pressure, including Save the Children and Médecins Sans Frontières.

The *Iuventa 10*, smaller and more nimble than other NGO ships, had a reputation for going further and doing more by getting closer to the Libyan coast. This meant a lot of the time, if there were too many dinghies for the *Iuventa* to reach all at once, there were no other rescue boats for them to rely on. Despite their ability to move with more ease, they also remained behind the nautical border unless directed by the Maritime Rescue Coordination Centre to do otherwise.

'Lives were definitely lost because of this,' Laura says. Laura is from the UK, but tells us that, there is a word in German that translates to the 'dark number': the true number that we can't know about. Laura says this applies to the loss of lives at sea. Just because a migrant drowns and nobody witnesses this, their death is no less violent and unnecessary. Laura tries to estimate the loss of life, a number that she guesses is 'just monumental'.

According to her, if one rubber boat sinks, that's approximately 130 deaths. If six or seven boats can't be reached by search-and-rescue vessels, the death toll is then in the thousands—and this scale can often be reached in only a day or a week.

But the importance of *Iuventa 10*'s work was not simply in fishing out those who would otherwise have drowned at sea; it was also about caring for those migrants after they had been rescued. Not only is the journey incredibly dangerous, but for women—some men too—there is another layer of danger added to the journey.

Laura prefaced her talking about the experiences of the migrants she met on the boat by saying she was uncomfortable speaking for these many migrant women by detailing what happens to them. But what Laura did tell us was that, of the women she got to know very well and spent a lot of time with in the ship hospital, every single one of them had been raped and sexually assaulted.

The rate of crime in Libya perpetrated against vulnerable migrants travelling to reach the channel is incredibly high. According to Amnesty International, 'tens of thousands of women, men and children are suffering horrific violations and abuses in Libya, only because they are refugees and migrants'.[12] One example of this from 2020 is when armed men opened fire on around 200 migrants being kept in a warehouse run by traffickers in the town of Mazda, southwest of Tripoli. Thirty men were killed, eleven injured and the rest were missing with the possibility that they were also killed or retrafficked.[13]

The women Laura met were kidnapped in Libya's port cities, and this is where their rapes often occurred. Laura tells us that many women she met in the ship hospital had 'gunshot wounds with scars or burns from being tortured'. She saw wounds that were so fresh they had clearly happened only days before. Some of the women were also pregnant from their assaults. She described this as 'an extra scar they had to carry with them'. Laura says the men are raped too. But the high rate of sexual violence women refugees experience in their efforts to find safe refuge makes it all the more important that women, such as Laura, are present during these search-and-rescue missions.

Laura describes the necessity of migrants' journeys by dinghy to Italy from Libya as 'a politically created situation. If there were safe routes for people to migrate and access routes to Europe, there wouldn't be this mass loss of life.'

At this stage, more and more centrist public figures were calling for stricter border policies. By the autumn of 2017, Pope Francis was asking whether Italy—'a country which has done so much'—had 'enough space'. The capture of *Iuventa 10* in August of that year and the criminalisation of search-and-rescue missions were a linchpin in the shift of anti-migrant sentiment from the far-right to the centre.

Riding a wave of neo-nationalist and populist political attitudes that reached a crescendo in the late 2010s, far-right politician Matteo Salvini ended up as Deputy Prime Minister of Italy and Minister of the Interior.

Although Salvini wasn't yet occupying this position of power in 2017, he had significant influence at the same time as *Iuventa 10* was battling to stay out on the waves. A *Guardian* article from September 2020 written by Daniel Trilling asserts that 'in the early months of 2017, Salvini transformed the fortunes of the party he leads, the Lega Nord, by helping bring the claim that NGO rescuers were collaborating with smugglers from the far-right fringe into the mainstream of political debate'.[14]

Italy is not alone in clamping down in this way. In December 2021, the British government announced a new bill that attempted to similarly criminalise humanitarian search-and-rescue efforts for migrants attempting to enter the UK.

On 2 August 2017, the crew on board *Iuventa 10* were asked to dock into port. There, they were met with Italian authorities and charged with people-smuggling. The *Iuventa* and its crew had been under secret surveillance for months. The ship was compounded, and so began a lengthy legal case that left these humanitarian volunteers in the lurch for years and wondering if they will end up being imprisoned for up to twenty years. At the time of writing, charges had been dropped against part of the crew, including Laura, but four people are still being charged.

When this happened, Laura was not on board the ship but instead at a small music festival in Germany. She got a text saying that the *Iuventa* had been seized. She wondered if it was a joke, but then received another text telling her that she needed to go straight to Berlin to meet with some lawyers. 'For ages we didn't even know the reasons. It went from zero to 100. The Italian press got hold of the accusations before the crew members, before the captain. It was very scrambled and created a lot of disbelief,' she says of those first few days after finding out.

The details of the case for Laura are 'hazy', and the most important and painful part of this for her is that they can no longer do their crucial work. 'It stopped us going back to sea,' Laura told us.

She drew a comparison between the criminalisation of humanitarian work by the Italian government with the same thing perpetrated by the government in Greece. There, and specifically on Lesbos island, volunteers have been imprisoned for 'people-smuggling'. This is the inaccurate label adopted by international governments for 'starting the motor on a boat', an example given by Laura, or rescuing drowning men, women and children.

While Laura exercised her freedom to travel around Europe for leisure, a founding member state of the EU was shutting down her and her colleagues' ability to help others with no such freedom. Her story shows that even those born with advantages of mobility can still be left powerless in the face of a bordered, bordering world.

POSTSCRIPT

SIX TIPS FOR CHALLENGING BARRIERS

People often ask us what they can do to help those whose mobility has been limited by the state, from those in refugee camps like Alphare and wheelchair users like Jessi to newly arrived refugees like Guli and displaced individuals like Minatu. The inspirational work of speakers and campaigners like Camilla, Jessi, Eva and Joey, and humanitarians, like Nadezhda and Najat, transforms lives—but not everyone has been forced into a position of advocacy by displacement or oppression and not everyone is able to devote their life to political or aid work.

Yet we've seen from stories like Patrice's, Guli's and Anka's that, no matter the context of a woman's migration or movement, the kindness of strangers and the power of community can be just as great a salvation. So what can each of us do to help?

We've written a list with the advice of our interviewees, but it is far from exhaustive:

Make friends—many people who arrive in a new country want community and support. Friendship is so important in helping people feel like they belong. Conversation is integral for helping people integrate, learn the language, find the support they need and, most importantly, feel at home.

Donate money, time, expertise, furniture, clothes, a room—resources such as money, furniture and clothes are integral for supporting people in a new country, but so is time and expertise. People who have specific knowledge, such as lawyers or accountants, are invaluable for offering expert advice. But this expertise could simply be helping someone navigate the NHS or find the nearest laundromat. Everything is a challenge to people moving to a new country, and you can help! Through many local councils you can find refugee centres, which can also offer advice on how to volunteer or where to find networks that provide services.

Write to and lobby your politicians—change cannot only be effected by individuals. It is primarily the responsibility of our governments to not only allow people to come to countries but also to support people when they arrive. Keep our governments accountable—the rights of everyone should always be defended.

At your place of work or at events, **ask about accessibility**. Make sure that this is a priority that people are considering at every level of our societies to make sure that everyone is included. Are there steps? Are there captions? Can you include a sign language interpreter? Questions like these will help to ensure that everyone is included from the very beginning.

Learn about people who have had different life experiences from yourself, especially those in our society who are more vulnerable. This will break down barriers between people and remove borders. Learn by reading, talking and, crucially, listening.

Advocate for and about the experiences of others, question the narratives of our media and governments and act to amplify the voices of those who need to be heard.

We believe that movement should be safe and legal for anyone who wants to move, not just those with the privileges of money, nationality, race, class, gender and good health. We believe that borders should be broken down on every level, not only litigiously but societally. Behind every label there is a face, a life and a story. Everyone should have a right to belong.

***

Wander Women took four years and dozens of interviews. We are so grateful to every person who agreed to speak with us, their families or friends who helped to organise these interviews and our own family and friends for supporting us through this process.

NOTES

INTRODUCTION

1. Her name has been changed for anonymity.
2. 'World FGM Map', National FGM Centre. http://nationalfgmcentre. org.uk/world-fgm-prevalence-map/ [accessed: 14/5/2022].
3. 'Female Genital Mutilation (FGM)', UNICEF Data (May 2022). https://data.unicef.org/topic/child-protection/female-genital- mutilation/
4. Ibid.
5. Ibid.
6. Melanie L. Straiton, Anne Reneflot and Esperanza Diaz, 'Mental Health of Refugees and Non-refugees from War-Conflict Countries: Data from Primary Healthcare Services and the Norwegian Prescription Database', *Journal of Immigrant Minority Health* (2017) 19:582–9.
7. Neil Quinn, 'Participatory action research with asylum seekers and refugees experiencing stigma and discrimination: the experience from Scotland', *Disability & Society* (2014) 29(1):58–70.
8. Valenta Marko, 'User involvement and empowerment among asylum seekers in Norwegian reception centres', *European Journal of Social Work* (2010) 13(4):483–501.
9. Giulia Turrini, Marianna Purgato, Francesca Ballette, Michela Nosè, Giovanni Ostuzzi and Corrado Barbui, 'Common mental disorders in asylum seekers and refugees: umbrella review of prevalence and intervention studies', *International Journal of Mental Health Systems* (2017) 11(51) (n.p.).
10. Straiton et al., 'Mental Health of Refugees'.

11. 'Working in the UK while an asylum case is considered', UK Visas and Immigration (21 February 2014). https://www.gov.uk/government/publications/working-whilst-an-asylum-claim-is-considered/working-in-the-uk-whilst-an-asylum-case-is-considered [accessed: 14/5/2022].

12. Linda Pressly, 'Resignation syndrome: Sweden's mystery illness', BBC News (26 October 2017). https://www.bbc.co.uk/news/magazine-41748485 [accessed: 14/5/2022].

13. We use the term 'transgender' or 'trans' in its broadest sense, including (but not limited to) our non-binary and genderqueer friends!

14. The reason we denote the 'refugee crisis' or 'immigration crisis' as 'so-called' is because of the way that this term is loaded to create a sense of hysteria and disaster, which more often than not alienates people from empathy and understanding and propels them directly into a kind of thinking centred around resources and fear.

15. Dina Nayeri, *The Ungrateful Refugee: What Immigrants Never Tell You* (Edinburgh: Canongate Books, 2019), p. 10.

16. Natasha Clark, 'Over 20,000 people have crossed the Channel in small boats to Britain this year', *The Sun* (14 August 2022). https://www.thesun.co.uk/topic/uk-immigration-crisis/ [accessed: 2/1/2022].

17. David Wooding, 'Dangerous foreign criminals to find it harder to dodge deportation as Dominic Raab tightens up human rights laws', *The Sun* (11 December 2021). https://www.thesun.co.uk/news/17013029/foreign-criminals-deportation-new-laws/ [accessed: 02/01/2022].

18. Clark, 'Over 20,000 people have crossed the Channel'.

19. 'The Sun is officially Britain's Number 1 newsbrand with a whopping 28.4 million readers', *The Sun* (29 October 2021). https://www.thesun.co.uk/news/16566639/the-sun-officially-britains-number/ [accessed: 2/1/2022].

20. 'What is a refugee?', UNHCR UK website (n.d.). https://www.unhcr.org/uk/what-is-a-refugee.html [accessed: 8/7/2022].

21. 'Asylum-Seekers', UNHCR UK website (n.d.). https://www.unhcr.org/uk/asylum-seekers.html [accessed: 8/7/2022].

22. 'Nationality and Borders Bill', Home Office (6 July 2021). https://www.gov.uk/government/collections/the-nationality-and-borders-bill#full-publication-update-history [accessed: 8/7/2022].

23. 'Priti Patel's racist Nationality and Borders Bill "drags the UK's reputation through the mud"', Amnesty Internation UK press release (27 April 2022). https://www.amnesty.org.uk/press-releases/uk-priti-patels-racist-nationality-and-borders-bill-drags-uks-reputation-through-mud [accessed: 8/7/2022].

24. Cameron Boyle, 'The Nationality and Borders Bill Is an Affront to Humanity', *Tribune Magazine* (7 December 2021). https://tribunemag.co.uk/2021/12/refugees-asylum-seekers-nationality-and-borders-bill-priti-patel/ [accessed: 8/7/2022].

25. 'What is the Nationality and Borders Bill?', Refugee Council (28 April 2022). https://refugeecouncil.org.uk/information/refugee-asylum-facts/what-is-the-nationality-and-borders-bill/ [accessed: 8/7/2022].

26. 'Channel migrants: Pushing back boats will increase danger, MPs warn', BBC News (1 December 2021). https://www.bbc.co.uk/news/uk-politics-59481143 [accessed: 8/7/2022].

27. 'Nationality and Borders Bill: Border Force powers to stop and seize small boats factsheet', Home Office (2 March 2022). https://www.gov.uk/government/publications/nationality-and-borders-bill-border-force-powers-to-stop-and-seize-small-boats-factsheet/nationality-and-borders-bill-border-force-powers-to-stop-and-seize-small-boats-factsheet [accessed: 8/7/2022].

28. 'An analysis of Channel crossings & asylum outcomes', Refugee Council briefing (November 2021). https://media.refugeecouncil.org.uk/wp-content/uploads/2021/12/24155629/Channel-crossings-and-asylum-outcomes-November-2021.pdf [accessed: 8/7/2022].

29. 'Nationality and Borders Bill', Home Office.

30. 'Nationality and Borders Bill', Home Office.

31. 'Convention and Protocol Relating to the Status of Refugees', UNHCR UK (n.d.). https://www.unhcr.org/uk/3b66c2aa10 [accessed: 8/7/2022].

32. 'The Nationality and Borders Bill has passed, what now?', Left Foot Forward (4 May 2022). https://leftfootforward.org/2022/05/the-nationality-and-borders-bill-has-passed-what-now/ [accessed: 8/7/2022].

33. Molly Smith and Juno Mac, *Revolting Prostitutes* (London: Verso, 2020), p. 62–3.

34. Smith and Mac, *Revolting Prostitutes*, p. 63.

35. Where some activists use 'prostitution' to reclaim the term, many others use 'sex work'. We assert the difference here between sex work and rape. Sex work is consensual work, and non-consensual sex, to pay a debt or not, is rape.

36. 'Population, female (% of total population)', The World Bank (2019). https://data.worldbank.org/indicator/SP.POP.TOTL.FE.ZS?end=2020&start=1960&view=chart [accessed: 8/7/2022].

37. 'Facts and figures: Women's leadership and political participation', UN Women (15 January 2021).https://www.unwomen.org/en/what-we-do/leadership-and-political-participation/facts-and-figures [accessed: 8/7/2022].

1. BEYOND THE BINARY

1. 'LGBTIQ+ Persons in Forces Displacement and Statelessness: Protection and Solutions', UNHCR Ireland (4 June 2021). https://www.unhcr.org/611e33704 [accessed: 12/5/2022].

2. Ibid.

3. Ibid.

4. Ibid.

5. Shon Faye, *The Transgender Issue* (London: Penguin Random House, 2021), p. 192.

6. 'Gender Identity Issues in the Asylum Claim', Home Office (n.d.). https://assets.publishing.service.gov.uk/government/uploads/system/uploads/attachment_data/file/257387/genderissueintheasylum.pdf [accessed: 12/4/2022].

7. 'LGBT claim and your asylum application', Danielle Cohen Immigration Law Solicitors Ltd website (n.d.). https://www.

daniellecohenimmigration.com/asylum-applications/gay-asylum-uk/ [accessed: 12/4/2022].

8. Jamie Grierson, 'Home Office refused thousands of LGBT asylum claims, figures reveal', *The Guardian* (2 September 2019). https://www.theguardian.com/uk-news/2019/sep/02/home-office-refused-thousands-of-lgbt-asylum-claims-figures-reveal [accessed: 12/4/2022].

9. Fox Odoi-Oywelowo, 'No, Uganda is not making it illegal to be gay (again)', Al Jazeera (6 June 2021). https://www.aljazeera.com/opinions/2021/6/6/no-uganda-is-not-making-it-illegal-to-be-gay-again [accessed: 4/8/2022].

10. Cowan, *Border Nation*, p. 112.

11. Ibid., p. 106.

12. Faye, *The Transgender Issue*, p. 193.

13. Jack Herrera, 'Why Are Trans Women Dying in ICE Detention?', Pacific Standard (4 June 2019). https://psmag.com/social-justice/why-are-trans-women-dying-in-ice-detention [accessed: 12/4/2022].

14. '"Do You See How Much I'm Suffering Here?": Abuse against Transgender Women in US Immigration Detention', Human Rights Watch (23 March 2016). https://www.hrw.org/report/2016/03/24/do-you-see-how-much-im-suffering-here/abuse-against-transgender-women-us#_ftn46 [accessed: 12/4/2022].

15. Emily Kenway, *The Truth about Modern Slavery* (London: Pluto Press, 2021), p. 50.

16. No person is illegal.

17. According to Merriam-Webster, a cisgender person is a person whose gender identity corresponds with the sex the person has or was identified as having at birth. https://www.merriam-webster.com/dictionary/cisgender [accessed: 2/1/2022].

18. Faye, *The Transgender Issue*, p. 9.

19. Haroon Siddique, 'Stonewall is at centre of a toxic debate on trans rights and gender identity', *The Guardian* (5 June 2021). https://www.theguardian.com/society/2021/jun/05/stonewall-trans-debate-toxic-gender-identity [accessed: 23/11/2021].

20. Faye, *The Transgender Issue*, p. 5.

21. Ibid., p. 6.

22. Chaka L. Bachmann and Becca Gooch, 'LGBT in Britain: Trans Report', Stonewall (2018). https://www.stonewall.org.uk/system/files/lgbt_in_britain_-_trans_report_final.pdf [accessed: 23/12/2021].

2. BATTLE SCARS

1. Bill Rolston, 'Democratic disruption: Ireland's colonial hangover', London School of Economics (5 July 2019). https://blogs.lse.ac.uk/wps/2019/07/05/democratic-disruption-irelands-colonial-hangover/ [accessed: 16/1/2022].
2. Ibid.
3. Flynn Berry, 'The Hidden History of Women and the IRA', CrimeReads (8 April 2021). https://crimereads.com/the-hidden-history-of-women-and-the-ira/ [accessed: 31/7/2022].
4. Simone Matassa, 'Women of the Irish Republican Army: Powerful or Powerless?', Rise to Peace (2019). https://www.risetopeace.org/2019/07/10/women-of-the-irish-republican-army-powerful-or-powerless/smatassa/ [accessed: 31/7/2022].
5. Amanda Ferguson, 'Closure of Marie Stopes Belfast clinic ends five years of hostility', *Irish Times* (8 December 2017). https://www.irishtimes.com/news/social-affairs/closure-of-marie-stopes-belfast-clinic-ends-five-years-of-hostility-1.3318970 [accessed: 18/2/2022].
6. The Northern Ireland Assembly is the devolved legislature for Northern Ireland. It has the power to make laws in a wide range of areas, including housing, employment, education, health, agriculture and the environment. It meets at Parliament Buildings, Belfast. https://www.nidirect.gov.uk/articles/northern-ireland-assembly [accessed: 18/2/2022].
7. Catherine Smyth, 'Abortion: UK "breaches NI's women's right"', BBC News (28 February 2018). https://www.bbc.co.uk/news/uk-northern-ireland-43167255 [accessed: 18/2/2022].
8. Article 41.1 of the constitution reads: 'In particular, the State recognises that by her life within the home, woman gives to the State a support without which the common good cannot be achieved.

The State shall, therefore, endeavour to ensure that mothers shall not be obliged by economic necessity to engage in labour to the neglect of their duties in the home.' Ronan McGreevy, '"Women's place is in the home": Citizens' Assembly again tackles thorny issue', *Irish Times* (14 February 2021). https://www.irishtimes.com/news/ireland/irish-news/women-s-place-is-in-the-home-citizens-assembly-again-tackles-thorny-issue-1.4484706 [accessed: 19/7/2022].

9. Michael Lipka, 'Irish vote highlights widespread popular support for legal abortion in Western Europe', Pew Research Center (29 May 2018). https://www.pewresearch.org/fact-tank/2018/05/29/ireland-abortion-vote-reflects-western-europe-support/ [accessed: 19/7/2022].

10. 'Health (Regulation of Termination of Pregnancy) Act 2018', Irish Statute Book, Office of the Attorney General (2018). https://www.irishstatutebook.ie/eli/2018/act/31/enacted/en/print#sec2 [accessed: 6/2/2022].

11. Ibid.

12. Sections 16 and 17 (1) of the Censorship of Publications Act 1929 ; sections 7 (b) and 9 (1)(b) of the Censorship of Publications Act 1946; section 10 of the Health (Family Planning) Act 1979. [6/2/2022].

13. 'Health (Regulation of Termination of Pregnancy) Act 2018', Irish Statute Book.

14. Camilla Fitzsimons, 'Abortion Access & Reproductive Rights' (January 2022). https://drive.google.com/file/d/1NsGHLQgb8BsYS SIBitZ1yBAabDWpeZOh/view?ts=61f93256 [accessed: 6/2/2022].

15. 'Health (Regulation of Termination of Pregnancy) Act 2018', Irish Statute Book.

16. Lorraine Grimes, Aideen O'Shaughnessy, Rachel Roth, Anna Carnegie and Deirdre Niamh Duffy, 'Analysing MyOptions: experiences of Ireland's abortion information and support service', *BMJ Sexual & Reproductive Health* (2022) 48:222–6.

17. Fitzsimons, 'Abortion Access & Reproductive Rights'.

18. Ibid.

19. Lauren Arrington, 'Constance Markievicz, the divisive revolutionary heroine', *Irish Times* (10 December 2018). https://www.irishtimes.

com/culture/heritage/constance-markievicz-the-divisive-revolutionary-heroine-1.3710763 [accessed: 14/5/2022].

20. Ibid.
21. Wendy Holden, *Born Survivors* (London: Sphere, 2020), p. 77.
22. Wendy Holden, *Born Survivors*, p. 81.
23. An exception to this rule was the 1933 Haavara Agreement, in which Jews could arrange the transfer of some of their assets upon their migration to British Mandatory Palestine. These assets were transferred by the purchase of essential items, manufactured by Germany, which were then exported. This agreement ran until 1939.
24. Holden, p. 87.
25. A pogrom is a violent riot with the intention of massacring or expelling a group of people. Kristallnacht, or the Night of Broken Glass, was a series of attacks by both Nazi forces and citzens on 9–10 November 1938. The name comes from the glass that littered the streets after Jewish businesses, homes and synagogues were attacked. The death toll was said to be in the hundreds, followed by 638 deaths by suicide.
26. Holden, *Born Survivors*, p. 92.
27. 'New monument unveiled in memory of those killed at Terezin', *Jewish News* (4 June 2018). https://www.jewishnews.co.uk/new-monument-unveiled-in-memory-of-those-killed-at-terezin/ [accessed: 7/5/2022].
28. Erin Blakemore, 'This Midwife at Auschwitz Delivered 3,000 Babies in Unfathomable Conditions' History (2 March 2018). https://www.history.com/news/auschwitz-midwife-stanislawa-leszczynska-saint [accessed: 31/7/2022].
29. Holden, *Born Survivors*, p. 187.
30. Ibid., p. 268.
31. Ibid., p. 292.
32. Ibid., p. 291.
33. Fernando A. Lopez Oggier, 'The Impact of Gender Discrimination on Statelessness: A Case Study of the Impact of Nationality Laws on Statelessness', *Enquiries* (2022) 14(4):1.

34. These countries are Iran, Kuwait, Brunei, Somalia, Swaziland, Qatar and Lebanon.

35. 'The Problem', Global Campaign for Equal Nationality Rights (n.d.). https://equalnationalityrights.org/the-issue/the-problem [accessed: 4/8/2022].

36. Shlomo Sand, *The Invention of the Jewish People* (London: Verso, 2020), p. 129.

37. The first sets of immigration rules in the UK and US were introduced in the early 1900s to control Jewish immigration from Eastern Europe.

38. 'Ravensbrück', Holocaust Encyclopedia, United States Holocaust Memorial Museum (n.d.). https://encyclopedia.ushmm.org/content/en/article/ravensbrueck [accessed: 7/5/2022].

39. 'Insiders/Outsiders: In Conversation with Monica Bohm-Duchen', Lund Humphries Publishers (21 April 2020). https://www.lundhumphries.com/blogs/features/insiders-outsiders [accessed: 8/7/2022].

40. Monica Bohm-Duchen, 'Artists: Contemporary Anglo', *The Shalvi/Hyman Encyclopedia of Jewish Women, Jewish Women's Archive* (London: Lund Humphries Publishers, 1996).

3.   MATRIARCHS IN THE DESERT

1. Cultures of Resistance Films, *Life is Waiting: Referendum and Resistance in Western Sahara*. https://www.youtube.com/watch?v=9QzRzm4uFxU&t=1486s [accessed: 11/4/2021].

2. 'Laayoune', Encyclopædia Britannica. https://www.britannica.com/place/Laayoune [accessed 11/4/2021].

3. It is worth noting that it is called the 'occupied territories' rather than the 'disputed territory' by those who do not recognise Moroccan sovereignty over the territory. Given that the UN and the International Courts of Justice maintain that the Saharawis have a right to self-determination, we are working from the premise that this is an occupation and will therefore be using the term 'occupied territories'.

4. Amnesty International's 2015 report *Shadow of Impunity: Torture in Morocco and Western Sahara* draws upon 173 reports of torture, ill-treatment and violence in police custody and places of detention between 2010 and 2014 in Western Sahara and Morocco. Torture, ill-treatment and threats, although prohibited in law, are used to obtain confessions. While the use of forced confessions in proceedings is also banned in Morocco, the report states that courts rely on such confessions as 'the main and sometimes the only evidence to secure convictions' (p. 9). The report also notes the weight that Moroccan legislation gives to confessions as evidence, including a line from Morocco's Code of Criminal Procedure that states that 'for infractions and misdemeanours, courts should assume police interrogation reports are trustworthy, unless proven to be inaccurate' (p. 27). It highlights the impunity security forces feel because of the deficit of investigation when claims of torture or other ill-treatment are made as a reason that such abuse is perpetuated. Further, it notes the unhelpfulness of the international community's tolerance for the discrepancy between declarations of human rights reform and failure to investigate claims. The report outlines measures that Morocco could take to confront torture.

Amnesty International, *Shadow of Impunity: Torture in Morocco and Western Sahara* (London: Amnesty International Ltd, 2015) <https://www.amnesty.org/download/Documents/MDE290012015 ENGLISH.PDF> [accessed: 11/4/2021].

5. Amnesty International, p. 7.

6. Ibid., p. 21.

7. Ibid., p. 54.

8. Ibid., p. 10.

9. bell hooks, *Yearning: Race, Gender and Cultural Politics* (Boston: South End Press, 1990), p. 384.

10. Cultures of Resistance, *Life is Waiting.*

11. The protest and its subsequent destruction, with 3,000 arrests, was noted by Noam Chomsky as the beginning of the Arab Spring.

12. https://www2.bfi.org.uk/news-opinion/sight-sound-magazine/ comment/festivals/fisahara-worlds-only-film-festival-refugee-camp [accessed 11/04/2021].

13. 'Country of Origin Information Report: Algeria', UK Border Agency (30 September 2008). https://www.ecoi.net/en/file/local/1343583/1226_1224671304_algeria-101008.pdf [accessed: 11/4/2021].

14. 'UNHCR Global Report 2009—Mauritania', UNHCR Ireland (2009). https://www.unhcr.org/4c09029d9.html [accessed: 11/4/2021].

15. RT Documentary, *Western Sahara: Determined, Saharawi Women Risk Their Lives to Clear Ancestral Lands of Mines*. https://www.youtube.com/watch?v=uYO_r-o-mPA [accessed: 11/4/2021].

16. Cultures of Resistance, *Life is Waiting*.

17. 'US Recognition of Morocco's Claims "Made Visible the Question of Western Sahara": Polisario', *The Nation* (18 December 2020). https://nation.com.pk/18-Dec-2020/us-recognition-of-morocco-s-claims-made-visible-the-question-of-western-sahara-polisario [accessed 11/4/2021].

18. Carne Ross, 'From conflict to compromise: Lessons in creating a state', *The Independent* (25 June 2019). https://www.independent.co.uk/news/world/politics/state-building-country-independence-plebiscite-palestine-south-sudan-kosovo-montenegro-a8888136.html?fbclid=IwAR0wH0DuZxs35yRBOgais9r4V3jWJpwdkl4xSeYF8NKGmy5EyTUZL39Coeo [accessed 11/4/2021].

19. Indeed, Moroccan media has levied this charge at the Polisario, suggesting that the 'Algerian-Polisario propaganda tries in vain to show "a war zone," through fake news, "war press releases," dispatches and daily reports of "imaginary clashes"'. They suggest that 'it is part of creating a media propaganda about the existence of war in Sahara'. If this is the case, perhaps this is just another form of non-violent resistance.

20. Manu Pineda, 'Increase in violence in Western Sahara following the end of the ceasefire', European Parliament, Parliamentary question (1 March 2021). https://www.europarl.europa.eu/doceo/document/E-9-2021-001177_EN.html [accessed: 29/7/2022].

4. WOMEN OF SYRIA

1. We suggest this as the exact details of whether he was required to have a permit vary, with some suggesting that street vending is illegal and some suggesting that no permit was needed at all.

2. Kim Sengupta, 'Tunisia: "I have lost my son, but I am proud of what he did"', *The Independent* (21 January 2011). https://www.independent.co.uk/news/world/africa/tunisia-i-have-lost-my-son-but-i-am-proud-of-what-he-did-2190331.html [accessed: 22/4/2022].

3. Faida Hamdy, the officer in question, has denied that she slapped Bouazizi. She was imprisoned twice, the second time allegedly for her own protection. She also, however, blames herself for everything that happened after. She is quoted as saying, 'I blame myself. Death everywhere and extremism blooming, and killing beautiful souls. Tunisians are suffering as always.' Some argue that she is a scapegoat in this situation. Ashley Cowburn, 'Faida Hamdy: Why a Tunisian council worker blames herself for the Arab Spring', *The Independent* (17 December 2015). https://www.independent.co.uk/news/world/middle-east/faida-hamdy-a-former-tunisian-council-worker-who-blames-herself-for-the-arab-spring-a6776866.html [accessed: 22/4/2022].

4. 'The Syrian conflict—10 years after the uprising', European Parliament resolution (11 March 2021). https://www.europarl.europa.eu/doceo/document/TA-9-2021-0088_EN.pdf [accessed: 22/4/2022].

5. Bethan McKernan, 'Rape as a weapon: huge scale of sexual violence inflicted in Ukraine emerges', *The Guardian* (4 April 2022). https://www.theguardian.com/world/2022/apr/03/all-wars-are-like-this-used-as-a-weapon-of-war-in-ukraine [accessed: 22/4/2022].

6. Arminka Helic, 'The world can't ignore Russia's use of rape as a weapon of war', *The Telegraph* (31 March 2022). https://www.telegraph.co.uk/news/2022/03/31/world-cant-ignore-russias-use-rape-weapon-war/ [accessed: 22/4/2022].

7. Dave Burke, 'Russian troops "using rape as a weapon" as woman forced to have sex at gunpoint', *The Mirror* (3 April 2022). https://www.mirror.co.uk/news/world-news/russian-troops-using-rape-weapon-26622596 [accessed: 22/4/2022].

8. McKernan, 'Rape as a weapon'.

9. Marlise Simons, 'UN Court, for First Time, Defines Rape as War Crime', *New York Times* (28 June 1996). https://www.nytimes.com/1996/06/28/world/un-court-for-first-time-defines-rape-as-war-crime.html?searchResultPosition=2 [accessed: 22/4/2022].

10. Ibid.

11. Elisabeth Jean Wood and Dara Kay Cohen, 'How to Counter Rape During War', *New York Times* (28 October 2015). https://www.nytimes.com/2015/10/29/opinion/how-to-counter-rape-during-war.html?searchResultPosition=3 [accessed: 22/4/2022].

12. Cécile Andrzejewski and Leïla Miñano, with Daham Alasaad, 'How the Assad Regime Used Child Rape as a Weapon of War', Zero Impunity (2 July 2017). https://zeroimpunity.com/how-the-assad-regime-used-child-rape-as-a-weapon-of-war/?lang=en [accessed: 22/4/2022].

13. Ibid.

14. Forensic doctor Dr Akram al-Shaar insisted, on Syria's only pro-regime TV station, that the marks were signs not of torture but of natural decomposition. https://www.aljazeera.com/features/2011/5/31/tortured-and-killed-hamza-al-khateeb-age-13 [accessed: 22/4/2022].

15. Hugh Macleod and Annasofie Flamand, 'Tortured and killed: Hamza al-Khateeb, age 13', Al Jazeera (31 May 2011). https://www.aljazeera.com/features/2011/5/31/tortured-and-killed-hamza-al-khateeb-age-13 [accessed: 22/4/2022].

16. 'New UN death toll: At least 350,000 people killed in Syria's war', Al Jazeera (24 September 2021). https://www.aljazeera.com/news/2021/9/24/at-least-350000-people-killed-in-syria-war-new-un-count [accessed: 22/4/2022].

17. 'Syrian war documentary "For Sama" makes history with 4 British film award nominations', *Arab News* (8 January 2020). https://www.arabnews.com/node/1609691/lifestyle [accessed: 25/8/2022].

18. Waad Al-Kateab and Edward Watts (dir.), *For Sama* (2019). https://www.infomigrants.net/en/post/25743/syrian-filmmaker-waad-al-kateab-i-dont-want-your-tears-i-want-action [accessed: 08/4/2022].

19. UNHCR tweet (23 March 2022). https://twitter.com/Refugees/status/1506574223032029185 [accessed 8/4/2022].

20. Rashawn Ray, 'The Russian invasion of Ukraine shows racism has no boundaries', Brookings (3 March 2022). https://www.brookings.edu/blog/how-we-rise/2022/03/03/the-russian-invasion-of-ukraine-shows-racism-has-no-boundaries/ [accessed: 8/4/2022].

21. Umar Farooq, 'How killing of Syrian refugee marks an alarming trend in Turkey', Al Jazeera (12 January 2022). https://www.aljazeera.com/news/2022/1/12/turkey-news-log-jan-12 [accessed: 7/5/2022].

22. Alex Howlett, 'Alex Howlett Meets Syrian human rights activist, Lubna Alkanawati', *Sister* (13 May 2019). https://www.sistermagazine.co.uk/blogs/sister/alex-howlett-meets-syrian-human-rights-activist-lubna-alkanawati [accessed: 7/5/2022].

23. Martin Patience, 'Syria War: Fall of Eastern Ghouta pivotal moment for Assad', BBC News (13 April 2018). https://www.bbc.co.uk/news/world-middle-east-43631838 [accessed: 7/5/2022].

24. 'Position Paper on Perspectives of Forced Displaced Syrian Women on Their Conditions, Rights, and Demands', Women Now For Development (28 April 2021). https://women-now.org/position-paper-on-perspectives-of-forced-displaced-syrian-women-on-their-conditionsrightsand-demands-pdf/ [accessed: 7/5/2022].

25. 'The UK's Syria Resettlement Programme: Looking Back, and Ahead', UNHCR UK (23 March 2021). https://www.unhcr.org/uk/news/latest/2021/3/6059f1fd4/the-uks-syria-resettlement-progamme-looking-back-and-ahead.html [accessed: 22/4/2022].

26. 'Zaatari Camp Fact Sheet', UNHCR (November 2020). https://reporting.unhcr.org/sites/default/files/Zaatari%20Fact%20Sheet%20November%202020%20-%20final.pdf [accessed: 31/7/2022].

27. May Bulman, 'Afghanistan: UK's refugee resettlement programme "confusing and disingenuous", experts warn', *Independent* (19 August 2021). https://www.independent.co.uk/news/uk/home-news/afghan-citizens-resettlement-scheme-unhcr-b1905230.html [accessed: 22/4/2022].

28. 'Afghanistan: 270,000 newly displaced this year, warns UNHCR', UN News (13 July 2021). https://news.un.org/en/story/2021/07/1095782 [accessed: 22/4/2022].

29. Helen Pidd, 'Hundreds of Britons offer to host Afghan refugees after fall of Kabul', *The Guardian* (27 August 2021). https://www.theguardian.com/world/2021/aug/27/hundreds-of-britons-offer-to-host-afghan-refugees-after-fall-of-kabul [accessed: 22/4/2022].

30. May Bulman, '"Enormous opportunity": Extend Homes for Ukraine scheme to include Afghan refugees, Tory MPs tell Gove', *Independent* (29 March 2022). https://www.independent.co.uk/news/uk/home-news/ukraine-refugees-afghan-sponsorship-scheme-uk-b2045796.html [accessed: 22/4/2022].

31. Philip Oltermann, 'Ukraine refugees flock to Germany after being put off by UK red tape', *The Observer* (30 April 2022). https://www.theguardian.com/world/2022/apr/30/ukraine-refugees-are-flocking-to-germany-and-shunning-the-uk [accessed: 30/5/2022].

32. Nadine White, 'UN admits refugees have faced racism at Ukraine borders', *Independent* (1 March 2022). https://www.independent.co.uk/world/ukraine-racism-refugees-russia-war-un-b2025771.html [accessed: 30/5/2022].

33. 'Policy on the dispersal of asylum seekers', Research Briefing, Parliamentary Library (29 April 2016). https://commonslibrary.parliament.uk/research-briefings/cdp-2016-0095/ [accessed: 30/5/2022].

34. Ibid.

35. Jonathan Darling, *Systems of Suffering: Dispersal and the Denial of Asylum* (London: Pluto Press, 2022), pp. 2–3.

36. Kate Lyons and Pamela Duncan, '"It's a shambles": data shows most asylum seekers put in poorest parts of Britain', *The Guardian* (9 April 2017). https://www.theguardian.com/world/2017/apr/09/its-a-shambles-data-shows-most-asylum-seekers-put-in-poorest-parts-of-britain [accessed: 30/5/2022].

37. Massoud Hamid, 'After 52-year ban, Syrian Kurds now taught Kurdish in schools', Al-Monitor (6 November 2015). https://www.al-monitor.com/originals/2015/11/syria-kurdistan-self-governance-teach-kurdish-language.html [accessed: 30/5/2022].

38. 'Who are the Kurds?', BBC News (15 October 2019). https://www.bbc.co.uk/news/world-middle-east-29702440 [accessed: 30/5/2022].
39. Ibid.
40. 'Anfal Campaign and Kurdish Genocide', Kurdish Regional Government, Representation in the United States (n.d.). https://us.gov.krd/en/issues/anfal-campaign-and-kurdish-genocide/ [accessed: 30/7/2022].
41. 'Group Denial: Repression of Kurdish Political and Cultural Rights in Syria', Human Rights Watch (26 November 2009). https://www.hrw.org/report/2009/11/26/group-denial/repression-kurdish-political-and-cultural-rights-syria [accessed: 30/7/2022].
42. 'Why has the Syrian war lasted 11 years?', BBC News (15 March 2022). https://www.bbc.co.uk/news/world-middle-east-35806229 [accessed: 30/7/2022].
43. 'Where do the Kurds fit into Syria's war?', Reuters (3 January 2019). https://www.reuters.com/article/us-mideast-crisis-syria-kurds-explainer-idUSKCN1OX16L [accessed: 30/7/2022].
44. Ibid.
45. Sarah Lazarus, 'Women. Life. Freedom. Female fighters of Kurdistan', CNN News (n.d.). https://edition.cnn.com/2019/01/27/homepage2/kurdish-female-fighters/index.html [accessed: 30/7/2022].
46. 'Analysis—Fires in refugee camps: A coil of neglect', Anadolu Agency (18 January 2022). https://www.aa.com.tr/en/analysis/analysis-fires-in-refugee-camps-a-coil-of-neglect/2477291 [accessed: 30/5/2022].
47. Ibid.
48. 'Zaatari Camp Fact Sheet', UNHCR.
49. 'Syria Refugee Crisis', UNHCR (n.d.). https://www.unrefugees.org/emergencies/syria/ [accessed: 30/5/2022].
50. Hamid, 'After 52-year ban, Syrian Kurds now taught Kurdish in schools'.
51. Emily Kenway, *The Truth about Modern Slavery* (London: Pluto Press, 2021), p. 81.
52. 'Syria's Women, Many Raped In Refugee Centres, Long To Return Home', *Huffington Post* (26 October 2013). https://www.

huffingtonpost.co.uk/2013/10/26/syria-women-rape_n_4166185. html [accessed: 30/5/2022].

53. Mie A. Jensen, 'Gender-Based Violence in Refugee Camps: Understanding and Addressing the Role of Gender in the Experiences of Refugees', *Inquiries* (2019) 11(2):1.

5.   THE MARRIAGE CONTRACT

1.   Her name has been changed to protect her anonymity.
2.   King's College, London, Migration Research Group.
3.   War Studies KCL, *Migrant Voices in London*, https://www.youtube. com/watch?v=C32CCqV-dto [accessed: 12/3/2022].
4.   These are states that exist in practicality but that lack formal or legal recognition.
5.   His name has been changed to protect his anonymity.
6.   'Russia—Country of Concern', Corporate report, Foreign & Commonwealth Office (12 March 2015). https://www.gov.uk/ government/publications/russia-country-of-concern--2/russia-country-of-concern#womens-rights [accessed: 31/7/2022].
7.   'Russia: Bill to Decriminalize Domestic Violence', Human Rights Watch (23 January 2017). https://www.hrw.org/news/2017/01/23/ russia-bill-decriminalize-domestic-violence [accessed: 31/7/2022].
8.   'Violence against women', World Health Organization (9 March 2021). https://www.who.int/news-room/fact-sheets/detail/violence-against-women [accessed: 31/7/2022].
9.   'Quick Facts about Domestic Violence in the United States', planstreet (20 June 2022). https://www.planstreetinc.com/quick-facts-about-domestic-violence-in-the-united-states/ [accessed: 31/7/2022].
10. 'Domestic abuse during the coronavirus (COVID-19) pandemic, England and Wales: November 2020', Office for National Statistics (n.d.). https://www.ons.gov.uk/peoplepopulationandcommunity/ crimeandjustice/articles/domesticabuseduringthecoronaviruscovid19 pandemicenglandandwales/november2020 [accessed: 31/7/2022].
11. 'Domestic Violence and COVID-19', United Nations Peacekeeping (6 May 2020). https://peacekeeping.un.org/en/domestic-violence-and-covid-19 [accessed: 31/7/2022].

12. 'UN supporting "trapped" domestic violence victims during COVID-19 pandemic', Department of Global Communications, United Nations (12 June 2020). https://www.un.org/en/coronavirus/un-supporting-%E2%80%98trapped%E2%80%99-domestic-violence-victims-during-covid-19-pandemic [accessed: 31/7/2022].

13. 'Convention and Protocol Relating to the Status of Refugess', UNHCR India (n.d.). https://www.unhcr.org/en-in/protection/basic/3b66c2aa10/convention-protocol-relating-status-refugees.html [accessed: 31/7/2022].

14. Ian Sanjay Patel, *We're Here Because You Were There: Immigration and the End of Empire* (London: Verso, 2021), p. 5.

15. Ibid.

16. James Trafford, *The Empire at Home: Internal Colonies and the End of Britain* (London: Pluto Press, 2021), p. 4.

17. Her name has been changed for anonymity.

18. Her name has also been changed for anonymity.

19. Leah Cowan, *Border Nation: A Story of Migration* (London: Pluto Press, 2021), p. 122.

20. Patrick Wintour, '"Go home" vans to be scrapped after experiment deemed a failure', *The Guardian* (22 October 2013). https://www.theguardian.com/uk-news/2013/oct/22/go-home-vans-scrapped-failure [accessed: 31/7/2022].

21. Cowan, *Border Nation*, p. 73.

22. Wei Ming Kam, 'Beyond "Good" Immigrants' in *The Good Immigrant* edited by Nikesh Shukla, p. 91.

23. Ibid.

24. Ibid., p. 91.

6. INVISIBLE BORDERS

1. The kyriarchy is an extension of the concept of patriarchy, as a system of oppression and domination, beyond gender to include intersections such as race and disability.

2. Melanie Close, 'Disabled People's Movement—History Timeline', Disability Equality (November 2020). http://disability-equality.org.uk/history/ [accessed: 31/7/2022].

3. John F. Helliwell, Haifang Huang, Shun Wang and Max Norton, 'Happiness, Benevolence, and Trust During COVID-19 and Beyond', World Happiness Report (18 March 2022). https://worldhappiness. report/ed/2022/happiness-benevolence-and-trust-during-covid-19- and-beyond/#ranking-of-happiness-2019-2021 [accessed: 31/7/2022].

4. Similar benefits are still very much in force in the US, and they even extend into health care.

5. While steps have been taken to liberate Employment and Support Allowance recipients from their finances being considered as tied to their partner, the reformed version of the benefit requires recipients to have paid tax, leading some critics to argue that this is a benefit designed for those who have become impaired, rather than those born impaired.

6. 'Disability and crime, UK: 2019', Office for National Statistics (2 December 2019). https://www.ons.gov.uk/peoplepopulationand community/healthandsocialcare/disability/bulletins/disabilityand crimeuk/2019 [accessed: 31/7/2022].

7. 'Disabled Survivors Too: Disabled people and domestic abuse', Safe Lives (March 2017). https://safelives.org.uk/sites/default/files/ resources/Disabled%20Survivors%20Too%20CORRECTED.pdf [accessed: 31/7/2022].

8. Maria Polletta, 'Many shelters can't handle domestic-violence survivors with disabilities', The Republic, azcentral (n.d.). https://eu.azcentral. com/story/news/local/arizona/2018/09/16/ada-domestic-violence- shelters-struggle-when-people-have-disabilities/771719002/ [accessed: 31/7/2022].

9. 'Disability and domestic abuse: Risk, impacts and response', Public Health England (November 2015). https://studylib.net/ doc/18295447/disability-and-domestic-abuse-risk--impacts-and- response [accessed: 31/7/2022].

10. 'Disabled Survivors Too: Disabled people and domestic abuse', Safe Lives.

11. Ibid.

12. Frances Ryan, *Crippled: Austerity and the Demonization of Disabled People* (London: Verso, 2020), p. 20.

13. Leslie Kern, *Feminist City: Claiming Space in a Man-made World* (Verso: London, 2020), p. 34.

14. Ibid., p. 12.

15. Jessie Lau, 'Hong Kong Is Still Waiting for Its Feminist Uprising', *The Nation* (25 February 2020). https://www.thenation.com/article/world/hong-kong-feminism-protests/ [accessed: 17/3/2022].

16. Wilfred Chan and JN, 'Hong Kong's Mask Ban Is Just a Cover for a Police Crackdown', *The Nation* (4 October 2019). https://www.thenation.com/article/archive/hong-kong-mask-police/ [accessed 17/3/2022].

17. Shelly Banjo and Josie Wong, 'Women Hong Kong Protesters Upend Gender Roles in Democracy Fight', Bloomberg News (6 February 2020). https://www.bloomberg.com/news/articles/2020-02-06/women-hong-kong-protesters-upend-gender-roles-in-democracy-fight [accessed: 29/7/2022].

18. *Do Not Split*, Field of Vision documentary, directed by Anders Hammer (2019). https://vimeo.com/504381953 [accessed: 25/8/2022].

19. 'Carrie Lam addresses extradition law controversy', *South China Morning Post* (12 June 2019). https://www.youtube.com/watch?v=HhgR6dCjKvg [accessed: 13/5/2022].

20. Hannah Ellis-Petersen and Rebecca Ratcliffe, 'Hong Kong protests: nearly 400 arrested as security law comes in; UK opens pathway to citizenship—as it happened', *The Guardian* (1 July 2020). https://www.theguardian.com/world/live/2020/jul/01/hong-kong-protests-china-security-law-carrie-lam [accessed: 13/7/2022].

21. *Do Not Split*.

22. 'Six-monthly report on Hong Kong: 1 July to 31 December 2021', Foreign, Commonwealth & Development Office (31 March 2022). https://www.gov.uk/government/publications/six-monthly-report-on-hong-kong-1-july-to-31-december-2021/six-monthly-report-on-hong-kong-1-july-to-31-december-2021 [accessed: 13/5/2022].

23. 'Joey Siu speaks at the Geneva Summit for Human Rights and Democracy', Hong Kong Watch (7 April 2022). https://www.hongkongwatch.org/all-posts/2022/4/21/joey-siu-speaks-at-

the-geneva-summit-for-human-rights-and-democracy [accessed: 13/5/2022].

24. 'Joey Siu testifies at Senate Foreign Relations Subcommittee on assault on freedom of expression in Asia', Hong Kong Watch (30 March 2022). https://www.hongkongwatch.org/all-posts/2022/3/23/joey-siu-to-testify-at-senate-foreign-relations-subcommittee-on-assault-on-freedom-of-expression-in-asia [accessed: 13/5/2022].

25. 'Women Leading in Crises: Joey Siu, Hong Kong', Community Democracies (n.d.). https://community-democracies.org/women/joey-siu/ [accessed: 13/5/2022].

26. 'Timeline of Arrests, Prosecution and Sentencing', Hong Kong Watch (10 August 2022). https://www.hongkongwatch.org/political-prisoners-database [accessed: 13/7/2022].

27. Sophie Elmhirst, 'Fall of the Palace of Pinks', *Tortoise* (1 December 2020). https://www.tortoisemedia.com/2020/12/01/fall-of-the-palace-of-pinks-2/ [accessed: 1/9/2021]

28. 'Women Making History', Oxford University (n.d.). https://www.ox.ac.uk/about/oxford-people/women-at-oxford [accessed: 27/12/2021].

29. S. P. Rosenbaum (1998). *Aspects of Bloomsbury: Studies in Modern English Literary and Intellectual History* (Hounsmill: MacMillan Press Ltd), pp. 113–15.

30. Turgay Bayindir, 'A House of Her Own: Alice Walker's Readjustment of Virginia Woolf's *A Room of One's Own* in *The Color Purple*', *Dialogue* (2009) 5:209–23.

31. 'Jamal Khashoggi: All you need to know about Saudi journalist's death', BBC News (24 February 2021). https://www.bbc.co.uk/news/world-europe-45812399 [accessed: 31/7/2022].

32. When a woman is seen in public in Saudi Arabia, her body must be covered by a long, flowing garment, an abaya. Priya Kaur-Jones, 'Reinventing the Saudi abaya', BBC News (13 May 2011). https://www.bbc.co.uk/news/world-middle-east-13372186 [accessed: 23/11/2021].

33. 'Gender Inequality Index (GII)', Human Development Reports (n.d.). http://hdr.undp.org/en/composite/GII [accessed: 23/11/2021].

34. 'Absher (application)', Wikipedia. https://en.wikipedia.org/wiki/ Absher_(application) [accessed 27/06/2021].

35. 'Women activists prepare to defy Saudi Arabian driving ban', Amnesty International (16 June 2011). https://www.amnesty.org/en/press-releases/2011/06/women-activists-prepare-defy-saudi-arabian-driving-ban/ [accessed: 2/2/2019]. Hillary Leung, 'What to Know About Absher, Saudi Arabia's Controversial "Woman-Tracking" App', *Time* (19 February 2019). https://time.com/5532221/absher-saudi-arabia-what-to-know/ [accessed: 2/2/2019]. 'Saudi Arabia: 10 Reasons Why Women Flee', Human Rights Watch (30 January 2019). https://www.hrw.org/news/2019/01/30/saudi-arabia-10-reasons-why-women-flee [accessed: 2/2/2019].

36. Jean Rhys, *Smile Please: An Unfinished Autobiography* (London: Penguin Classics, 2016).

7.   UNLAWFUL ACTIVISM

1. 'The Calais Jungle: Three Years On', Choose Love (24 October 2019). https://chooselove.org/news/the-calais-jungle-three-years-on/ [accessed 15/11/2019].

2. Through the publication of comprehensive legal analysis and media statements, the UNHCR warned that the bill undermines the 1951 Refugee Convention, the agreement that has protected refugees for decades, and of which the UK is a signatory. 'UK Migration and Economic Development Partnership with Rwanda', UNHCR UK (n.d.). https://www.unhcr.org/uk/uk-immigration-and-asylum-plans-some-questions-answered-by-unhcr.html [accessed: 26/7/2022].

3. Ibid.

4. There are no limitations or compulsory requirements on someone advising in a legal capacity for a case in Russia. Valeriya Kachura and Aleksandr Kuznetsov, 'Regulation of the legal profession in the Russian Federation', Thomson Reuters Practical Law (1 May 2021). https://uk.practicallaw.thomsonreuters.com/1-633-8957?transition Type=Default&contextData=(sc.Default)&firstPage=true [accessed: 6/3/2022].

5. David Litvinova, 'Human rights activist forced to flee Russia following TV "witch-hunt"', *The Moscow Times* (20 October 2015). https://www.theguardian.com/world/2015/oct/20/russia-activist-flee-nuclear-tv-witch-hunt [accessed: 6/3/2022].

6. Alex Howlett, 'Iara Lee, "Burkinabe Rising: The Art of Resistance in Burkina Faso"' *Polyester* (n.d.). https://www.polyesterzine.com/scrapbook/iara-lee-burkinabe-rising-the-art-of-resistance-in-burkina-faso [accessed: 4/5/2022].

7. The Gaza Strip was put under a blockade by Egypt and Israel after Hamas, a nationalist Palestinian militant organisation, took control of Gaza after the Battle of Gaza in 2007. In the eyes of the EU, USA, Canada, Japan and Israel, Hamas is classed as a terrorist organisation. The UK, Australia, New Zealand and Paraguay consider only the military branch of Hamas to be a terrorist organisation. The United Nations General Assembly in 2018 rejected a US resolution to condemn Hamas and their actions.

8. 'Moria migrants: Fire destroys Greek camp leaving 13,000 without shelter', BBC News (9 September 2020). https://www.bbc.co.uk/news/world-europe-54082201 [accessed: 6/5/2022].

9. 'Number of civilian casualties in Ukraine during Russia's invasion verified by OHCHR as of May 4, 2022', Statista. https://www.statista.com/statistics/1293492/ukraine-war-casualties/ [accessed: 6/5/2022].

10. 'Number of civilian casualties in Ukraine during Russia's invasion verified by OHCHR as of July 24, 2022', Statista. https://www.statista.com/statistics/1293492/ukraine-war-casualties/ [accessed: 26/7/2022].

11. 'Mariupol fighting: More evacuations from besieged city on Friday, UN says', BBC News (6 May 2022). https://www.bbc.co.uk/news/world-europe-61342436 [accessed: 6/5/2022].

12. 'Nowhere Safe: Cycle of Abuses Against Refugees and Migrants in Libya', Amnest International (n.d.). https://www.amnesty.org/en/latest/campaigns/2020/09/nowhere-safe-cycle-of-abuses-against-refugees-and-migrants-in-libya/ [accessed: 26/7/2022].

13. Ibid.

14. Daniel Trilling, 'How rescuing drowning migrants became a crime', *The Guardian* (22 September 2020). https://www.theguardian.com/news/2020/sep/22/how-rescuing-drowning-migrants-became-a-crime-iuventa-salvini-italy [accessed: 26/11/2021].

INDEX

INDEX

INDEX

INDEX

INDEX

INDEX

INDEX

INDEX

INDEX

INDEX

INDEX